CW01636527

I'M GAY AND DRINK WATER

A MEMOIR

BY ALLY NIKOLAUS

I'M GAY AND DRINK WATER
a memoir
by Ally Nikolaus

Edited by Dana Alsamsam
Cover design by Ally Nikolaus

Printed in United States of America

Paperback ISBN: 979-8-9894965-5-6
eBook ISBN: 979-8-9894965-6-3
Turn Your Page, LLC
An Independent Publishing Company
St. Louis, MO 63119
www.allynikolaus.com

Dear Reader,

Thank you for picking up my book, whether that's electronically or physically. Much like my time playing soccer, I left it all on the field, and as I hit the final button to print this final draft, I can honestly say after 7 full years of writing this, I left it all on the page.

My main goal for you in reading this is to feel a little less alone in the world. Please note before you begin reading, the following topics are mentioned and/or detailed in this work of non-fiction: sexual assault, suicidal thoughts, depression, anxiety, self-harm, identity issues, death of a loved one, and substance abuse.

This is how I remember the things that happened. While the following events are true to me, they may be interpreted differently from others mentioned in this book. I hope that you learn something about yourself from my story or learn something about a loved one, helping you understand them or yourself more. I'm proud of you for taking the time to read this and being open to absorbing the words bound within this book. I have lived these words and carry them with me almost every day. Now, they finally live on this page. I am honored to pass my words along to you and those whom you share parts of my story. So, take a sip of water and turn that page, my friend.

XoXo,

Ally

CONTENTS

Introduction **6**

AUGUST 2010 – DECEMBER 2011

Chapter I 11
Chapter II 20
Chapter III 33
Chapter IV 37
Chapter V 44
Chapter VI 49
Chapter VII 61
Chapter VIII 67
Chapter IX 71
Chapter X 77
Chapter XI 81
Chapter XII 86
Chapter XIII 95
Chapter XIV 99
Chapter XV 105
Chapter XVI 110
Chapter XVII 118
Chapter XVIII 123
Chapter XIX 133

JANUARY 2012 – MAY 2014

Chapter XX 140
Chapter XXI 147
Chapter XXII 156

Chapter XXIII....161
Chapter XXIV....170
Chapter XXV....177
Chapter XXVI....184
Chapter XXVII....194
Chapter XXIX....201
Chapter XXX....209

MAY 2014 – AUGUST 2015

Chapter XXXI....213
Chapter XXXII....216
Chapter XXXIII....222
Chapter XXXIV....226
Chapter XXXV....230
Chapter XXXVI....234
Chapter XXXVII....244
Chapter XXXVIII....250
Chapter XXXIX....254
Chapter XL....263
Chapter XLI....272
Chapter XLII....286
Chapter XLIII....293
Chapter XXLIV....307

Looking Back....315
Acknowledgements....321
Works Cited....323

INTRODUCTION

In the late spring of 2023, I went to see a psychic. I was living with my parents at the time and in need of a little spiritual guidance. The psychic told me my aura was cloudy. I wasn't surprised. I've never intentionally cleansed my aura before, and by the time I was thirty-one, the lavender haze needed to be swept away. Well, the haze needed to be, but the lavender I will keep forever.

The day after my reading, on the lunar eclipse on May 5th, I performed a cleansing ritual to let go of anything I could think of that would have truly clouded my aura or held me back over the last year and beyond. I wrote a single word on every few lines of a legal pad piece of paper: certain people, money, strangers, anxiety, microaggressions, discrimination, and so on. I ripped each word into its own piece and shuffled them. In the four corners of the bath stood four different crystal towers. I lit four candles and dumped salts, baking soda, and lavender oil into the warm water. The sun was getting ready to leave the western hemisphere.

Before I entered the water, I took nine deep breaths and set my intention: to let go. In my workspace where I wrote drafts five and six of this book, I have a blue post-it on which I'd written: *let go of this to open space for bigger and better things.* Around nine weeks later, I met my life partner. Well, we re-met. We went to the same high school and grew up in the same zip code.

In the water, with a lighter from my parents' kitchen, I burned those little ripped pieces of paper one by one. And with the warm, salted, oiled bath water in which my skinny ass sat, I let the flame go out and the ashes sink.

Water is not a privilege. It's a human right even so many do not have. I took a moment to acknowledge the clean water I've always had access to. Grateful and humbled, I left the bath with a massive headache. My headache meant the work I'd just put in was working. When your brain is not used to deep meditation, expect a headache. I viewed this headache as my third eye actively chipping away at the eye crusties it built from being closed longer than it should have been.

The anxiety I had felt in the two months prior especially was awful. It was so awful that it forced me to cut back on my second favorite beverage right after water: coffee.

The day after my cleansing ritual, my anxiety fell from a nine to a two out of ten. The eczema on my hands had nearly cleared completely five days later.

This cleansing meditation has become a part of my daily routine. It is vital for my existence in this life.

I am a more spiritual being these days—a more intentional, on purpose spirit. But I had to write this book. I had to live through the experiences and people herein to get to where I am. It is within these pages I began to lift my higher being out of uncharted waters, sometimes letting myself get familiar with those unknown waters. It is important to me to no longer swim (or run) away from what I do not know. Then, it was as if I was plunged down to the ocean floor, sometimes feeling like I couldn't breathe. And at times, it would be so dark I would not know which way was up.

To find our way, we must find an ebb and flow of standing still and moving. If we're doing just one and not the other, then we really aren't going where we are supposed to go.

It is in the stories I share here, through therapy, through living, through grieving, through laughing and playing and writing and praying and moving and sitting still, that I have actively chosen to walk through the fire of trauma, pain, and toxic traits that live within me. I say walk, not run, because running, speeding things up, is not how I heal. It is only slowly through the flames that we may feel and taste the sweet nectar that the next drink of water brings to our tongue.

I'm Gay and Drink Water is a linear collection of memories and moments from the time I was eighteen, a freshman in college, to shortly after I came out at age twenty-four. Being gay in a heteronormative world is one thing while you're trying to find your voice and your place. Having a drinking problem on top of that escalates all of it.

To truly appreciate what water can do for us, we must feel the burn of the hurt we've received from others, but more importantly, feel and forgive the hurt which we bestow upon ourselves.

I thank God I love water.

I thank God I have the bravery of letting go of the edge.

And I thank God that I'm a damn good swimmer.

> *"We are our most productive, happy, and successful when we are our authentic selves."*
> **– Billie Jean King**

For anyone who is afraid to live their truth.
It gets better. Keep going.

Part ONE

AUGUST 2010 – DECEMBER 2011

CHAPTER I

I can count on one hand the number of times I had fun and felt okay while being drunk. Only a few times did I feel as though I was a responsible drinker. Only a few times did I feel like I was collecting *good* memories with friends that I would have for the rest of my life. Only a few times was not enough to keep drinking like I was. It didn't matter if I drank nights or days away or if I had just one or two beverages at a time. I was almost always consuming alcohol for the wrong reasons: drinking intentionally to hide myself, like the alcohol was filled in a tank around me to fit into this world pretending to be heterosexual. It was as if the tank acted like a thick glass shell, keeping me safe and providing a barrier between me and others where no one could *touch* the real me. When I started drinking at age sixteen, I did not realize what exactly I was doing, creating that shell with what I thought was liquid gold. Once I figured out what I was doing, I never thought that that glass shell would eventually break. But it did, and I'm glad it did. The glass tank would only break shortly after the ceiling had been sealed.

Alcohol would always be *there*. When things were good, I thought I could start drinking again. So, a lot of times, I did…even after weeks or months of taking what I told myself was a "break." There were a few nights I only consumed one glass of wine, one beer, or a glass of whiskey, but more often than not, those drinking days and nights were spent binge drinking myself stupid.

I used alcohol to drown my truth and avoid the uncomfortable feeling of, well, feeling my feelings. But the thing about that is while I may have quieted my truth by drinking, it is impossible for it to drown completely. It is impossible for the truth to die, especially when the tide rises as the years go on. The longer I suppressed, the longer I chose to drink, the harder it was to keep it all underwater… to keep myself under the influence. To keep it all under the influence.

I didn't drink too much in high school, but that changed shortly after I started my college soccer career as a freshman on the University of Mississippi Women's Soccer Team.

On September 4, 2010, I wrote in my journal, a Labor Day tournament at Notre Dame:

"I never even dreamed that I'd be where I am today. D1 soccer in the SEC! We play #8 Santa Clara tomorrow morning. This is my life now. I have dreamed of playing college ball since I was a little girl. I dream a dream, but I exceeded my expectations. I never expected to be playing D1. IN THE SEC. Dreams do come true. And you make the most of it more than you ever imagined. I am thankful every day to not take anything for granted. This opportunity comes once in a lifetime."

Yeah, I'm that girl who hopelessly believes dreams can and will come true. However, I am not a fan of the phrase "once in a lifetime." I think it's pessimistic, but I find it true in rare cases. The opportunity to play soccer in such a competitive conference only comes once in a lifetime.

September 6, 2010; Labor Day:

"At High Point now studying, got an iced mocha and working on my English paper due Wednesday. It's absolutely beautiful in Oxford today. I don't mind the studying when it's outside a coffee shop on an amazing day like this. I love Oxford Mondays. [St. Louis Cardinals] are tied 2-2 - end of the 6th. Hopefully, they will get it together and start winning again. My parents are coming in town this weekend! Excited for the food! We play McNeese State on Friday and Memphis on Sunday. Goals for this week: church, smile, meet new people, and make headway in acting class."

While those were just two of the several high points of my time at Ole Miss, I wrote these entries to remember happier times. It was only a tiny sliver of the huge truth I had been struggling with. I wrote them because I wanted something to hang on to and remind myself that I was happy at one point in Mississippi. Or more so, trying to convince myself that I was happy there. At times, I was, but overall, I really wasn't. I cannot write things down for them to come to fruition. Manifestation is about patience but also about putting in the work. I put in the work physically during my freshman year, but mentally, there was no healthy work being done. Wanting to want to be there was a hopeless wish.

I did not know the how's, when's, where's, or why's; I just knew what was. And that was the long-term goal of playing soccer in college. I certainly did not give myself enough credit back then nor allow myself much of a break. I was always the hardest on myself—to do better, to be better—because a. I held myself to that high standard, and b. I believed I was capable of so much more. Coming into Ole Miss, I never thought I would actually be a starter in my freshman year, let alone be granted any playing time as a freshman on a book scholarship.

Less than 8% of high school athletes will go on to play at the collegiate level and in the NCAA. Less than 2% of those athletes will play at the Division 1 level. Those stats were published on NCAA.com in 2012, so I imagine the numbers have changed since then.

Upon arrival to Ole Miss, my only goals were to pass my fitness tests and not get redshirted. I ended my freshman season starting three games and appearing in eighteen of them. Honestly, not too shabby, considering I came in at the beginning not expecting to ever make it off the bench.

I wanted college to be the time of my freakin' life. But I'd soon find out that my mind is prone to cyclical, sometimes major depression, which led me to make poor decisions and turn to alcohol as a way to numb the feelings I didn't want to deal with.

I'd soon find out that I have a drinking problem.

It was barely 6 a.m. in Oxford, and my shirt was already spotted with sweat. It was the first day of preseason as a freshman on the Ole Miss Women's soccer team. The team reported to preseason a month before classes started.

My plan was to play soccer for Ole Miss and earn a theatre degree. I chose theatre because that was the one thing that I dreamt about most outside of soccer. As a child, I often played songs as I fell asleep, envisioning myself singing on stage. Whenever I watched a musical or an episode of "Parks and Recreation," I pretended it was myself on the stage or as Leslie Knope. I wanted to trade in the soccer field for the stage as soon as time allowed. After graduation, I had my heart set on moving to Chicago to continue my studies at The Second City theatre. Being the class clown of my high school class and hearing others laugh at something I said or did always felt magical. I felt noticed and needed. I felt seen. Those laughs always made me feel like I belonged.

However, before I got to Chicago and before my journey as a theatre major started, I had a month of preseason to get through first.

The team met at the Track and Field Complex for my first official fitness test as a college athlete. I'd prepared for the last eighteen years plus one summer for this moment. Butterflies flipped in my belly. I was nervous and excited but cool, calm, and collected on the outside.

I was excited because I was finally living a childhood dream. I was excited that I was playing soccer for a team in one of the most competitive conferences in the country. I was excited and proud that I was one of the 8% of high school athletes who made it to play at the next level: college.

I was nervous because it was the first day of my college career and because these were new coaches. The coaches who recruited me left Ole Miss to take over the program at the University of Georgia a few months prior.

The team met wearing mismatched Ole Miss soccer gear. It was the only time acceptable during the season to not match at team gatherings. I smoothed my loose t-shirt against my belly to soak up more sweat. I bent down to retie my running shoes and stood back up for a bullshit warmup.

A few high knees. Quad stretches here. Calf stretches there. I swung my arms a bit and made a conscious choice not to smile. Smiling might've come off as cocky. I needed to be serious right now. My nerves and I only cared about one person at that moment, and that person was me. *You trained and prepared as much as you could. You got this, Ally.*

Up first was the Cooper test: around the track as many times as possible for twelve minutes. The passing goal for this test was seven laps. Two weeks before I left St. Louis for Oxford, I ran the Cooper at a training session and timed just under twelve minutes. My body felt heavier in the heat that morning despite only eating a banana on the way across campus. The bloat of my belly also suggested I drank too much water. I took one long deep breath in and one long one out. I stepped up to the line with the first group and took my ready stance, trying my best to ignore the butterflies that continued to flap in my gut. They flew away as soon as I did after the coach yelled, "Go!"

I purposefully paced myself on the first lap, wanting to work my way up to a faster pace. After the first lap, I lengthened my strides. I was like a racehorse. No, a cheetah. No, BOTH. I stood five feet, nine inches and weighed nearly 160 pounds. Coaches allowed a generous handicap for incoming freshmen. The champion mentality in me struggled to accept that handicap. I wanted to be held to the same standard as upperclassmen.

My legs grew heavier with each stride. My cheetah/horse slowly turned into a pony. Still fast, yet not as strong. As I approached the last curve of my seventh lap, the butterflies returned. No, they felt more like a car speeding over gravel this time. Me being the gravel.

Other than passing this test, my only goal for it was not to stop. To keep going no matter what. The car chase in my belly was stopped by a waterlogged and broken-down banana coming up my throat and then out of my mouth. I threw up to my left, only slowing down briefly but never stopping. Puking cost me to be passed up by another teammate, Emily. I crossed the finish line in 12:32, with just a few seconds to spare and just a few seconds behind Emily, but I still passed.

As soon as I caught my breath, I told our trainer that I threw up on the far corner of the track.

She shrugged and said, "I'm not cleaning it up."

She didn't ask if I was OK, and neither did anyone else, for that matter.

Clearly, I was fine since I'd continued running.

I passed all the tests, getting me out of the dreaded "breakfast club" for those who did not pass the fitness tests the first time. The club was reserved for players who required extra strength and conditioning. I passed enough of the fitness tests to not be redshirted, which was my main goal during preseason. In fact, it was my only goal throughout the season.

I didn't want to be left behind, and I expected no playing time. I just wanted to be there, to be a part of the team. Wherever they went, I wanted to go. I wanted to be there.

When I met with the coaches during freshmen orientation, they asked me if I had a preference for my number. I said #13, but it was already taken, so I replied that I had no preference.

After the first day of testing, gifts waited in the locker room. A new soccer season meant new gear.

The Ole Miss women's locker room at the time was a near perfect rectangle with an Ole Miss rug in the center that touch of any kind was forbidden. It was out of respect to not touch the rug or perhaps a superstition. I never received a direct, definitive answer. Lockers lined the permitter of the room. I scanned the numbers on each of them. #17, Kelly. #18, Maren. #19, Candice. That's when I saw my name written on a plate above my locker: Ally Nikolaus #20, St. Louis, MO. I had never worn #20 before. I was honored.

I loved my spot. I loved that I had a senior sitting next to me, and on the other side of her was Maren, a teammate who quickly became one of my best friends. Our little corner had very good energy.

It smelled good in there that first day: free from sweat, mud, grass, and blood. Everything smelled new. New bags, cleats, running shoes, hoodies, sweatpants, clothes, and more clothes. Our reward for a hard day's work. Our reward for making it this far.

New beginnings. Some of which I couldn't even see, nor did I know were on their way.

As I opened a box of white and navy Nike running shoes, I was stopped by the most genuine laugh I'd ever heard. I looked up and saw the laugh belonged to Lauren, a junior defender. The way the numbers ran, she was across from me and slightly to the right. Eyes shut with her head tossed back, she continued to giggle at a joke I only wish I would've heard so I could laugh with her, too, but quieter so hers would shine.

"Ally!" Maren said. My eyes didn't move.

"Ally!" Maren said again.

I jumped as a bundled pair of socks hit me in the shoulder. I looked up and tossed the socks back to Maren as she mouthed, "What the fuck are you looking at?"

I mouthed back, "What? Nothing."

"Okay, sure. Sureeeeee!"

"Shut up," I said with a laugh and returned my focus to a different box, this one with black and white cleats.

I had met Lauren before that day, but that was the first time I heard her laugh. I was unable to name what I was feeling at the time. I ignored those feelings and convinced myself that it was best for me to keep my distance from her. Gravity, however, had other plans.

The structure Ole Miss provided was a high point for me, but it was also a low. I loved routines. I loved high school for that very fact that I knew exactly what would happen on a day-to-day basis, the biggest element of variety being the days and times of practice.

Childhood summers were spent at various camps, followed by a plethora of pool time. As I got older, summers were spent with equal amounts of pool time, a part-time job babysitting, and, of course, training after the State Cup. During the school year, even in winter, I trained several times a week in the evenings and on weekends: practice, games, and scrimmages. School, soccer, rinse, repeat. That was life for twenty years. If you take out parent politics, it was pretty awesome most of the time.

I've had an incredibly privileged life. Being white and straight-passing, I never had to face adversity because of my skin color as some around me did, and even later, I rarely faced harassment and hate because of my sexuality.

Soccer made me believe that if you work hard and are consistent, it will pay off. Well, that's if you have a lick of talent to begin with. Luckily, I was fucking great at it.

A lot of attention came with being a great athlete, and while I didn't allow that to go to my head, subconsciously I began to assign a large part of my self-worth to sports. I realized this because I was rewarded for good playing. I was rewarded for scoring goals. I was rewarded for winning. Who doesn't want to be recognized for a job well done?

I kept soccer close, too, because it bought me time and granted me space to neglect other areas of my life and mind. With soccer, there was hardly any time to think about dating guys, although I did date a few before college. Soccer acted as an excuse to get out of social events I was too anxious to attend without drinking.

Soccer kept me focused. I'm not a big troublemaker, but soccer kept me out of *bad/real* trouble. It gave me something to talk about. It gave me attention. It gave me so much, but what it gave me when I was younger didn't help as much as it did when I reached college. I started to get tired of running. And I'm not just talking about my tight, crunchy knees on a long run, but I started to get tired of running from myself, from something greater than soccer. Something deeper. Running from something as simple yet as complex as who I am at my core. Athletes are so much more than physical specimens to win championships. We are so much more than the goals we score. We are so much more than the person we must become to win. Being an athlete is only one part of us.

During my freshmen season in Mississippi, I found myself afraid and alone in my thoughts. That routine that worked so well for years and years started to not work anymore. I suddenly couldn't find my footing. I was angry. Why now? Why here? Why was I struggling so much?

I think collegiate student athletes have it harder than regular students. Not just because of the pressure to perform in the classroom and on the field but also because we are trying to figure out the rest of our lives while starting to say goodbye to a game that most likely we'd been a part of for most of our lives. 2 percent of NCAA athletes move on to professional sports. My 9-year-old dreams of becoming the next Mia Hamm faded over time. I realized I had other interests and wanted to pursue them someday.

While I spent countless afternoons daydreaming about what my theatre career would be like, I never once considered the grief that would come after soccer ended.

No one talked about the loss of playing your sport. It was almost taboo. We all knew we were running out of time, but no one that I know of was preparing for ways to deal with it when the clock stopped. We were sad, but we didn't talk about it.

"Don't say that!"

"I don't want to talk about it."

"Let's not talk about it."

Most choose to tuck away any feelings that reared their heads as we neared hanging up our cleats for good, only to bring them down here and there for a scrimmage or a local co-ed league.

We all lose games, and athletes know how to deal with that, but what about when we lose the game for good solely because we graduate? We may not be pros, but we still retire. No one prepared us for that retirement. No one prepared us for the months following the final whistle. *What now?*

Rarely do we talk about the loss unassociated with the death of a person. We don't talk about the loss of moving states. We don't talk about the loss of switching jobs. We don't talk about the loss of who we used to be: athletes, drinkers, pretenders, etc. Sure, we talk about the adjustment period, but rarely the mourning during that adjustment. The discussion around adjustment remains surface level with comments like:

"You'll get used to it."

"Give it some time."

But never "How are you really feeling about this change? What were you feeling right before the change took place?"

Maybe those talks about loss are true for some people and some athletes, but not me. My stomach churned at the thought of talking about my feelings. The rare times I found myself about to speak my feelings, I'd swallow it with a beverage or spit out a joke instead. Sometimes both. I didn't deal with most of my non-death related losses until years later...when I stopped running from those, too.

CHAPTER II

The early days at Ole Miss were incredible. I was going to finish my soccer career playing in the SEC. The same conference Abby Wambach played. I was able to settle in before the rest of the student body came. I got to play soccer nearly every single day at an intense level, which I was grateful for and loved. I got to hang out with teammates and not worry about school yet. It was summer camp that I never wanted to end.

Labor Day weekend was the first time the team could really do something social. Sunday evening, just a couple of hours back from our tournament at Notre Dame, a group of Juniors hosted a team get-together at their house off campus. Half of the team dressed up, including me.

My hot pink miniskirt and white camisole with 5-inch black heels screamed 2010. I looked like I was ready to hop off MTV's "Next" bus, competing to win a date with a guy who had bleached tips.

Heels were another way that I made sure I was seen by others. As I got ready that night, a thought popped into my head: "I want Lauren to see me in these." The thought left as quickly as it came like a goalie dropkicking a ball immediately after picking it up, soaring it across half field. Lauren wore short jean shorts, a white T-shirt and a pair of Toms shoes, looking effortlessly adorable and beautiful.

Maren and I were each handed a beer upon our arrival at the house. We both chugged them and as soon as I leveled my tilted head, Lauren's eyes caught mine. I smiled at her, and she smiled at me.

I was already much taller than Lauren without shoes on my feet. Noticing the height difference, a teammate held up their Nikon

Coolpix digital camera and suggested Lauren and I take a picture together.

For once, I was happy to do what I was told. I strutted over to Lauren, careful to balance myself on the gravel driveway. Before my feet completely lost their footing, Lauren was wrapped in my arms with her own around my waist. Although the touch was brief, it made a lasting impression on me.

And there was that laugh again. That stop you in your tracks, can't help but smile, contagious laugh. Her laugh made me laugh, too. Not in the *ha-ha this is funny* way but in that breathless, wholesome, warm way that everything might just work out better than I could have ever imagined.

The next morning, I woke up feeling weird. I was a little sad and didn't have an explanation as to why. My eyes and head felt full as if I'd slept only a few hours opposed to the nine I just got. I shook it off and blamed it on staying up too late, not taking into consideration how much alcohol I had the night before.

I didn't want to waste a beautiful late summer day in bed. So, I got my ass out of bed. I put on some clothes, grabbed my laptop, grabbed Maren, and headed across town to High Pointe coffee.

At the coffee shop, I finished two papers. One was due the next day, and the other was due two weeks later. My keyboard let me escape from whatever the hell I felt that morning. But escapes are temporary. Back at the dorms, I sat on my bed and starred at the floor. The feeling I woke up with came back as soon as the distraction left.

Once classes were fully underway, social outings like that Labor Day weekend were far and few in between. The standard student-athletes were expected to mirror was that of a full-time job plus over time—at least at the D1 level. So, in that aspect, I didn't have time to navigate these new feelings that came up. I had a job to do, so I pushed the feelings down, ignoring them. The structure and full schedule were grand distractions, but it came at a price.

I was all for it, but meeting that standard, at least for me and I'm sure many other student athletes, meant sacrificing my voice. Sacrificing my voice meant suffering in silence despite not truly knowing how to speak up. I wanted to, and I *knew how*, but I didn't know how to start the new habit of speaking up. I thought I would be perceived as weak if I ever said what was truly on my mind. I thought I'd be seen as someone that just makes excuses. A complainer. I also didn't want to be yelled at. The few times in the past when I had spoken up in my soccer career, I was yelled at in response.

Before college, the few times I spoke up for a problem I was facing on a team, I was not met with listening, compassionate ears. I was met with "Get on the line" or "Well if you didn't do x, y, or z" or "Well maybe if you weren't laughing during warmups, then you would have performed better the rest of practice."

Early in my junior year of high school, I had asked my coach why I hadn't seen much playing time when I'd been performing in practice so well. And during games, I thought I demonstrated quality play that would earn me more minutes. The coach replied with a heightened tone, "Seriously, Ally? You go up to your opponent and just knock them down. I can't have that every time you go out on the field. You think I should trust you?!"

Five years before that, I confronted my U-12 club coach regarding why I didn't play at all one game. He said: "Because you don't know how this team works. You needed to see them play first before you can play against them. Can't you see that?"

If I could've seen it, I would most certainly not have asked. Believe me.

Out of all the coaches I've had over the years, there were only a few who knew what they were doing in terms of the game AND were kind and approachable. Maybe coaches should be more responsible to check in with our mental wellbeing, especially in our youth. Sure, we were young adults who needed to be taught responsibility and discipline, or whatever, but every human needs help. It's a team effort, right? We cannot go it alone and expect to thrive. Going it alone barely means we survive. Some of us don't. **Too many of us don't**.

While we weren't directly pressured or ever told we couldn't speak our truth, it kind of felt like an unspoken rule. Especially in the south. The loudness of what was unspoken felt huge to me and made my ears ache. It felt heavy, as if no one wanted to rock the boat. Sure, we technically had a job to do. To keep our scholarships. To keep our playing time. But at what cost? What were we sacrificing that mattered more? Our mental health and wellbeing? True balance? Not learning how to communicate our thoughts and feelings better or more efficiently? College sports should teach us more about life and life after college, not condition us to be more afraid of it because of the fear to speak up. Even though there are mental health resources at each college in America, it does not mean those resources are accessible and approachable.

My playing time was well earned that freshman season. I didn't play in every game, but I was grateful and accepted any playing time I got. But I wanted more. I felt that I had so much to prove. Not only to the new coaches but to those in my past who told me I wasn't good enough to play D1. I so badly wanted to be seen. Well, I suppose I wanted to be seen more than I ever had been before. Because the more I was seen on the field, the more I could hide other parts of myself that were starting to surface, parts I didn't want to show.

Parts that no one could see beyond the athletic front most people saw when they first looked at me, and not a college student who hid her feelings deeply and didn't yet dare to explore those feelings: depression and the feeling of being different. A different feeling that I could not quite name yet.

I felt like myself in a lot of ways, but I knew that the parts I hid were so different that I didn't want to show them. I also didn't know exactly what I was hiding. I hadn't realized yet that the different part of me was the fact that I'm gay.

Suppressing the feeling of being different reminded me of water on a stove with the heat on low. Anytime I felt the water starting to bubble inside, I tried my best to get it to remain still like a lake without a breeze. However, if the lake was in a warmer climate, I couldn't help but also pine for a breeze to make the hot stillness bearable.

It was all starting to turn into a constant push and pull. The more pull I felt to my pot heating up and feeling my truth coming out, the harder I'd run. The more I felt the steam rise, the more I would obsess over the game, training, and practice.

That dedication came with a reward. And the reward granted me a distraction from the looming thoughts crawling their way up inside me. I also knew there was a risk of losing that reward if I had let my sexuality boil over the pot.

This bubbling, though, remained in my thoughts as a feeling of being different. I wouldn't realize the exact 'different' feeling had a name until I allowed the water in the pot come to a boil. At first, I thought the 'different' parts of me were directly related to my mind and being depressed—not related to the fact that I found myself looking for or at Lauren during most bus rides to away games, team meetings, and even around campus.

We played Vanderbilt away in Nashville that year. I was awarded a whopping fifteen minutes of playing time towards the end of the first half. This was the moment that triggered my mind to start self-sabotage. The fifteen minutes to me made me think that I was only worth fifteen minutes as a player. I was only worth fifteen minutes as a person. *Did I suck that bad?*

My dad drove to the Vanderbilt game, and I felt guilty for having wasted his time; he drove all that way only to see me play for a whopping fifteen minutes.

At that game, the team got their shit together and we made two penalty kicks. Ole Miss won 3-2. Coach wanted to celebrate. I so badly wanted to leave after the game. I just wanted to get back to campus, back to my bed and sleep or watch a movie. I wanted to be by myself. At that point, I couldn't remember the last time I had time that was just mine—me, myself, and I.

After a quick hi and bye to my dad, we went to P.F. Chang's. I mean, where else would we go to celebrate a W? I wasn't hungry, but I ate anyway because that's what I was supposed to do. I said barely two sentences at the dinner, which, to me, felt as if it went on for several hours. *Why can't we celebrate with a nap? I would love a goddam nap. It's Sunday afternoon. Prime napping time.* I was too tired to think about school the next day and mounds of homework I needed to finish up before morning came. The NCAA bylaws state: "During the playing season, all countable athletically related activities (per Bylaw 17.02.1) shall be prohibited during one calendar day per week..." Thank goodness Mondays were off days. I needed one immediately.

We finally loaded the bus, some of us carrying boxes of leftovers. On the way back, I was relieved to not have to share my seat with another freshmen. At least I had that space to myself. I plugged my headphones in and listen to the same song repeatedly—Colbie Caillat's "Realize." And while I'm pretty sure the lyrics are about not telling someone else that you love them, I interpreted the song that day as realizing my own pain while others didn't—and I never spoke up.

I leaned my head against the window, catching a quick glimpse of myself in the glass. I was too sad and tired to even hold my own gaze. I pretended to sleep. As desperately as I wanted a nap, my body was not cooperating.

At some point during the bus ride, a junior on the team ran down the aisle of the bus. Cackling from behind me seeped in over the headphones and into my ears. The upperclassmen appeared next to me, standing.

"Hey, Ally!"

I turned my head.

"What?"

In her hand, there was a leftover piece of lettuce soaked in some kind of white sauce. I looked over at her just as she slapped the piece of lettuce in my face and then let it fall to the floor of the bus, left for a freshman, of course, to clean up when we got back to Oxford.

I have a good sense of humor when it comes to most things, even when I am depressed, but when I was as depressed as I was that day, her action shattered me. I wiped the ginger soy sauce off my face onto the sleeve of my formerly clean pullover.

I had no energy in me to cry or retaliate, but my insides fumed, tattooing this bad memory in my mind right alongside unbalanced chemicals. I wanted to scream, but I couldn't.

My insides did the screaming for me. *I am exhausted. CAN YOU NOT SEE ME? DO YOU NOT*

SEE HOW MUCH FUCKING PAIN I AM IN? I AM NOT EVEN PUTTING ON A BRAVE 'SMILING' FACE AT THIS POINT. I rested my blank face back against the window without outward reaction. *How dare you.*

The upperclassman ran to the back of the bus so fast, sure I'd chase after her as if she actually heard what my mind was screaming. I wish I could run from it. All of it. But for the next few hours, I was there, sitting, waiting, and wishing for the storm to pass. I turned the volume back up on my headphones and stared out the window as if nothing happened.

At some point during that bus ride back to Oxford, I pulled up the notes on my phone and wrote:

Driving along, driving along

Almost 3 hours repeat on the same song

Don't understand, don't know why

Wish someone would hear my silent cry

It could go one way or it could go another way

I have the voice, but I must choose what I want to say

Having everything I could ever ask for and even more than is given

I just go every day trying, livin' No one knows. No one sees.

Dear god, will you please?

Do not know why it comes and goes.

Mad at people, the one person that actually knows.

Need someone more than just a bystander, I'm a friend, a sister, a teammate, and daughter.

Do I act for me?

If I do will someone finally see?

Something is not right. Something is very wrong.

I try not to cry. I try to stay strong.

Don't want to disappoint those who have done so much.

But they disappointed me for not looking through the fake smiles and such.

I see with my eyes everything as a movie, I see what my life could be.

Over a thousand to choose from,

How come am I only hearing this one?

I probably won't say anything.

I'll just keep writing, keep laughing, and maybe sing.

Lots of rough times

How are people so fucking blind?

On a bus full of people,

Thoughts have crossed wanting to hang from a steeple.

I won't ever do it because I am thankful more than once a day.

I am beautiful and different in a beautifully different way.

Not sure why. Not sure when.

I don't believe only the good die young because those words were not truly sung. I will still wake up in the morning sun even though I truly see gray everywhere I run. Run. Run. Run.

Don't want to waste anymore days in bed.

When I'm 30, I want to be alive and 30 and not dead.

I'll let them all down if I don't follow my dreams.

I'll let down my sisters even though they didn't understand my seems.

Sit and think. Sit and think.

Feel like my boat is about to sink.

Just breathe. All I can do is breathe.

Frozen. Body is frozen for so long.

Over a thousand songs to choose from, how come I only listen to just one?

Those words flew out of me like a cloud that could no longer hold the weight of rain. I had forgotten about releasing words on a page, or in this case, words on a phone screen. I didn't feel much better after writing that little ditty above. However, I did sense a form of safe escape in writing those words. If only I remembered to write down my feelings more consistently, maybe I would've had a slightly better go of navigating the hard parts of that season—or any season of my life around that time.

Soon after I hit 'done' on my note app, Lauren texted me from the back of the bus. I don't remember how often we texted before that message popped up on my screen. The communication between us, though, became more frequent after that.

The vibration of my phone gave me a fuzzy feeling in my hand, but seeing a message from Lauren on my screen gave me a warmer, fuzzy feeling in my chest.

Her text said, "Are you okay?"

She was the first person to ask this question since I stepped foot on campus that summer.

I replied: "No, but I will be."

Lauren was, and probably still is, the embodiment from Shakespeare's *A Midsommar Night's Dream*: "Though she be but little she is fierce." She was stronger than me and had a matching work ethic to my own. She was kind and vulnerable and adored her family. She shut down every opponent that season, even when her ACL tore during an away game against the University of Florida in Gainesville.

I suddenly had the opportunity to step up and not only earn a starting spot but also show up for Lauren, who had just suffered a huge loss—bigger than our losing 3-0 that day.

When she went down, I pushed aside my off-kilter mind and the other issues looming inside me. That didn't matter at that moment. That could wait. Stronger feelings came in as she held her knee, laying on the hot turf. My heart sank for her. I felt compelled to hold her. To take away her pain. I wanted to take her ache away. Not just the physical ache of her injury but also the sadness that came along with a season ending injury.

When the trainer helped her off the field, I inched my way over to her on the sideline, a cup of water in my hand. I reached it out for her to take.

"Here," I said.

Our hands briefly touched as she took the cup from me. She took a sip and quietly said, "Thanks."

Her eyes drained, but she still looked beautiful. She put on a strong front and continued being an incredible teammate as she cheered the team on until the final whistle blew.

I rested my hand briefly on her shoulder and gave her a few gentle taps before stepping away. I slide a few feet down the bench but didn't go too far.

The game continued. As I tried to cheer on the team and focus on what was happening on the field, my mind was elsewhere. My mind was now occupied with what I could do for Lauren. I wanted to be there for her in a more intimate way, but I didn't know how to do that exactly.

So, I did what I knew how. I kept showing up for her as a friend. I sent encouraging texts and checked in with her. I'd type out longer messages, but the ending of those paragraphs was always met with backspace arrow held down by my thumb. I was afraid to say anything more. Afraid of rejection, probably. Afraid of a label I was not ready to accept.

Thoughts of dating Lauren really did not cross my mind. I felt an attraction to her that I could not shake. That attraction to her math-minded, mouse-loving, coffee drinking, kindhearted brilliance only grew as we were in each other's lives that semester. Those feelings and thinking about those feelings did not turn into thoughts of dating her.

Even if I did have thoughts of dating her, not only was she still a teammate, but dating teammates was frowned upon—another one of those unwritten, unspoken rules…Lauren was also seeing someone on and off that semester, a softball player named Cori. Cori was cute but tried too hard to be masc.

One evening after Lauren's procedure, Maren and I stopped by Lauren's apartment to check on her. Lauren's mom was there, having flown in to help her recover. She had cozied up in bed with her leg wrapped and propped on a leg support pillow.

Maren and I entered the room. Lauren's mom was sitting comfortably at the foot of the bed. And in a white t-shirt and basketball shorts with the lanyard to her car keys hanging out of her pocket, Cori stood right next to Lauren's nightstand.

Lauren looked tired and sad, although she managed to smile and laugh with us during that brief visit. Maren set the Get Well Soon balloon down next to the other Get Well Soon gifts. I said goodnight to Lauren and told her mom that it was nice meeting her.

We walked out of the room, and I turned around to give Lauren a smile, but a tiny crack in my heart formed when Cori had already moved closer to Lauren, blocking her view of me.

I was quiet the entire ride back to our dorm. I sent Lauren a text before bed saying it was good to see her and hoped she slept well. She replied the same and thanked me for stopping by with Maren. The last thought before I drifted to sleep was that Lauren hadn't lost any of her glow. Although she was going through a hard time, her warm energy and light hadn't faltered.

It was clear that night that Lauren and Cori were *on* again. I didn't want to meddle with that and knew I needed a distraction. So, I threw myself back into soccer even more than before, and I did the one Cori couldn't do: step up for Lauren on the soccer field.

After a pep talk with my dad, I mustered up the courage to call my coaches. Physically, the coaches could see that I was prepared for this starting position. It was now a matter of not just asking for what I wanted but demanding it. Even though I'd be playing defender, not my go-to position, I still fucking deserved it. As I passed through The Grove on the way to class, I dialed the coach's number. I told him I'd like to meet with him about the lineup, and he responded that I had beaten him to it. Calling me was on his to-do list that day, and he would like me to come meet with him and the rest of the coaching staff to discuss it further. I hung up the phone and entered the class with the most determination and focus I'd had since starting my journey at Ole Miss. At that moment, the deep depression I'd been under cleared for just a moment—hope, optimism. I totally thought I had it all figured out. LOL!

I was ecstatic, excited, and proud of myself. That was the first time in my life I'd spoken up for what I truly wanted: I asked for the ball off the field. Well, it was the first time I asked and didn't get yelled at in response. Someone finally saw my worth. Not only was I good enough, but I believed that I was good enough. I realized my talent and that there's no harm in asking for what I want, because the person answering just might say yes.

I met with the coaches before the next practice and was one step closer to securing a starting position ON A TEAM IN THE S.E.C. I couldn't believe it. My high school and middle school coaches would melt from regret that they ever told me I was not good enough to be a starter. As I walked into their offices, I said a silent *fuck you* to some former coaches because I knew I was about to make it happen. That said, I had one more obstacle before any final decisions were made: I had to compete with another teammate for the starting spot. Emily. The same teammate, one year earlier, that passed me up during the Cooper test as I threw up a banana.

Challenge accepted.

Only three practices were in place for me to make this happen. Well, 2.5 because

Thursday's practice was short. The starter would be announced at Thursday afternoon's meeting.

At Tuesday's practice, we did a one-on-one drill. The way the lines fell, I ended up going against Emily. I didn't let her beat me. I didn't give her the chance to even think about beating me.

That Thursday, it was announced that I would be the new starting defender. *I put myself here. I deserved to be here. I earned this.* I felt on top of the world, and I laughed because, at that moment, I truly believed that getting that starting position meant I had beaten my depression. I thought from this giant win that all the heaviness I'd been feeling would go away.

I was wrong. Depression didn't go away. It just got scared of my light and hid a little further inside of me until the light dimmed enough, once again, for it to return.

At that moment, however, I wasn't thinking about the inevitable return of the darkness within; I was riding on the high of rising to a challenge—of kicking ass in practice.

We can always do so much more than we think we can. The human capability can be pushed. We are all resilient, but not all humans rise up to what they are capable of. During practice that week, the realization sunk in that I was capable of more than I'd ever thought. I realized I liked who I was when I rose up. I made a mental note to always rise up as much as I can. If I was going to be there and continue my time with the team, I might as well make the most of it. With my newfound focus and energy, I let go of what had been holding me down, or I thought I did, but really, I just suppressed it more and more. Looking back, it's clear that I wasn't actually dealing with it at all. To deal with it meant to truly go inward, a place I didn't wish to go just yet. No matter how hard I focused on the sport or how hard I studied outside of it, that inkling of sadness still sat inside me.

At the starting announcements before the first whistle, the whole team formed two lines before each game. One across from the other that left a pathway about a yard and a half wide in between. When a starter's name was announced, she ran down the pathway, did a special handshake with a teammate at the end, then ran back up the path out on to the field to line up for the national anthem. My leg shook with nervousness as the announcer began. My first start as a college athlete right underneath the Friday night lights.

We were playing Georgia, and their coaches were the ones that recruited me to play for Ole Miss the summer before. Just like the freshmen, Ole Miss's current coaches were in their first year with the program, too.

The announcer finally got to my name, and I sprinted down the aisle as fast as I could. I didn't even think to slow down and enjoy this moment. Due to my nervousness, I went way too quickly and completely messed up my handshake, which Katie and I had spent the last twenty-four hours perfecting. Shit. And then I had to pee again. I told myself that I'd just sweat it out during the game and joined my teammates at midfield.

On a fall Friday night, both of my parents attended the game. I saw my dad at the opposite end of the field, holding an umbrella like a cane. During a lot of games, my dad could be found standing in a different area than my mom. He and I are alike in that way: standing away from the crowd, enjoying certain events in solitude. I heard my mom in the stands before I spotted her exact location. I did not mention to either of them I was starting that night. It was a surprise. My gift to them, showing that all our work and all their support had gotten me somewhere.

I beamed toward each of my parents, eyes wide, not saying out loud how awesome this was but feeling it together...experiencing it together. My focus flickered from the field back to each of them, stealing glances and trying to see if their reactions mimicked how I felt.

Just like that first day of preseason, I acted cool amongst my teammates. I stood a little taller that night during warmups and during the national anthem.

I was living, running proof that hard work pays off, and I will never forget that moment and how it made me feel despite rushing the opening.

Earning the starting position made it much more worthwhile than if it were handed to me. I had two goals for my performance during that game. The first was to give my mark a living hell. I would not leave her side. At least she wasn't lonely. You're welcome, sweetie.

The second is to not let Lauren down.

I played my ass off in that game and the few that followed. I believed I could, so I did. Nothing could get me down...except losing what I had worked so hard to earn.

CHAPTER III

Somewhere in the middle of the season, another freshman told one of the coaches that myself, Maren and another player spread a rumor around campus that she was a lesbian. First of all, we hadn't. My heart broke about the entire situation. I was angry and sad. Sad that this other teammate would tell on us without saying something to us before. Angry that someone would do this when I had been in so much pain for months. Angry at myself for not letting someone in. Angry that my coach didn't ask us if we had a side of the story. I had other shit to deal with. I stayed silent most of the meeting.

Sure, in some ways I was on an all-time high, but I was confused. Was that high just an escape? Was I in denial? Was I running away from my mind by clinging on to a few good times?

Being accused of spreading a rumor about someone else's sexual identity forced me to let go of the bad parts I was suppressing. However, this anger was directed at a situation and my teammate[1]. I wasn't dealing with my own feelings, but I was using the situation to lash out. I had an opportunity to release what I had been suppressing.

I was upset, of course, but grateful to be released finally after trying to shove that nagging voice inside me further down. The voice that crept in slowly and randomly and never left. The voice that told me I shouldn't seek help. The voice that choked me any time I wanted to say how I truly felt. I appeared happy on the outside, but on the inside, I was struggling deeply.

---

1 I am happy to report that the woman who told on us is now happily married to a woman.

After the meeting with one of our coaches, I sobbed to Maren on the concrete just outside the entrance of Gillom. I didn't have the space to deal with being accused of rumors. Even though I was ignoring them, I had my own battles to fight.

As tears fell, I yelled at Maren because of what happened, not because I was mad at her. I'm grateful she was there for me. As I calmed down, a thought entered my mind. One I had never thought of since the first time I kicked a soccer ball. I started to wonder if quitting was my only option to finally escape the pain in my insides. Not playing soccer any more would give me the free time to rest. Rest my body from all the sports I played since I was a child. I could rest my mind, get to know myself, and dig deeper into the root cause of feeling inadequate and why.

Now, this is when the structure of soccer became a double-edged sword. The familiarity of it was comforting because it was what we all knew, but I was starting to get burnt out from the repetition. I was running out of distractions, and the other side of the sword started to sharpen...and fast.

Things got worse after I lost my starting position. I frequently contemplated leaving the team.

But if I left the game, then I would be stepping into the unknown. Was I willing to give up the comfort and safety of soccer? I wasn't sure right then, but I thought that soccer was the sole reason for making me so sad. So, I did a math equation...the simplest of them all, and thought I had my answer. Life - soccer = happy.

I was starting to convince myself that if I eliminated the external issue, then my mental health would be fixed. I spent days going back and forth with myself: *If I quit, am I wasting my talent? Am I giving up too soon? Does it even matter that I'm good? Who am I good for?*

Am I still playing for myself or am I playing for this coach I just met to win him games? To win him over? To win more playing time? To make him look good?

Am I playing to prove others wrong?

Will I miss it?

What would I do if I quit?

I thought of quitting many times my freshman season. I dreamt of an autumn without soccer. A summer without two-a-days. A winter without strength and conditioning. I dreamt about what I'd do with those days. I dreamt of another path. But those dreams were tarnished while I struggled with letting go of something I wasn't going to finish.

I still loved the game. I still love it today. At different points during my freshman season, though, the hope was dwindling. Earning playing time. Winning games. Scoring goals. It still mattered, but I found myself questioning that maybe there were other things that mattered more. Maybe it was time to move on. But I wanted so badly to finish what I'd started, not just a few months ago when I stepped on campus but fifteen years ago when a little girl fell in love with the game and wanted to play it at the highest level her body would allow.

I had now less than four seasons left, and I wanted to see it through. I wanted to graduate from Ole Miss with a theatre degree and four years of soccer. Surely, I could find a way to suck it up and push through. That's what I was taught to do. Push through. Push. Push. Push. Never sit and feel. If things get uncomfortable, gotta push through it. There is some good truth to that, and my habit of *keep going* has gotten me through more bad times than I can count. However, as I still hadn't yet understood, pushing through also meant pushing feelings down. They had to go somewhere.

With as much excitement as you feel when you daydream about another life, the other edge of that sword's sharpness comes from the unknown. *How could I break away from something like that? Would I be betraying the game if I left before I saw it through to my finish line? Would I be betraying myself? What happens if I don't execute the biggest dream come true for me?*

As time went on, the sword sharpened on both sides. I ignored the fact that despite soccer being the greatest known in my life, it was also filled with unknowns each year. I didn't know what team I'd be playing on after I got unexpectedly cut from my club team when I was twelve. I didn't know how high school tryouts would go. I didn't know what team I'd call home when I moved from St. Louis to Pittsburgh back to St. Louis between ages nine and eleven. I figured it all out, though, and it wasn't as scary as I thought it'd be.

A lot of those unknowns were out of my control. That was OKAY, but I didn't take into consideration that I had survived so many unknowns before. I didn't see it because the unknowns were masked by a greater known, which was always soccer.

LIFE is the greater unknown, but what we fail to realize a lot of the time is that there are so many knowns within life. And the thing about the unknown is that it becomes less unknown as time goes on, and eventually, you find your new normal. The narrative we build up becomes this scary gross dragon, but who are we to say that we can't do it? Look at all we've done so far. Look! LOOK! LOOK! LOOK! If you can't see it, ask someone to tell you, to show you. I don't always see things for myself, but having someone else point it out helps a hell of a lot.

CHAPTER IV

After one grueling practice, I set out for a long drive. I didn't tell anyone I was leaving or where I was going—I didn't know myself. My head was in dire need of clearing. I needed to feel free. The speed limit on campus was eighteen miles an hour, and nowhere in town did the speed limit exceed forty unless you were driving on the highway. So, that's where I went: the highway. I was still careful not to speed; the speedometer reaching sixty satisfied me enough. I'm not an adrenaline junkie, far from it, actually, but the high that speed gave me is something I struggle to describe. I dreamt for a moment of driving down to the coast, to the water. Dipping my toes in the sand and feeling the coolness of the saltwater swaying over my feet. That was a short-lived fantasy. My lack of adventure and money forced me to turn the car around. I may have been a runner, but I never ever went too far.

Back on campus, I turned my phone back on and was reassured of my spot in the world when a handful of texts and voicemails appeared on my screen. Maren and some other teammates were at the FedEx center, a facility for student athletes to study and work. I grabbed a protein bar from my dorm and my schoolwork and left again to meet them. I entered the building with a smile on my face, laughing as Maren lovingly yelled, "where the heck have you been?" I told her the truth: "I just went for a little drive is all."

The next several days were good days. I laughed and goofed around with my friends. Classes were fun and I was engaged in discussions and spent more focused time in the library. I made an effort in my friendships outside of soccer. I reconnected with some friends from back home that also went to Ole Miss. I was finding balance. I thought, *Look at me. I'm doing okay. No way I'm depressed! Right?*

Wrong. I was so so so so wrong.

That great week and good morning I had going for me ended abruptly, and the walls of distraction I built came crumbling down immediately, when, without warning, I lost my starting position. It was given to Kelly.

Talk about a punch to the gut.

I was devastated, not just because my distraction from my depression was taken away abruptly, but also because I knew the ignored feelings would start coming up faster and louder. I didn't want to feel any of those feelings. Not even a little.

Throughout the season, the coaches held scouting report meetings to watch films from upcoming opponents and to strategize. At one particular meeting, the coaches announced that Kelly would be a starting defender, replacing me. My throat immediately tightened. My tear ducts readied to open. I shoved my hands in my pockets. The tears, though, stayed behind their gate and didn't storm my cheeks until I was alone. I didn't dare let them see me lose composure.

Kelly smiled and nodded her head, accepting congratulations and high-fives without as much as a thank you in return. It was like she knew they were going to announce this. Not only did I lose that starting spot, but I was also sent back to square one: getting little to no playing time. It truly felt like the end of days. Yes, I appeared in eighteen games, but just like my mood that semester, those appearances were up and down. The inconsistency played was jerking around my mind, which was already on an internal rollercoaster. It was all becoming way too much.

Of course, I was thankful that I was still given any playing time at all, and I was grateful and humbled. But without an explanation or warning that Kelly would be taking over my starting position, I was left to think that I was an awful sack of dog crap stinking up the house but hidden out of sight.

I suck. I am not good enough.

My hard work paid off, but it didn't last long enough for me to fully enjoy it. It wasn't enough. It was taken away from me too soon. The inconsistency of that season made me feel incompetent and worthless on that team and in the sport.

Was it the inconsistency or the depression? Was the inconsistency a result of the depression, or was the depression a result of the inconsistency? And since when did I need consistency and routine? I had never realized that routine was all I knew: sleep, eat, school, soccer, repeat. The good at that time did not outweigh the bad. I feared what this news would do to my already hurt mind.

There were absolutely zero conversations about me not starting the next game. Sure, I'd had a terrible game against Tennessee the weekend before, and in the world of competitive soccer in America, a lot of times, that meant this player goes right back to the bench. *That'll teach 'em.*

Bench them without explanation. Without warning. HA!

But I truly wish the coaches had thought highly enough of me to at least have an individual conversation.

At the meeting where the change was announced, there was no energy left in me to fight back and demand the ball again. Not this time. I just wanted to be done. I felt that I had nothing left to give.

After the meeting, we were told to go to a different facility to take ice and hot baths. I dragged myself there, crumbling within, while Kelly was having the time of her fucking life—laughing with the upperclassmen and other freshman starters. She felt the same way I had felt just a few weeks ago. I wanted to slap her. I wanted to slap that smug smile and dumb laugh right out of her stupid body. Sometimes people need to be slapped. I knew I wouldn't, though. I never fought dirty like that—except for a few times ON the field against an opponent.

I left the rehab center early and went outside to cry on the curb. A minute or so later, I heard the door open and shut. Strong footsteps approached me. I sat on the curb with my knees to my chest and my head tucked. The footsteps stopped, and LC, another teammate, sat down next to me. I briefly looked at her and shook my head.

"Yeah, I know," she said to me, patting me on the shoulder. A simple gesture that took away some of the loneliness at that moment, making the pain slightly more bearable. Perhaps some of the hurt evaporated with that little touch.

"I don't understand," I blubbered. "I was totally blindsided."

LC nodded. Her long brown hair was in a low ponytail with baby hairs sticking out of her hairline. Her red soccer socks bunched at her ankles. She crossed her feet.

"Don't let them get to you," she told me.

"Feels like they already have," I said.

"You'll be alright. It's a shitty thing, but you are stronger than you think you are."

"I guess," I said with a pathetic nod.

I had no jokes to shake this like I did in the past. Going through a hard time? Here's a joke to cope.

"You are. Come on. Let's go back in," LC said as she stood up, pulling me up with her.

We walked back inside as I wiped the rest of the tears before they dried on my salty face. I had never felt lower than that afternoon, but having another teammate see my pain eased it. Even if our interaction that day was only for a few minutes, I still think of it often.

Up until that point, soccer had always been an outlet. My outlet. Anytime I had a bad day at school or later when depression appeared in my life, soccer made everything better. Soccer made everything easier until it didn't.

Depression was the only one to blame for my poor performance. Soccer had failed to be my distraction. I found this all sorts of fucked up. Working out releases endorphins. Working out helps with depression. Eating healthy helps with depression. I was not consuming alcohol during the season except once or twice. Nothing I was doing felt like enough to not feel that awfulness. My quick fixes slowly stopped working. Soccer would be the one thing that had to go, but what was I going to do without it? Who would I be without it?

Contemplating quitting brought up new anxieties and fears. I did not know how to separate my soccer life from my regular life. Soccer was my life. Soccer was my priority, even more so upon entering college. As the rest of the season went on, I continued to see little to no playing time. On a line chart, my freshmen season was sketched with several zig zags. I started with some playing time, shot right up to the top with lots of playing time, then catapulted down to riding the bench, which I clawed the sides of, a meager attempt to hold onto my previous high.

How did I get here? My body could take it. My body could play great soccer. But my mind was not connected to my body. Negative thoughts prevented me from moving my legs and body the way that she should do to compete. To win. To thrive. I deserved both. I deserved all of it.

At practices, the coaches split the team up. The starters and frequent subs on one side, everyone else on the other. To keep the "everyone else" group in shape, those players are conditioned harder during practices since they don't play much in games. During preseason, the coaches kicked one woman off the team because she failed the fitness tests too many times in a row.

I was put back in the group with everyone else. During keep away, I hit an invisible wall, a wall that would present itself again and again throughout the next decade of my life. This was the first time I felt it. I stopped. I tried to move, but my legs became heavier, and the grass then felt like hardening mud. One coach was particularly annoyed by my lack of drive. I knew it was not my best play, but my mind forbade my body from doing as I was told. Sports are 90% mental after all.

Come on, Ally. Get it together. ***But you can't. You suck. You shouldn't even be here. Just give up.*** *But I don't want to give up!* ***I'm not giving you the choice today. Today, I win, Ally.***

But you don't deserve to win, depression. ***Then why am I still here?***

I made a mistake.

"Ally, what are you doing?" Coach says.

I dove in for a ball.

"Come on, Ally!"

I passed a ball to no one, and it rolled out of bounds.

"Jesus Christ!"

I stopped, took a deep breath and stared at the ground.

"Ally? What is wrong with you today?"

Today. What is wrong with me today? **What's wrong with her today? Ha. I've been here all along, Coach.** *How about what's been wrong with me for the last two months? I am done.*

Mhmm. You are done. I win.

I wondered if my coach even noticed the difference in my outward appearance: my eyes were puffy from crying and always on the verge of new tears. My hair resembled a rat's nest. My skin broke out more than usual. The only reason I had not lost weight yet was because this depression at least let me keep my appetite. I jogged off the field toward the locker room—before practice concluded.

"Sure, walk off! Just go."

In the locker room, I immediately took off my gear and changed into my running shoes. The rest of the team came in, only a handful aware that I skipped on the last ten minutes of practice.

"Hey, you okay?" Maren asked.

"Drive my car back to the dorm and take my bag, will you?" I tossed her my keys and put my bag in front of her locker.

"Yeah, but are you okay?"

I responded with silence, which answered the question well enough: no, I was not okay.

I left Gillom. I stretched my quad as I overheard some teammates talking about me.

"What is she doing?"

"What's with her?"

"Where's she going?"

"Does she know practice is over?"

Anger boiled up inside me as some of them laughed. I never verified if they were, in fact, laughing at me, but my mind convinced me they were. I sprinted the mile and a half back to my dorm, failing to make eye contact with Lauren, who watched me leave and ignoring her as she called after me.

I didn't understand how I could run by myself just *fine*, but I couldn't continue practice. My legs were not working like usual.

Or was it my mind?

When I got back to the dorm, I took a shower and directly went to bed. My thoughts wandered like the zig zagged line chart of my playing time. Eventually, I fell into a deep sleep.

I counted the days until our season ended. I convinced myself that the soccer season had made me that way. Made me depressed. Most of my teammates counted down the days until they could drink. I would drink, too, on that day, but in my mind, I counted down the days until the season ended so I could go back to feeling like myself, whoever she was, wherever she was. *Once season ends, so will my depression.* I held on to that logic for years, not realizing that external gratification and external things would never help my mental health.

Although external validation is needed and valid during many occasions and for many reasons, it was internal work that would be the key to my healing.

As I sprinted back to the dorm that day, my thoughts raced along with my feet. There I was, again, running away, but my mind was just as quick. I could not escape it this time. I could not escape the darkness I wished to push down, could not acknowledge that others did not see the depression behind my eyes, and could not see that soccer was not the reason I felt the way I did. At that moment, all I could do was run until my body and brain were too tired to continue.

CHAPTER V

A week or two earlier, Lauren met me for lunch at the student union. I trusted her more than my coaches or anyone else in Oxford. Lauren and I had been texting frequently, always as friends. There was never an ulterior motive with either of us. Our feelings for each other were natural and grew slowly over time, starting as teammates and then becoming good friends.

I didn't want to turn to my coaches for help. I didn't want them to see me as weak or for them to think that I couldn't handle the pressure, that I wasn't strong enough to keep up with the demands of being a division one student athlete. I ordered a sandwich but barely touched it. I was nervous and grateful that someone was there who understood what I was going through. She shared her own story with me with ease, and as she spoke, I became hopeful. What she went through during her freshman year two years prior mimicked what I felt right then. I started to believe that I, too, could get through this. As she was speaking, though, I found my attention slipping away from her words more than once. She was kind, funny, patient, and human…and adorable and pretty.

Although she was still claiming her truth at that time, I could tell that she had a strong sense of self; she was well on her way to living her truth. I, however, had a long way to go to get there. In that moment, even with her company, I felt stuck, unable to seek that strength or a truth of my own. Here in this body. Here with this mind. My feet sank in black tar that dried faster than I could pull my feet out.

I tried to lift my feet using all the muscles from my calves to my quads to my glutes and abs, but I couldn't move. There I was, in the best shape of my life, unable to move. All I could do was keep trying to free my feet until the tar finally broke. Oh, and it would certainly break at some point, but not without leaving pieces of it Gorilla glued to my skin.

With Lauren there, I believed I could be unstuck. I felt different around her. Better. Lighter. Comfortable. Happy? Maybe. I had forgotten what exactly that felt like. However, even with Lauren next to me, I still found it hard to verbally open up. Typing my feelings out on a tiny screen was so much easier than hearing them come out of my mouth.

"Have you thought any more about telling your parents?" she asked.

"Yes, I have," I said as I took a big bite of my sandwich. Not because I was hungry, but so I could use it as a tool to keep me from talking about my feelings.

"I just," I started to say.

I took a long drink from my water bottle wishing it was something even slightly stronger than water. I swallowed then exhaled.

"It's so hard to talk out loud about it," I confessed.

Lauren put a hand on my shoulder and said, "I understand. Maybe you don't have to say it out loud. You could write it out. Maybe in a letter or an email.

"Email. A letter would take too long to get there, and I need them to know now."

Lauren gave my shoulder light squeeze. I smiled at her and held back my tears by forcing myself to finish my lunch.

I wanted to tell my parents how I was feeling, but even with Lauren's support and kindness, I was afraid to speak up. How was I supposed to tell my parents that I was so unhappy when they'd done so much for me? With each inhale, I anticipated saying how I felt and before I could speak an imaginary avocado pit lodged in my throat. At that time, I was capable of only yes or no questions. I took a bite of my sandwich and drank a long drink of my water to wash down the seed.

Later that night, I drafted an email. I finished editing and rewriting it in Maren and Kelly's dorm on their futon. It took me all of twenty minutes to write but over three days to send.

I sent the following e-mail to my mom on October 17, 2010 at 7:22pm.

Hi Motha,

Bare with me.

I really do not know how to put any of this, but it's been on my mind and in my heart for a while now. We both know that recently, it has been hard for me, but I do not think you understand how hard it has been. I can't fall asleep at night because I don't know how I am going to feel when I wake up. I have not laughed like I normally do in a really long time, and I have not been myself. I get so angry at the dumbest things, and it's just not me. I'll be on the verge of tears if I forget to grab a cup of water before class, and I get so mad if the line at the union is too long when it's really not even long, to begin with. It's not your fault, it's not my fault, it's not soccer's fault, it's not anyone's fault. It's not about the roommate, it's not about not being able to go out, and it's not about being away from home. It is getting to the point where it's affecting everything I do. I can't laugh or make someone else laugh because I simply just do not want to. I do not want to do anything. I take naps when I'm not even tired. I just do not care if I yell at someone or get mad at them. I know you want me to have fun, but I can barely have a conversation with someone, let alone a funny one. It's not that I don't want to be here or that I am homesick, but I just am not myself, and I hate being like this. I have to force myself to do well at practice, and I am not myself in my classes. I am the weird girl that doesn't talk that much. I keep thinking all of the sadness I am feeling will go away, but it hasn't. Sometimes, I will randomly get bursts of energy and be in a good mood, but it won't last long. Whatever it is, it's taking over me, and it is not going away. I hate this. I do not have any reason to feel this way. You and dad give me everything I could ever ask for and more than that, and I cannot be happy. I do not want to worry you or make you upset, but I cannot live in this slump any longer. I know I will have some bad days, but this is bull shit, and it's been going on way too long. It isn't because I haven't been meeting people, it's because I don't talk to people. It's not because soccer is time consuming. If I didn't play soccer, it could be worse. Honestly, I think my grades have been so good because that's all I do is schoolwork outside of soccer, and I am not messing around in and outside class because my mind and heart simply just cannot do anything more than the homework or the soccer or the simple motions. I wasn't going to say anything, but [Lauren] helped me a lot and talked me through it because she went through the same stuff her freshman year, too. I figured this was my one major fault. I'm not perfect; nobody is, but I just assumed that it would be something that would come and go throughout my life and will never go away. I will not get anywhere in life if I always feel like this. Lauren helped me realize that I don't have to feel like this. Sure, there will be some bad days here and there, but I can't laugh, I am frozen, and it's been like this for so long. I'm sorry I didn't say anything sooner, but I thought that it would go away. I don't know what to do. I'm scared. I need help, more than you and dad can give me. I cannot wait until the season is over. I'm not even sure if it would just go away after the season, but if it can get any worse than it already is, I don't want to take the risk. Today was a good day, though. I am not sure why, but it was a better day than it has been lately. I was myself a lot more, but not fully. It was a good day today.

Love you!

- AL

Instead of replying virtually, my mom called me minutes after hitting send. She cried so hard I could not hear what she said, but I cried instantly.

Through tears and 355 miles she asked, "Are you suicidal?"

"No," I replied, and that was the truth. Had some suicidal thoughts crossed my mind? Yes, but they were very few and only lasted a moment. I did not want to act on them. It wasn't an option.

"Do you want to come home?" Mom asked.

"Now?"

"Yes, now."

"No. I want to stay."

If I ran home to my mom and dad, then I'd look like a baby. That would be weak, and I was not weak. Leaving would also mean failing, and I did not want to fail. Not once did my mom deny my feelings or my pain, though. She understood my pain. While telling this story in hindsight, I refer frequently to my depression. However, at that time, I did not have a name for the feelings I was feeling…or not feeling. That was until my mom said it—the word "depression" associated with my experiences for the first time.

Before that, I did not know there was a name for what I was going through. Sure, I had heard of depression. Who hasn't? But me having it? That was a tougher pill to swallow than the pit of an avocado.

I had (and still have) depression simply because my brain's chemicals were imbalanced. The adjustment to college may have triggered it. That's the only reason I can think of…other than soccer. My mental health was not where I wanted it to be. I found I was constantly reminding or convincing myself that I wanted to be there, that I couldn't go home. But I couldn't truly parse whether it was my surroundings or just my own mind that I wished to escape from. Even though I was grateful for the support from my mom, I was more confused after talking with her because that was when treatment options came into play.

It felt foreign to think about treatment and medical professionals as if I had some disease. I hadn't even yet wrapped my mind around the fact that something was wrong with me, so to think about treating that something caused me to disassociate immensely.

Of course, I did not protest my mother's help. I obliged. She made me an appointment with a psychiatrist for when I'd be home for winter break. I texted Lauren and let her know how it went with my Mom. I thanked her for her support and encouragement, expressing that I truly didn't think I could've hit send without her ongoing support.

I did not understand depression. I did not understand how I had worked so toward a dream, and when I arrived at that dream, I became depressed. I had friends, a loving family, and hopes; I was in college, playing soccer for a school in the SEC, studying theatre. How did depression wander in when my life was so wonderful?

CHAPTER VI

Our very last game of the season was against Mississippi State. A restaurant's disorganization in Starkville lead to a lengthy pre-game dinner. They had ample time to prepare our meals that we preordered. Famished and desperate to feed the beast inside me, my hangriness reached a whole new level. A teammate picked up on this and asked: "Ally, what's wrong?"

"Nothing."

"Come on, what's wrong?"

Let's see…my food is late. And I'm depressed. Like really fucking depressed. I honestly do not believe it will ever pass or that I'll amount to anything in this life, but hey, I had a good run, I guess: D1 soccer, haven't murdered anyone yet, and I am making your life so much easier by not saying all of this. Oh, and MY FOOD IS LATE.

What I actually said: "Nothing. I'm fine."

Pretending I was fine was becoming harder and harder. I may not have said it out loud, but I said it with my face, my hair, my attitude, and body language. Depression wrote itself all over my body now.

Since arriving back in August, I had not felt cold in Mississippi, but this trip to Starkville was different. One of the reasons I chose to go to school in the south was the warm weather. I loathe the cold. My body aches in the cold and shrinks my blood circulation. That day in Starkville, it was so cold that they broke out the winter parkas for us. I didn't see a second of playing time until there were two minutes left in regulation when coach told me to go in. I muttered, "What's the point?" Just loud enough for Carlee and Maren to hear.

Carlee said, "Just go. End on a high note. It's bullshit, but in two minutes, it'll all be over for a while." Favored to win, we were down by one. The coaches were not happy, and everyone could feel the tension waiting for us on the ride back to Oxford. With Carlee's support, I took off the warm parka, jogged down and back a few times on the sideline, and then headed to midfield to sub in for Kelly. I called Kelly off the field. She's one of those runners that swings her head from side to side when she runs, usually looking down. I jogged toward her and stuck out my hand, not for sportsmanship but more out of instinctual habit.

She slapped it as we passed each other.

I ran around on the field for those last 120 seconds before the final whistle blew. I touched the ball once or twice. Our season ended and Mississippi State celebrated their 2-1 win. Ole Miss, on the other hand, all looked like dogs with our tails between our legs afraid of our angry, disappointed owners—otherwise known as our coaches.

After boarding the bus, we were given our usual *top notch* postgame meal, Domino's pizza, passed out by our team manager. Gatorade shakes were passed out to players who played half of the game or longer, a usual postgame beverage that's sipped on as coaches give a rundown of the game. As silence overcame the entire trip back, I silently cried. It was over for now, and for now, I could be free…or so I thought.

I have always been a loving fan of this Latin quote by Ovid: "Perfer et obdura, dolor hic tibi proderit olim." Which translates to: "Be patient and tough; someday this pain will be useful to you." I was born tough, so now I just needed to perfect patience. Easy peasy…right? I discovered the quote during a Saturday in between episodes of one of America's greatest high school dramas, when I'd spent the entire day in my dorm on my hot pink futon binge watching *One Tree Hill* snuggled up on my hot pink futon.

My door was open. Some friends and floor-mates passed by on their way out and asked why I wasn't dressed to tailgate in the Grove. I told them I was skipping the Grove and the football game, but I might meet up with them later. I had more important things to do: watch a show that I had seen at least half a dozen times already.

Fortunately, they accepted this and did not protest my decision not to follow a day of drinking with a night of it. Soccer season was over, and all I wanted to do on this fall day was sit and do nothing. I had been overworked mentally and physically in the last few months, but not academically. I looked forward to the rest of the semester. I would then have the time for myself to focus on my studies and also hang out with friends from class. I hadn't had a day to myself in months. I needed to be free of chatter and bodies everywhere I turned. It was a perfect day to stay in, too. It was cloudy, making my room a little darker in the daylight. I loved that. Between episodes, I googled different quotes about pain to see if anything resonated with me that would give me hope. The one I just mentioned was one of the first quotes that came up on my search. I immediately wrote it down in my planner and copied and pasted it into my notes on my laptop. It wasn't much, but it was something for me to hold on to.

I liked going where the crowd was not. I was utterly jazzed when the entire town was a few hundred yards from my dorm tailgating in The Grove, getting ready to attend a football game later that day. That meant the floor was empty, all mine for most of the day.

After half a season of OTH and a nap, I gathered enough energy to shower. I returned from my shower to several texts and missed calls from Maren and some teammates wanting me to join them. I looked at the safety and comfort of my dorm and took a deep breath. I texted them back, ignoring my own wants yet again, and said I'd meet them within an hour. However, I refused to wear a dress to tailgate.

Ole Miss tailgates are legendary and notorious for being *fancy*. Fans dress in their Sunday best, cater food, and set up satellite TVs. Some even bring nice silverware and dishes. I've even seen *modest* chandeliers hanging from the center of some tents. I never really cared for football. While I understand why they take the ball through a pile of men in the middle of the field, I don't understand why they don't go long and wide more often. It's all about strategy, I'm told.

In lieu of a dress, I wore jeans, a long-sleeve pink shirt, and boots. I borrowed Maren's black pleather jacket and black and white animal print scarf. I didn't care that I was casually dressed compared to the majority of tailgaters. I was comfortable. Earlier in the football season, the team went to a game. I wore a bright yellow, flowing mini dress, but I later changed into shorts and a polo top. Wearing dresses to a football game just didn't make any sense to me. It is football.

Not a school dance. Not a wedding reception. Not a damn polo match at Windsor. It's fucking football.

As soon as I entered my friends' tent, I was handed an opaque plastic cup from Newk's filled with alcohol. The Grove was littered with underage college students holding these kinds of cups from local eateries. I hadn't asked for this cup. I did not want this cup. The person handing it to me thought it was fun. Assuming, maybe? Why isn't anyone asking me what I want? I would've rather had some water, maybe mozzarella sticks, then gone straight back to binge watching. Instead, I graciously and enthusiastically accepted the cup, just as expected of a college student.

I was playing the part.

"What's in this?"

"Just drink it, freshman!" someone yelled.

I sniffed and sipped; to my relief, it was just a sweet white wine. Ninety minutes later, though, I was hammered.

We stopped at the campus Subway to carb up before we went out. I needed to eat something.

Anything. I hadn't eaten that much during my One Tree Hill marathon. *It has only been an hour, Ally—go back to the futon where it's safe. Chug some water. Go back and watch a movie. Sleep!* But I did not do what the better part of my mind told me to. I didn't listen to my inner voice, which actually had my back for the first time in months. That wasn't the depression talking. That was me. Depression said **all you need is a sandwich. Rally, Ally. Eat. Drink some water and then rally. You deserve to have fun.** *But fun for me is staying in and basking in a quiet room only filled with noise coming from a rom-com.*

Instead of briefly disappointing my teammates, I chose to disappoint myself again. A small part of me worried that my mind would take a dip into unknown waters if I were to stay in by myself that night. If I entered those waters of deep thoughts, I knew I'd wish for a substance to suppress them. I wasn't ready to think too much about my attraction to Lauren and how I had become so unhappy with soccer. So, I caved in annoyingly easily, and instead of waiting for my mind to wish for a substance, I went out and got it.

I may have gotten started drinking early that night, but this head start came with an inkling of the smallest possibility that this night would be different.

And it was different but badly different.

Eating some type of bread or a large meal was all part of the pre-game ritual. I loudly announced my order, but in my drunken stupor, I ordered the wrong thing, which I ate anyway. I changed my shirt into a more party appropriate top but kept the jacket and scarf. I touched up my makeup and filled up a different Newk's cup filled with a fresh bottle of white wine. Three or four different songs blasted from dorm rooms throughout the floor. We danced between sips while taking photos with our laptop's cameras.

I can handle this right now. This is fun. We should just stay here. MAYBE if I announce we should play a game instead tonight, they'll go for it. I am so tired.

I didn't say anything.

"Alright! Let's go! Y'all ready?" Kelly shouted as she passed my room.

"Hell yeah!" I yelled back.

"Damn right! Hotty Toddy gosh almighty who the hell are we? Hey! Flim. Flam. Bim. Bam.

Ole Miss by damn!"

And then ten minutes later, we were back on The Square in line for a bar called the Library. I kept drinking, knowing very well I should have stopped hours prior. The first time I truly binge drank in college, I didn't know how to stop. One drink was handed to me after another, and I was far from comfortable saying 'no' to other people, especially ones who were my teammates and/or those who claimed to be my friend. I didn't have a fake ID my freshman year because I didn't need one. While some bars in Oxford had 21 and over sections, all of them were 18+. So, getting in the door was not an issue. Upperclassmen would purchase drinks for us, or I'd pretend to flirt with a guy to get him to buy me one.

I didn't need to learn how to act like this. I felt pre-programmed to take the drink I was offered and dance with any guy who asked… or any guy who *didn't* ask. Conversations with female friends in high school dreaming about going to college parties. Movies and TV shows that portrayed high school and college kids getting drunk.

Like in *Mean Girls* when Cady Heron throws a party when her parents are out of town and is totally overdressed, and drinks too much to win over Aaron Samuels. Or in *One Tree Hill*'s early seasons, when Brooke Davis does anything at a basketball game after party.

Just like a lot of those TV and film scenes, as I looked around me at other bargoers, most if not all of them college students, everyone seemed intoxicated on some level. I always felt I needed to be on one of those levels. There was not much else to do socially in this small town in 2011. Not as a student athlete. Not for a tall, beautiful blonde like me. However, like I just mentioned, I didn't know how to stop drinking once I started. It also didn't help that I loved the taste of beer and whiskey. I guzzled it a lot of the time like it was water.

The more alcohol that entered my body, the more my mind told me I needed it. No one was going to stop me, either. I scanned the bar, and the first guy I made eye contact with bought me a drink. Like most guys I met in bars, I gave him a real phone number, but it was not mine. I usually gave out a former childhood friend's. Sorry, Dani.

I wished the Library was a real library, wished I was surrounded by books so neatly aligned and ordered, the comfort and hope of endless possibilities waiting to be explored. But this was the opposite of a real library. Instead of growing, I was killing braincells and heightening the anxiety in my body, trying to fit in but making myself more depressed in the process. What a big price to pay. But hey, at least I was being a college student. How does one go to Ole Miss or almost any college and not party? I told myself it was necessary. And it's not lost on me that I could have spent more time at real libraries.

A week later, Maren and I were leaving Lauren's apartment, and the guy I gave the wrong number to that night at the bar was walking up the stairs. He called me out on it, but I laughed and ran away. I was always running from confrontation, literally—the only place I ran toward it was on the soccer field. I faced conflict head on when I played.

I felt I had to participate in a night out simply because it was the Saturday night of Halloween weekend. Halloween may have been the excuse, but we weren't dressed in costume.

Well, I was okay until Maren did something she had done dozens of times before and would do a hundred times again: she took a drink from my drink. This time, though, I hit the Wall.

The Wall is what I refer to as the point of no return when I was intoxicated. The point I inevitably hit after binging too much. The only true way to outrun the Wall was to stop myself from getting there, but stopping myself from drinking too much did not happen often.

As Maren handed me my drink back, I looked at her like she'd killed my dog. I slapped the cup out of her hand and sprinted out of the bar.

There was no rhyme or reason as to why that triggered me to run. Maybe my mind was just looking for another excuse to run.

I ran directly to a different bar up the street on the corner: Taylor's Pub. I didn't want to pay the $5 cover, so I climbed through the window like I normally did. This was one of my prouder party tricks.

Two minutes after I stuck the landing inside the bar from window to floor, I stole a shot from the bar top while I made my way to the dance floor. Seconds later, some frat bro in a breathalyzer costume started kissing me and touching me. The mouthpiece of the costume stuck out of his crotch. He pinned me against a wall near the DJ booth. Two girls from my acting class pulled him off me, thank God, because I was no longer in control. I thanked the girls, but as soon as I saw an exit, I took it and ran again. This time, I went across the Square and back toward my dorm, which was over a mile.

I slowed down and stopped in front of my dorm. I stared at it, knowing I should go inside. Get that water and food then shower and cry if I still felt like it. *Go, inside*, a whisper said to me, but the loudness of my legs taking off drowned out any help I could give myself. Going back inside meant there was a chance I'd admit something I was not able to admit. I felt that to not question any hard truths about myself, I needed to wear out my mind and body. If I did that, then I could pass out before my mind had the chance to wander.

As I ran, I called at least two of my guy friends to tell them what I was up to. Miraculously, I still had my phone and wallet. I ran toward two other dorms at the bottom of a huge hill. That's where the guys were. I remember my friend Tim pulling me away from cars that I kept kicking and punching. He held me, trying to calm me down, trying to keep me from running. Drunk me did not like this. His grasp felt like a tight rope, even though it came from a place of care.

They tried to help, and I was later grateful for that, but on that night or any other night, no one ever asked me why I was running. They just told me not to drink so much next time. Or pace myself. Or not to mix alcohol. Or to drink water with my liquor.

Or Or Or Or.

The best alternative that someone could have suggested to me at the time? Not drinking at all. But we were all just college kids, giving in to the college life. Booze. Drugs. Sex. Booze. Drugs. Sex.

I wasn't having sex yet, but stay tuned, my friend...we'll get there.

I wish college for me would've been: Books. Coffee. Laughter. Writing. Learning. Books.

Coffee. Laughter. Writing. Learning. Books. Coffee. Laughter. Writing. Learning. Books. Coffee. Laughter. Writing. Learning. Twelve years after that drunken 5k, I am finally living a life with just that: Books. Coffee. Laughter. Writing. Learning. But it took a long hard road to get there with rough terrain, high winds, and unpredictable speeds and turns.

That night as I continued my escapades, I escaped from Tim's grasp and sprinted away again. Neither of those guys were in half the shape as I was. It was easy to outrun them. It was not so easy, however, outrunning my problems. As I sprinted back toward my dorm, Maren was there trying to catch me—my only real competition. Her grasp was much harder to break, but I did. She was strong as fuck. The scarf I'd borrowed from her flew off my neck in slow motion. I saw it flow in the air and gracefully fall to the street.

As a car drives by, my perception ebbs into slow motion. The car swoops it up, spits it back out and it lay there in a tangle on the ground. I briefly wished I was that scarf.

I stared at my dorm again. Logically, I knew I needed to get my drunk ass inside, but my body didn't listen. I took off once again, not knowing where I was headed until I was a few hundred yards away from Lauren's apartment complex, at least two miles away from campus. Earlier in the evening, I texted her that I'd hit rock bottom. She was fast asleep and didn't return my text or calls until the following morning. Before I landed in front of her apartment building,

I called Carlee. She was asleep, but she answered. It wasn't even midnight, and I got upset. *Why couldn't I be in bed sleeping right now? Why couldn't I be more like her?*

Carlee calmed me down a bit as I looked on to three campus police cars sitting outside, waiting to scoop me up and take me somewhere. I could only imagine that incoming call: "I've never seen a drunk person run so much in jeans. Good for her but girl needs to drink some water and go to bed."

I cannot outrun my drunkenness until I am sober. I cannot face the depression that swims in my head if there's alcohol swimming along with it. The only way to get better is to face the fire head on, but I didn't know that yet. I didn't even know how to begin fucking knowing that. I didn't have a clue. I surrendered just as I was about to enter Lauren's apartment complex. I couldn't get in anyway. I got into the campus police car, and they drove me back to my dorm. My friends were there, worriedly waiting.

I probably locked in close to five miles that night. The next morning, I forbade myself from eating anything until the sun went down again. Maren tried to get me out of bed to go eat breakfast with her, Tim, and Cody. I refused but let them take my car. Laying there in my hungover state, feeling the soreness of my feet from running, I wondered why I kept putting something into my body that I did not like, knowing it was not good for my body, mind, future, or soul.

I had no business being drunk. I was an underage college freshman who already had no idea how to do college without alcohol. If I had looked deep within myself, I would have realized I had no genuine desire to be drunk, but at that time, it didn't feel as if there was another way. Society, media, advertisements, and everything around me was telling me that this lifestyle was the acceptable path. I had no idea yet how to even socialize without alcohol in the equation.

When I did go out and drink, it was the same routine each time: I'd wish for a night alone to take care of myself and recuperate. However, the moment someone asked me to join a social function, I went. I dressed up, put on makeup, and drank as if on autopilot. Feeling disgusting during and after drinking became normal. Feeling exhausted became normal. I could almost sense some friends feeling the need to press the breaks, too, but none of us spoke about it, and so we kept going this way. *Why do I keep doing something I don't like?*

I'm not sure I fully understood it at the time, but I now realize I was afraid that if I didn't go, there would be backlash from peers. As an eighteen-year-old who didn't love confrontation outside of the soccer field, I seldom stood up for myself. It was easier in that moment to say yes and tag along. I was also afraid and not ready to explore my mind in stillness.

Being still would have revealed truths about me I was not ready to explore. It would have also given me time to think about Lauren.

I was not yet at the point of not letting alcohol wash down the truth.

Goddamn, I felt like absolute shit. I felt gross and a different kind of tired. I felt like a damp rag left at the bottom of the bucket left to mold. I needed some tender, loving self-care. I needed some water, a good cry, and a nice hot shower. I preferred a hot bath, but the tubs in a dorm? Insert puke emoji here.

Growing up, adults in and out of school told us that we can say no. No to alcohol. No to sex. No to drugs. But it was easy to declare prior that you'd say no; once you were in the situation and you're the only one not drinking, it was a completely different story. I knew a few people who didn't drink in college, but we didn't have much in common to sustain a friendship. And all but one of them ended up starting to drink alcohol before graduation.

I lacked queer role models in my day-to-day life, and in 2010, the only representation that was easily accessible to my knowledge was found within the cast of *The L Word*. And that was watched only in the secrecy of my dorm room. I didn't have a group to discuss and analyze episodes. I didn't have or even know where to look to explore more about sexuality. A self that was clearly gay but never had a thought of that label. I knew I was attracted to certain women, but I didn't do the math. Romantic attraction + sexual attraction to women = lesbian.

Maybe having more role models or even one or two and hearing more stories I could relate to would have helped me put two and two together. Maybe then I would have had a label for my sexuality sooner. At the very least, having more LGBTQ+ role models on TV and in movies would have made it more clear to me. Sure, there were dozens of gay soccer players to admire, but I wanted to connect to shows and characters with life-like storylines. Not just watch professional soccer players kick ass. At the most, I absolutely believe that I would have been less lonely had I had more queer worlds to escape to other than the heterosexual world in which we all roam.

Looking back, it was clear to me I was gay, but I never thought I was. I just knew I was attracted to certain women. I also didn't feel the need to go searching for other shows, books, or stories about LGBTQ+ folks. All I knew for sure is that I cared deeply for Lauren.

I stopped watching *The L Word* after season one. The feelings the show gave me only made my feelings for Lauren stronger. I wasn't sure what to do with those feelings, so I kept them inside and found other ways to distract myself.

Other than confirming my feelings for Lauren, *The L Word* brought out ugly feelings—feelings that I kept secret until I wrote them in this book. Feelings that I also didn't fully understand at that time.

I was jealous that the women in the show could live so openly and freely. I didn't understand why I was jealous, but I didn't look for a deeper meaning or reflection as to why. I just felt the way I felt. I envied the confidence most of those women portrayed. I was pissed off, so I suppressed my feelings. I was angry I didn't have a group of gay friends. I yearned for an older gay like Bette Porter to take me under her women-loving wing. I coveted for pointers from the coolness of Shane McCutcheon. I pined for a friendship like Alice and Dana's. I would've paid good money to visit The Planet café even if it was for five minutes.

Instead of sitting in my anger and jealousy, I went after what society told me would make me happy and admirable. I skipped dwelling on whether or not my feelings for Lauren were mutual. Thoughts of taking Lauren on a date didn't enter my mind, nor did thoughts of taking any woman on a date.

I forbid myself from going there by thinking about literally anything else. It's like I beat myself to it before my physical attraction turned into mind wandering.

Instead of fantasizing, I'd text a friend asking about a guy in her class, Riley, whom she said we'd be perfect together. I'd go shopping with Maren on the Square. I'd Skype friends from high school. I'd text my ex-boyfriend.

I had teammates there who were openly homophobic. My gay friend, Finn knew another gay classmate was yelled at for being queer...walked to the other side of the sidewalk in 2010.

Even with hearing those remarks and stories and even with my fear of being *out* in Oxford Mississippi... even with running away from my sexuality...The L Word gave me a little bit of hope...maybe. Just maybe. I could have a part of something that was my own here. Something that rang true to who I am...

I was too afraid to even try to be *out* in Oxford, Mississippi, but even with running away from my sexuality, I felt that maybe I could have part of...a little bit of my own L Word there...

CHAPTER VII

I woke up early that Monday after my drunken 5k to get a jump start on running from my problems. If I was productive and focused on school, then I could make up for my bad behavior over the weekend. I looked in the mirror briefly. My eyes were caked with yesterday's mascara. I got in the shower, not waiting for the frigid shower temperature to turn hot. I was in and out within two minutes. I threw my hair into a bun on top of my head, not taking the time to dry it. I quickly tossed my belongings into my backpack, grabbed my student ID, and left my dorm just after 6:30 a.m. Once I got outside, I checked my phone. No missed calls yet. I tapped the do not disturb button and walked to High Point. As I'm writing this, I realize half my visits to High Point were extremely low points for me. Oh, the irony.

I sat and drank my coffee for about an hour before heading over to the FedEx center. Other than a handful of football and basketball players cramming for tests, I was the only one there. I printed my paper for my English class and walked to my acting class. I checked my phone to see a few texts from Maren: a picture of her sitting on the toilet making a funny face made me laugh. It felt good to laugh. Strange. Familiar but distant. But Good. There was a text below the photo asking where I was and how I was feeling. I told her the truth. I was okay, but I had been better. We then made plans to grab food later that day.

I set my phone back to do not disturb when I arrived at my acting class. My acting classes and the theatre may have been my only true happy place in Oxford. I failed there, and I did not care that I failed. I learned that I needed to fail in order to succeed, especially if I was going to have a long-standing career as a writer and actor. Not only was failure accepted in my theatre classes, but it also came with minimal to no repercussions. Each failure in class was an opportunity to grow and learn. Failing in those classes helped me learn to accept failure outside of the classroom. However, that acceptance did not come easily, nor did it come quickly. I was quicker to accept that soccer may have failed me at some point that fall semester. I was quicker to blame anything else on my depression than sit down and reflect on any other potential reasons. The most obvious of which would be the simple fact that my mind is prone to depression. That is just how my brain works.

Everyone in my class had experience with acting prior to attending. The only experience I had was being voted Class Clown during my senior year of high school. I did exactly one short play in high school and a few skits for student assemblies. I wasn't cast the following year for the One Act festival because I failed to memorize my lines the first time. Other than that, I didn't have an ounce of experience past co-starring in a school musical when I was twelve.

Performing on a stage or in front of a camera was what I thought about most when I wasn't thinking about playing soccer. The possibility of acting in shows in front of an audience thrilled me. It was a consistent daydream that I wanted to make a reality. I was drawn to the idea of creating something out of nothing or creating something sparked from one sentence, one word, an object, or an interaction.

I loved creating stories. Much like building off ball movement in a soccer game, the same could be said for building stories in a play or television show. The goalie throws it to the left defender. She knocks it over to the center midfielder who turns and switches the field, finding the feet of the right-wing midfielder. She takes it down the line and crosses it. The ball finds the head of the striker, who sneaks it passed the goalie. The crowd erupts in applause.

Also, much like ball movement in a soccer game, stories are strung together from practice and repetition. Stories are on every inch of the field, along with each player who runs on it. Just like stories are on every inch of a stage with the actors who grace it.

I loved the chance to use theatre as an escape from my reality. An escape from the uninvited roommate living in my head who left me to pay their portion of the rent. Depression weighed me down like an anchor at the bottom of a boat. Theatre was a chance beyond soccer to set me free from that weight, if only for a little while. A little while because like soccer, the escape usually came only when I was performing in those classes.

Most of the time in class, with each line I spoke or any laugh I got, I felt my anchor being pulled back up to surface. I felt like I could breathe easier with each class I attended. However, my anchor was let go after practice or class once I was by myself again. With my anchor left for only me to carry, the weight of it would send me back down to the bottom of an ocean. My teammates, friends, and classmates helped carry that anchor, that heaviness, and they probably had no idea.

I got to escape in that class. But still, I was acting. I was not facing my truth. *How could I play a different role when I am still trying to figure out my own?*

Our fifty-minute class ended too soon, like always. I checked my phone, instantly dropping it after reading the screen. Anxiety ran back toward me. When we push our feelings down, like anxiety, for example, sometimes that just means we are pushing it back until it's ready to catapult and slam back into us. It's hard, but I discovered later that it's ultimately better to deal with things. Face them.

Two new missed calls and two new voicemails. Both with a 662 area code. I rushed back to my dorm, threw my bag on my futon, and plopped down on my desk chair, thankful my roommate was out. One voicemail was from the campus police officer from Saturday night. One voicemail was from student counseling services telling me I was required to make an appointment with them as soon as possible. *Fuck that.* I laid down in bed and pulled the covers over my head and slept through my next class.

When I woke, I checked my e-mail. Shortly after the counseling services called me, they also sent an e-mail stating that if I did not comply with them, they would have no choice but to tell my coaches what happened over the weekend, a bit of a pre-calculated threat. *Dammit.* I called the number and made an appointment for the next morning. I wanted to get this shit over with.

Lying to yourself is one thing, but lying to others is just bad karma. At dinner, Maren took one look at my face and knew something was up. So, when she asked, I was honest and told her I had to meet with a counselor. If I didn't go, they'd tell the coaches, which could get me kicked off the team or cause some other sort of trouble. The last thing I ever wanted was trouble.

Shortly after telling Maren, I texted Lauren to give her an update. She had texted me earlier in the day to check-in, but I hadn't replied yet. She encouraged me and reminded me that a counselor helped her a whole lot when she needed it. Maybe they could help me, too.

The next day, I put a hat on and made sure I had my sunglasses with me on the trek across campus to my therapy session. A couple hundred yards before I reached the building, I looked around—no one I knew in sight. I cautiously approached the front door of the counseling center and opened it.

Inside, I kept my jacket on, not in protest of being here, but because this office was freezing. As the counselor rested his elbows on his legs, he revealed perspiration from his underarms that traveled down the sides of his torso. I will call him Matt. If I had to guess, Matt was in his early 30s. He was slightly taller than me and appeared physically fit. I briefly wondered if I could outrun him if needed.

I could not tell if Matt's stance was a comfort thing or if he had to air out his armpits. The man put on a pair of brown wooden glasses. *Okay, this guy LOVES brown*, I thought to myself.

I swung my backpack around and held it like a pillow, protecting my bubble and comforting my own discomfort. The small office smelled of pine. I assumed it was his body spray until I saw the pine scented air freshener plugged in behind a plant in the corner.

An oak-colored, leather chair was my sole seating option. It squeaked even if you barely breathed while sitting on it. Matt's glasses slowly moved down his nose, I assumed because of perspiration.

I tried to make a joke inside my head because humor was my number one coping mechanism aside from alcohol. I remained still, only hugging my backpack in a little tighter, pretending it was my dog, Heidi, and not a bag of books.

"Are you comfortable with your jacket on? It's a little toasty in here." It is not toasty in here.

I don't know what to say, so I spat out, "I have Raynauds."

"What?"

"Raynauds."

He looked scared…or confused. I couldn't tell. I wanted to talk about anything other than the incident over the weekend.

"Raynauds is an autoimmune disorder. Particularly in my hands and feet. When I am cold, the arteries or capillaries shrink, and blood flow stops to the tips of my fingers and toes."

"Ah. I see. That sounds like quite the annoyance. It must be better, though, living in a warm climate, right? And you're from…"

He glanced at his notes.

"St. Louis."

"It can be, but usually when I enter a building, the AC is blasted. However, this office is comfortable for me."

"I have the opposite problem," Matt replied as he ever so slightly gestured to his armpits, making me wonder if he meant to do that or not.

He gave me a soft smile as he crossed his legs and pushed his glasses back up his nose.

"Just to let you know, we at student counseling services are aware of all incidents with campus police. It's our job to follow up with students when something like this occurs."

"Mhmm. I understand."

I'll make this easy for him.

I knew what I needed to say to get out of there without anything more than a slap on the hand. These therapy sessions felt like a punishment, but even with the thought of making it easy on him, I surprised myself.

He said, "talking these issues out would help tremendously for someone like me."

"Like *me*? You don't even know me."

"Well, they'd be helpful for anyone in that kind of situation."

"Right. Well, I got stupid drunk, and most people laughed about it, but I don't find it funny at all."

"Why didn't you think it was funny?"

I hugged my backpack tighter.

"I, um. I just don't like how I feel when I drink alcohol."

"What does it make you feel like?"

"Woozy, I guess. Not in control."

Wow, that was honest.

"Do you not like being in control?"

"Well, not when it comes to another substance making me not control myself."

Wow, that was too much honesty.

"I can understand that. What made you run that night?"

My shoulders shrugged and my eyes diverted contact with his.

We sat in silence for several minutes, and then Matt asked, "Can I ask you a question?"

You just did.

"Sure," I said.

Eventually, he asked me, "Have you considered antidepressants?"

I slowly shook my head 'no' and said nothing, looking at him like he was the one with the mental illness. My coaches never found out about that night nor the follow up sessions with Matt. My first fear was that I would get in trouble for drinking. My second fear was that I would not be supported through the rough time I was having. Since I went to see a counselor that day, my coaches never found out. I believe my teammates were left thinking I was some crazy drinking legend that knows how to have a good time. In all honesty, they probably haven't thought much of me or that night unless they found this memoir. If they ever find it. I hope they do, and I hope they're all doing well. My 'legacy' at nineteen was backed by booze and the ability to outrun strangers and friends. I was a depressed college student who self-medicated with alcohol, and just so happens, I couldn't handle my liquor, either. Thankfully, later in my college career, my legacy would begin to change—but this journey was not easy, nor was it fast.

CHAPTER VIII

Things got worse after meeting with Matt. While I should have continued to see Matt, I didn't. I did the required three sessions and never saw him again. It was enough to get student services and campus police off my back. I just wanted to get back to moving my body. I didn't necessarily want to go back to soccer, but it was what I knew. So, that's what I did. It's easy to keep going back to things that you know so well. Plus, I was still great at the sport. It's rewarding to excel in something you're good at, and at that time, soccer was all I felt I knew how to be good at.

A handful of optional practices were set up before winter break. I went to these optional practices in hopes of finding a positive distraction from my mind. I was still at battle in my mind about soccer's place in my happiness and depression, but still, I laced up my boots and showed up. I didn't drink the night before any optional practice because I had an excuse, I knew I wouldn't back down from. That and I had class right after, at 8:00 a.m.

None of this planning, however, prepared me for how depressed I'd feel when I got out of bed that morning. My alarm woke me up just after 5:00 a.m. I rolled out of bed, grabbed my keys and a granola bar and left. Most of my gear remained in my car or sat in my locker, so I don't think to do a quick scan of my dorm for anything else. It never occurred to me that we would need to match for an optional, unscheduled, out of season, come as you please practice. Only six of us showed up that morning. As I scanned my locker, I quickly noticed two items missing: a navy pull over and navy joggers—the exact same uniform of every other person that was there.

I had pants. I always had pants. I had my black Adidas pants, the ones that still fit since I was in sixth grade. As I pulled them on, an upperclassman asked, "Are those the pants you're going to be wearing during practice?"

They're on my fucking body. So, yeah.

"Mhmm."

"If you don't match everyone else, then you need to take those off."

You've got to be fucking kidding me.

I understand the value of a uniform. I had worn one for the last fifteen fucking years. Another avocado pit made its way into my throat. I wanted to cry, but I didn't. I didn't answer her. I looked in a few other people's lockers, but the ones that did have the joggers were two sizes too small. Also, the importance of having pants was tremendous. If I was not warm enough, I jeopardized my performance. My body did not function well in cold weather, and I desperately needed to have a good training session. If I didn't, I knew it would only make me feel worse. We were a Nike sponsored school; how dare I wear a competing company's attire? The tiny fact that my pants were Adidas quickly escalated into detrimental territory. If I wasn't depressed, I'd easily and calmly not give a damn, but I was depressed, and I needed the goddamn layers! It wasn't even 6:00 a.m. It was offseason. We had NEVER worn the pants my teammates were wearing that morning. Never. Not one time. Instead of standing up for myself or forgoing pants altogether, I ran back to my dorm to get the other pair. That was how depression presented for me: getting upset over little things that do not compare to the grander things in life. Some say, "Oh, you shouldn't let that bother you. It doesn't matter." Well, it did matter. It does matter. It matters to someone who doesn't understand how their mind chemically imbalances itself when she's done nothing to make it that way. At least she didn't think she'd done anything. This moment mattered because I still remember it over ten years later. This moment mattered because if this upperclassman was even the slightest bit nicer, then I would not have been triggered to do what I did next.

I left the locker room and sprinted to my car, passing my coach along the way. If he was just getting here, I had enough time to get the pants and get back before I was punished with sprints for being late. I sped back to my dorm, certainly well over the eighteen-mph speed limit. I was screaming. No one passing me noticed. I was going too fast for anyone to realize that I was hitting myself in the head as I screamed about how fucking stupid I was. If only I'd woken up ten minutes earlier. If only I had gotten everything I needed out the night before instead of laying in bed unable to fall asleep until 2 a.m. If only I wasn't such a fucking loser, then I wouldn't be depressed. Right? If only. If only.

If only.

Wow. So glad having matching attire was worth it this morning. Totally saved all of our lives. You're so welcome.

I grabbed my pants and sped back to the field. I joined the group in matching attire and did not speak a word during practice nor a word during my 8:00 a.m. class. After that class, I grabbed a sandwich to take back to my dorm. I ate it and slept until Maren's light knock on my door woke me up for dinner.

Although I was miserable, at times, I was proud to be on a D1 soccer team, and I willingly let everyone know it simply by repping my team's gear. I knew soccer better than I knew myself. In soccer, I received approval from all if I played with fury on the field, a fury that matches the way I feel within when I'm off of the field. But the soccer field was the only place where this fury was acceptable or celebrated. Depression, I've learned, can be and mostly is an invisible illness.

Is a person's only worth how athletic they are? How talented they are? How can I be so seen when I played and barely be seen at all as soon as the game or training was over? Surely, I had other talents. Surely, I would not suffer forever, right? Soccer would not last forever. I only had a few years left. I did my best not to think of what was next, but I couldn't help it consuming most of my daydreams… or nightmares.

I guess I can live this way, I thought. My childhood was amazing. High school was a blast. I had it good up until then. I guessed I had to settle for depression. I would just keep going, I assumed, because, on paper, my life was amazing. On paper, I played soccer for a school in the SEC. On paper, I wanted to be there at that school in that small town. On paper, my future looked bright, but I did not know what the fuck my future held. No one did. Would I or wouldn't I fulfill my dreams? Whatever happens, I would be depressed, I thought.

So, I supposed soccer was better than no soccer. I'd probably be more depressed without it than with it. But would I grow to detest that love of soccer if I become depressed at my prime within it? I was so incredibly confused. *Do I still love soccer? What do I love? Who do I love? How do I love?* If only someone could have told me all of the answers. I had a long way to go before I realized that those answers lived within me.

A few weeks later, I was finally home for winter break. Right before Christmas, I met with the psychiatrist. He prescribed me an antidepressant, but I rebelled, thinking my brain did not need that. I struggled to accept taking them and only took them when I *felt* like it, which is not how that shit works. It would be years before I began taking them regularly enough to see a positive impact.

A month or so later, I wrote in my journal about that night: "Here I go again, about to keep it all in. I ran away as far as I could, but they stopped me. Someone always is stopping me. Something is always there, holding me back." Later, I'd find out that the someone holding me back was myself.

CHAPTER IX

I thought that the only thing worse than going back to Ole Miss was not going back to Ole Miss and staying in St. Louis. Taking a semester off or only going to school part-time was not something I was interested in doing. I needed to be a full-time student and wouldn't allow myself to half-ass my journey. I wanted to graduate in four years, no matter what. This was partly due to parental and societal expectations and partly due to the fact that I was extremely hard on myself. I was also afraid staying home would make me look like a failure. I was afraid of being left behind.

I finish most things I start. It was in my nature, even if it meant sacrificing what I truly wanted, but my decision was made. I was quitting soccer and would tell the coaches the first day back from break. I decided that maybe soccer was, after all, the reason I was so depressed. I mean, I had played the sport since I was three years old. Maybe I had over played my welcome. Maybe it was time to hang up my boots and utilize my other talents. In my first semester of college, I played soccer more than I went to class or spent time studying or trying new things.

I was struggling to find my voice while new feelings came up that I hadn't experienced before—leading the pack: my lingering attraction to a woman.

I texted Lauren and wished her a Merry Christmas. I wanted to call her. I wanted to text her all day, but I didn't want to be that girl. To my delight, she replied, wishing me a Merry Christmas, followed by another question: When would I be back in Oxford? I told her not soon enough, and I also told her that I would no longer be playing soccer for Ole Miss. She gave me a reply, which I really needed at the time—instant support. No questions asked. I was so relieved to have support from a teammate and a friend. It meant the world to me. She helped me a lot that year and taught me a ton about myself. She was extremely patient. Never judged and always listened. She made me feel seen.

I don't remember anything else from that specific Christmas Day other than her texting me. She was all I can remember thinking about that day.

With the horizon of a big change coming up, I started to dream more about what life would be like without soccer. I allowed my mind to actively wonder about what it would be like to date a woman. Not just any woman, but Lauren! She was open and caring and funny as hell.

I hadn't come out as gay to myself yet, but I had admitted to myself that I had feelings for Lauren. I didn't want to live in secret. I didn't want to live a lie, but I also was far from ready to have those conversations about my sexuality with other people. Plus, I had a bigger announcement to take care of first.

I waited until the last week of winter break to break the news to my dad about quitting soccer. The confrontation was eating away at me, and it was difficult to bring it up in conversation. I tried to say something two separate times, but I choked on my words. Another time I tried, the words didn't even come. I stopped trying until I absolutely needed to speak up. So, I decided to wait until I was about to head back to Mississippi to avoid any change in dynamics or mood from my big news. I didn't want to disappoint my parents. I wanted to run away from the outcome, no matter what it was.

My parents loved watching me play sports. As a naturally gifted athlete, I felt that I was doing both of them a disservice, taking away the last few years that were planned for me to continue playing. I felt guilty, but I knew they'd respect my decision and love me no matter what. They never forced me to play the sport. They never forced me to do anything. They just wanted me to always do something I loved and to work hard at it.

My dad is calm, cool, a little disorganized but mostly collected. I never wanted to disappoint my parents, especially my father at that time. He worked his behind off to give my brother, mom, and I the life that most only dream of. My mom worked just as hard, too, as a businesswoman herself and homemaker. She remarkably supported him when he started his own company during the 2008 Great Recession.

I was mostly devastated because my plan to earn a bigger soccer scholarship would no longer happen. I planned to earn more scholarship money as my time on the soccer team progressed, as a tribute to my parents for all they had done for me, taking some financial load off my family.

This was another reason I struggled with having depression. I had more than enough, more than most people. My parents were always involved in my life and my brother's. My parents were always around. There was laughter and very little yelling in our household. They showed up with love and guided my brother and I the best they could. We had dinner on the table nearly every night promptly at 5:30 p.m. My brother and I were both sent to private school, and we vacationed most years. On top of all that, I played a sport that had me traveling all over the country. We were, and still are, extremely privileged and blessed.

Just shy of fifteen years in the game, it no longer made me happy or fulfilled. Before dinner one evening, I finally told my dad that I'd be going back to Ole Miss, but I would be terminating my soccer career. I felt that at that time, that decision was best for me. He told me he'd miss seeing me play, but he understood and said I shouldn't sacrifice my happiness for something that no longer makes me happy.

Quitting soccer means my depression will go away. Duh. I was so excited going back to school without the burden of what soccer had become.

I would be finally free to have a truer college experience, whatever the hell that meant. I would be free to hang out with other people. I would be free to get closer to Lauren, whatever the hell that meant.

I decided to put soccer behind me to finally start focusing on the other things I came to college for: writing and theater. Not having soccer would open up more time for auditions and writing.

I returned to campus for my second semester, excited for what was ahead of me and utterly and totally convinced I was about to cure my depression once and for all by quitting soccer. I had figured it all out with little to no help from people that actually know what the fuck they're doing.

I felt more excited than when I arrived on campus back in August. I was determined to make things work. I might have been about to quit soccer, but I was not about to quit Ole Miss. Not that easily, at least.

I thought I was ready to leave soccer behind and accept and embrace a true college experience, even if that true college experience didn't truly represent what I wanted. So much alcohol. Not enough books. Well, the books were there, but it was easier to say no to that than chugging beers and taking shots. It was less lonely that way.

I thought, without soccer, other doors would open, but in actuality, more bottles were opened. I was not strong enough to see the other opportunities around me. I rarely looked beyond the cup in my hand.

The Saturday before I officially quit, Maren and I headed out to town. We met up with other team members on the Square for another night dancing and drinking. I hadn't spoken to Lauren in the last few days, but she was the first person I saw when we walked into the bar in the basement of the Rib Cage, a local eatery that has since been permanently closed.

Lauren found me, too, which wasn't hard. I had on five-inch heels and looked hot. On top of my heels were tight black jeans and a white T-shirt. I like to think I brought a jacket out with me that night in January, but let's be real, I didn't. Very few of us did, and the ones who did regret it as soon as the dancing started at The Library. I didn't care if I was freezing outside when I had whiskey and dancing to keep me warm.

We drank beer at the first bar before being topped off with a round of Rumple Minze Peppermint Schnapps that an underage sophomore, Carlee, charged to her dad's credit card. The dozen or so of us were each handed a shot glass. Rumple Minze tasted good but was dangerous. Rumple Minze after a few beers, and I was good to go, but 9/10 times, I kept drinking when I shouldn't. Fortunately, this wasn't one of those nights. This was one of the few nights I had fun being drunk, and by fun, I also mean that I didn't run nor hit any kind of Wall…I did, however, fall a few times, but it was followed by laughter, and I got back up.

We all raised our Rupplemint shots. Carlee toasted, "To a new year! To a new semester! To never growing old! And to being back home! Hotty Toddy!" *Home. They all feel at home here.*

The thought was interrupted by dozens of WOOO!s that followed from all directions.

I couldn't help but notice Lauren standing close to me the second the evening started. I carefully bent down with my shot glass to get eye level with Lauren. I already towered over her barefoot let alone in my five-inch heels.

We looked in each other's eyes a moment longer than *just friends* or *just teammates* would. I felt the tension thicken between us, wondering if Lauren felt it, too. I wondered if her knowledge of me quitting the team would give her permission to explore our relationship beyond platonic. I would've kissed her right then and there if all those other people weren't around. Never had I ever want to kiss someone so badly before that moment.

We tapped our shot glasses on the bar, tapped them together, then rose 'em back up and tossed 'em back. After we took the shot, our eyes met again once we finished squinting from the burn of peppermint. I smiled at her and thought, *Home. Lauren feels like home. Oxford doesn't though...* I ignored that feeling of Oxford not feeling like home. My feelings for Lauren with this liquor were strong enough to push away what was looming deep inside me: depression and something I wasn't fully ready to admit yet: gay, gay, gay, gay, gayyyyyyy!

There was the usual amount of dancing, but this night was filled with more laughter, love, and fun. It easily became one of my favorite nights at Oxford. Lauren and I were quietly holding hands briefly during favorite parts of the songs that played. At one point in the night, I fell while dancing from abruptly twisting my ankle. I crawled a few feet away from the crowd before Lauren helped me up. I joked about my soccer career being over. She laughed with me, being one of the few people besides Maren that held the knowledge of my leaving the team.

One of our other teammates, Emily, picked us up as she got back into town. One thing I did love about Oxford was that the bars closed early there. Most of the drunken nights allowed me to pass out by 1:30 a.m. or sooner. As Emily pulled up, we all hooted and hollered like we had just cheated death, and she was saving us from our demise. Me, Maren, Lauren, and another freshman, Megan hopped in Jenni's navy-blue Range Rover. Maren sat shotgun, and I was sure to sit next to Lauren in the backseat. I think Lauren had the same idea because she sat in the middle seat immediately, leaning closer to my side of the car, our legs touching.

Lauren scooped her hand into mine and held it the entire way back to my dorm. We took turns tracing lines on each other hands. The drive from the Square to Hefley Hall was short, just like most drives in this small town, but that one certainly felt like the shortest one of my freakin' life! I didn't want it to end.

Emily pulled up to mine and Maren's final destination; I didn't move. I didn't want to say good night to Lauren yet, and I felt she didn't either. We hadn't seen each other in over a month! Either of us leaned in, and we kissed for a long time, but not long enough.

This was not my first kiss with a woman, but this was the first kiss that meant something. I had kissed a few of my best friends before, but this was my first kiss with a woman I had feelings for truly.

Megan squealed, "Oh my god, Ally!"

I smiled, but my lips never left Lauren's.

I understood Megan's confusion because, at that moment, Lauren and I were still technically teammates, but in less than forty-eight hours, Megan would figure it out. I only broke the kiss when I heard Maren yelling at me from outside the car to quit making out and to get my ass inside. I obliged. I said goodnight and thanked Emily for driving us. I ran up the front stairs in my heels to the dorm, drunk on booze and high off Lauren's lips.

We lived on the second floor and always ran up the stairs, always racing with no reason. I miss that energy of my youth. Maren got upstairs first because, for the second time that night, I wiped out after my toes missed the final step. We laughed so hard that eventually, Maren was on the ground laughing, too. I finally unstrapped and took off my ridiculously high heels. A shiver ran through me. I was freezing. After brushing my teeth and washing the make-up off my face, I put on sweatpants, a hoodie, and fuzzy socks and crawled into bed. I checked my phone and smiled when I saw a text from Lauren had come through, telling me she got home safely and that she had a lot of fun. I replied I had fun, too, and that I missed her. I wished her a good night just before I fell asleep. *What a good kisser.*

CHAPTER X

Before heading back to school, I e-mailed the coaches and asked for a meeting on the first Monday of the spring semester. I was ready to get this over with and wanted to do so ASAP. I didn't want to grieve the loss. I just wanted to move on from it all. I didn't want to feel worse than the low points of the fall semester.

I don't blame my coaches for my quitting. It was honestly no one's fault. My mental health issues were normal even though I felt alone with those issues then. I felt that I had to do it on my own like the independent boss I was, but just because strong folks are strong and independent doesn't mean we shouldn't ask for help from time to time, especially if we don't think we need it. Asking for help always fell under the burden umbrella for me. I didn't want to worry anyone or have them take time out of their own troubles and busy schedules. I didn't want to be in the way.

Monday. The first day of the second semester. Not even forty-eight hours after Lauren and I kissed for the first time. I was nervous as I walked into Gillom for what I thought was the last time. As I opened the doors, I stepped in, thinking that eliminating soccer would not make me depressed. I wasn't nervous because of that part. I was nervous because I had to say what was on my mind.

The conversation went a little something like this:

"So, I've really been struggling this semester," I said.

My voice started to fade. I cleared my throat and sat up a little straighter.

"I guess, I'm just unhappy, and I've decided to no longer be a part of the team going forward," I continued.

"Okay. Are you going to transfer and play somewhere else?" One coach asked.

"No. I've decided to stay here. Just be a regular student and focus on my mental health outside of soccer."

I felt myself putting on another front. These words coming out of my mouth were mine but also felt like someone else's.

"We had no idea you were struggling so much. Is there anything we can do for you?" The assistant coach said.

What's the point?

"No," I said slightly shaking my head.

But you could have been more aware. I know there were times when it was written all over my body how much hurt I was carrying on the inside. You saw it and mistook it for a bad attitude or a lack of effort.

"Are you getting help, at least?"

"Yes."

"Well, good luck to you. We wish you the best," the head coach said.

"Th ank you," I said as I got up and walked out.

I wish I would have told the coaching staff what they could have done differently—that a major turning point for me was being blind-sided when I lost my starting position.

It's not that I felt entitled to have a conversation; the thought just never crossed my mind that the ones in charge would not at least give me a heads up.

I bent the truth and told them what I thought they wanted to hear so they'd think I was and would be okay. I wasn't okay and didn't know if I'd be okay. But I was more concerned with convincing them I was okay than anything else. It was already hard enough, and I was scared to open up my wounds further and show other people my pain. I wanted to hide. I wanted to run.

"I am on medication. I saw a psychiatrist at Th anksgiving and have been seeing a counselor on campus regularly." *Maybe I would not be here, quitting, if mental health was a priority in student athletes. Th ey say sports are 90% mental, don't they?*

I did not want to leave them worrying when I walked out of the office. I did not want anyone worrying. Because then I'd have to talk about it, and I did not know how to talk about any of it. I did, however, know how to drink about it. It isn't so easy opening your mouth and speaking painful things. Washing the pain down with alcohol? Now that was easy!

I was polite to them and gave them a small speech on how grateful I was for the opportunity to play for Ole Miss. This obviously was not the outcome I anticipated when signing with Ole Miss. That's the thing about plans, though, they rarely work in the favor of the player. Maybe the outcome is the same, but the getting there can be a goddamn gamble.

As soon as I got in my car, I texted Lauren and told her how it went. I typed: *It went well. Short and sweet...just like you.*

She replied with a smiling emoji and: *are you going to tell the team?*

Me: *Yeah, I think I'll send a text or something soon.*

I wanted to let the team know before we all met to pick up our books for the semester. So, later that day, I copied a message from my notes into a group text. I typed out my farewell message days earlier. I hit send before giving it a once over to let my team know that I quit. The message started with a very bad joke. Oopsie.

Even though I was no longer on the team, my book scholarship was still covered. The next day, the team met at the Student Union Bookstore to pick up their books for the semester.

There was no protocol for quitting, however, I didn't want to just not show up to spring training without saying anything. A handful of other teammates quit or transferred by the time the school year ended. Why did I have to tell them anyway? I certainly did not owe them anything. If anything, some of them owed me an apology for smacking me in the face with lettuce! I forgive, but rarely do I forget.

I stood near Maren and mostly everyone else didn't seem to care that I was there. Very few of my now former teammates wished me luck. When I say very few, I mean two or three out of the twenty-five or so girls on the team even acknowledged me. Maren didn't wish me anything because she doesn't have to. She wasn't going anywhere.

Standing there, I felt resentful that they could provide some books but not more compassion or attention for my mental health. I knew it was not up to anyone else but myself to deal with my depression.

However, D1 athletes were catered to on a daily basis with food, clothes, and academic assistance—rightfully so in a lot of ways. They work their asses off. Unless I was completely not paying attention one day, not one time during my time in a Division 1 program was mental wellbeing supported or acknowledged.

Unless, on the off chance, I blocked it from my memory. If there was, in fact, any mention of mental wellbeing, it was certainly not amplified.

I was able and willing to gather my books like a regular student, but I was unable to speak up on behalf of my emotional and mental struggles. I grabbed my books and left, never having felt more invisible in my life.

CHAPTER XI

Lauren and I were in our own little world for a while. We would sneak away for mid-week lunch dates followed by late afternoons and evenings studying at High Point, a local coffee shop, sipping on marble mochas. Maren usually tagged along to those coffee dates.

Lauren and I fell asleep together more nights than not and spent afternoons in each other's arms as winter heated into spring. We spoiled each other on Valentine's Day with our favorite drinks and candy. Diet Coke and flowers for her. Balloons for me. Chocolate for both of us.

I held her hair when she had too much champagne during a pre-game one night. While everyone else went out, we stayed in. I took care of her and cleaned her entire apartment, grateful to be completely sober. I loved how she fit around my arms as she perfectly rested her head against my chest.

I visited my cousin in Memphis for a volleyball tournament, but I left early to go spend the night with Lauren. Even though they begged me to stay for the night, saving me a ninety-minute drive in the dark, I insisted on getting back because there was light waiting for me when I got there.

My ID went M.I.A. during a wild night out in February. Finn, Maren, Rachel, and I prepared all week for a rave only to get there and be the only ones dressed in rave attire. Somewhere between the shots and songs, my ID was gone. I drove home the following weekend to get a new one. One of the nights at home, I Skyped Lauren while my parents were at an event. While I was still on the call, my parents came home and then into my room to say goodnight. I told them I was talking to Lauren. They thought it was a Lauren from high school, so they shuffled right on over to say hi. "No, this is Lauren from the soccer team and..." I said.

My girlfriend.

I so badly wanted to tell them, and I almost did. I screamed it in my head, but nothing came out of my mouth.

I pretended I had a stomachache so I could call her from the bathroom during a spring break trip in Montana. I was with another friend that I was convinced wouldn't approve of me having a girlfriend. The service sucked, so our calls and texts were sporadic and short. That week was the longest we'd spend apart since December. I missed her.

We made out in her car. Our feet touched any time she sat across from me. There was nothing else but tunnel vision from my eyes to hers. It was just her, me, and the electricity between us. The pacing of our physical relationship was beautiful. Nothing was rushed. Nothing was forced. We were enjoying each other slowly.

We had fooled around but never got naked until one Thursday night after hitting the Square for a few hours. I wasn't drunk, but I was pretty buzzed when we had sex for the first time.

When I had sex for the first time.

My first class the next morning started at 9:30. I didn't want to miss it since it was my favorite class, especially since I was in such a good mood—maybe the best I'd felt since I stepped foot on campus.

Getting to class that morning, I made my most questionable fashion choice of my eighteenth year: extra-long, bright red soccer shorts with a too-tight Bob Marley T-shirt and shiny copper cowboy boots. It was my one and only walk of shame, and I had never been prouder.

I never questioned where to kiss her or where my hands should go. We didn't speak. Our bodies did all the talking for us. It was the most natural act of love I had ever done.

Lauren always made sure I was comfortable from the very beginning of our sexual relationship, and after we made love, we always talked for a while before finally falling asleep—either her in my arms or our hands interlaced beneath the sheets.

Sex with her felt like lightening in the middle of a summer storm, intense flashes of light, strong and beautiful: a light in the darkness of depression. Sex with her was euphoric and delicate but filled with fire. Our bodies are two matching puzzle pieces snapping together with ease. She was better than whatever first time I had dreamt of in my head.

Like I said, we were in our own little world, and the people who knew, knew, and the people who didn't, well...they had no idea.

Finally letting myself surrender to the feelings we had for each other felt incredible. No longer resisting and finally giving in was one of the most honest and best things I had done for myself up until that point. When you wait your whole life to feel a connection like that, and one that is indescribable, you don't want to question it. I didn't at least.

I knew Lauren had experience with other women before, but she was my first. While she could have showed me the 'ropes' of lesbian sex, I didn't need her to do that. We fell into each other's arms and bodies with grace and ease. The bit of alcohol in my system may certainly have helped any nerves that I would possibly have come up without it. I was not that drunk, though. For weeks, I recalled everywhere her lips touched my body and how her legs intertwined with mine. I recalled the slowness of how things got started when we got back to her apartment. I replayed her soft, small but strong hands on my hips and other places.

I had never felt more free. I had never felt more true and more myself, but I sensed my bubble threatening to pop one evening in Lauren's bed weeks after our first night together.

We were both standing on our knees, chest to chest. My long arms wrapped around her. Her shorter but stronger arms wrapped around me. I kissed her slowly at first, and then she kissed me back, picking up the pace.

Lauren inhaled deeply, and with her eyes closed, she said, "I think I'm falling in love with you."

At first, I smiled and gave her another kiss. Briefly, I rested my forehead on hers before we made love. I put my body before my thoughts, wanting to say 'I love you' back. If I hadn't done something physically in that moment, my body would freeze, conflicted. Part of me wanted to run and run far, far away. Part of me wanted to scream I LOVE YOU from the rooftops right before and right after whispering it in her ear as we fell asleep. A tiny part of me wished I wasn't in this position at all.

Even to reciprocate the "I love you" scared me. My world would change. I was comfortable without being fully *out*. It may have been harder on me to stay in the closet, but I thought that if I stepped out of the closet completely, then it would be harder on others in my life. My mom and my dad being the top of that list. Reciprocating those three little words would have made it too real, even though I would have meant it.

If I couldn't hide with her, then I would have to run. I could only be with her in secret or else I'd have to face a lot of things I didn't want to face. I was afraid to face them. So, I did what I did best back then. I stayed in my comfort zone even though it was dangerous and ran. Lauren didn't deserve someone who was still hiding. She deserved so much more than I could give her.

Lauren never truly gave me an ultimatum, but I internalized that that's where the relationship was heading. So, I pushed her away. I concocted such a story that made me believe an ultimatum was coming, but truthfully, I was running away from the truth…again. When things became too hard or too real: I ran. I either ran away emotionally or distracted myself by literally running miles and miles.

I was grateful and excited that she wanted me just as much as I wanted her. However, I never put a label on my sexual identity. I never felt nor thought of a reason to do so. Naming my sexuality wasn't important. What was important was experiencing my first love with someone regardless of their gender. She was the one that opened a door that I worked so hard to keep shut. After Lauren, though, that door never fully closed no matter how hard I tried to keep it bolted with a key I could toss in the water. However, what I didn't realize, though, was that the key to my door could float, and it would always find its way back to the lock to open back up.

Right before my birthday, Lauren and I ended things. I was not ready to come out, and I didn't want to risk the pressure of it, even if it was only put on me by myself. The wounds from quitting soccer were still raw, and to come out right after that seemed like too many big things to handle at once.

I hadn't even accepted the fact that I was gay. I never put a label on myself when I dated Lauren. She was my girlfriend, yes, but I didn't think I was gay because I was with her. She is a person that I cared a lot about. I never thought about being gay or straight or bi;

I just followed my feelings until following them became too close to the truth, and continuing to follow them became scary. Labels are a great way to identify oneself, but at the end of the day, does it really matter?

The hardest part of our break-up was the awkward air in my dorm when Lauren started dating another freshman up the hall from me: a softball player. They started talking the summer before and dated earlier that school year. I acted like it didn't bother me, but it did. Neither of us three ended up together in the long run, but damn, that other girl had NOTHING on me. You never forget your first lesbian love triangle, do you? Good times. ;)

My memory is a little fuzzy on whether or not I ever told Lauren that I loved her. I think I would remember if I had. If I hadn't, my only regret is not telling her that I loved her, too. So, Lauren, if you're reading this, I loved you back then. I was in love with you and I am so happy for you now.

It took me years to realize that no matter how free I'd felt, I couldn't truly be if I was keeping myself in a bubble.

CHAPTER XII

Springtime at Ole Miss in my day meant themed day parties at frat houses, Rebel baseball, and the Double Decker festival. The town had to do something to pass the time until the next football season. One particular frat house, Sigma Nu, hosted an annual crawfish boil they called "Woodstock."

Maren had come down with a cold, so she spent the weekend resting. We, Finn and I, assigned her to pick us up from the crawfish boil later that afternoon because we knew we'd be drunk and, god forbid, if we walked more than five minutes back to the dorms. Finn was a friend of a friend who became one of my good buddies at Ole Miss. He was hilarious and welcoming, and so quick witted, we couldn't compete with our comebacks in his presence.

I wore dark gray cutoff shorts, some gray converse, and a pink and white tie-dyed tube top. It doubled as a crop top, as well, because I cut off a strip at the bottom of the shirt to use as a headband. How fashionable of me. I know. I might have been depressed, but I was a trendy, depressed college freshman…at least some of the time. The backyard of the frat opened up to a horseshoe-shaped courtyard with a pool at one end with questionable, murky, gray water. A porch wrapped around both the second story and the first. The only difference between this Woodstock and the actual Woodstock was the music and partygoers with handheld devices called cell phones. And also, a shit ton of crawfish covered a dozen tables. I wonder if any crawfish were, in fact, present at the real Woodstock…

There were trashcans full of beer—hundreds of beer cans. A line extended from the outside entrance to the party. At the gate, a frat bro collected money from silly little freshmen willing to pay to have fun. Finn and I noticed a side door that occasionally opened and closed with a big, strong college dude pushing another trashcan full of beer outside.

"Oh my gosh! You poor thing," I said.

"Let us help you with that, sweetheart!" Finn added.

"Right on!" the frat bro eagerly replied.

Finn and I performed the one-person job of opening a door, and the college dude pushed out the beer bin. He thanked us by tossing us a beer each. Once he was out of our way, we ducked inside the frat house and found the FREE entrance to the food and fun. As usual, Finn and I danced through the crowd together after I spotted two friends from high school gnawing away at crawfish. Dancing with Finn and Maren were some of the better drunken memories from college. Riley, the guy I was supposed to be having a "thing" with, was nowhere to be seen. I smiled. Relieved. *Maybe he's not coming.*

To remember the moment forever, I took out my phone and started to take some pictures. Mid-click, Riley ran across the yard right towards me. I tossed my phone to Finn, and he caught it and celebrated as Riley scooped me up, threw me over his shoulder, carried me to the pool, and tossed me in it. I plugged my nose and kept my lips as tight as humanly possible. I had been to several frat houses, but this was the first one with a pool. Frat house pools were much like the inside of the frat houses: murky and full of unidentified liquids that you don't ever want to identify because the truth is better left unsaid.

Riley. *sigh*

Riley was from a small town near the most southern part of Mississippi. Although from the deep south, he talked like the midwestern boys I had grown up with. He was adorable and fun, so some friends who knew him thought we'd make a good match since I am also adorable and fun. For months, I heard from friends, "You have to meet Riley." "Seriously, Ally. You two are meant for each other." After things with Lauren turned south, I finally caved and gave permission to a friend to give the boy from the south my number. Riley was in RROTC and a hard worker. When he wasn't training, we spent many nights watching movies in his dorm, like *Nacho Libre*, *Superbad*, and *Clerks*. I assumed that I liked the movies, despite them being extremely sexist and with males as the target audience, because I'm the cool girl. I'm the girl that can look the way I do and also enjoy these movies.

Another assumption: Riley assumed I could swim. Thank God that was correct. So, there I was, in a dirty pool with a boy from Mississippi and my friends cheering outside of the pool. As I swam up, I thought: *Great. Here we go, back to pretending. Now, more energy will be taken away from me because now I have to pretend.* I swam back up for air but oddly found comfort in the gray water: finally, a tangible resemblance of what I'd felt on the inside for the last eight months. Murky. Gross. Swimming through the unknown.

Heads above water, Riley and I kissed. It could have been anyone, but someone threw us each another beer, and with my athletic ability, I jumped up and caught it with ease. I immediately cracked it open and chugged half of it, impressing all of the straight white cis men with my abilities. They cheered me on. I'd gone from winning soccer games to winning drinking games—being cool and tomboyish, my only defense to stay in the public graces.

So, when Riley said, "Get on my shoulders! Get on my shoulders!" I did. Someone threw us another beer.

I had always been accepted by male peers for my athleticism since grade school. So, of course, Riley and I chugged the beer down. As soon as I crushed the can and tossed it out of the pool, Riley sank down and fell into the water, taking me down with him. We rose back up, laughing hysterically. I looked over to see that we had gathered quite an audience. We kissed again and finally got out of the pool, only to be tossing each other in and out of it throughout the rest of the afternoon. I rang out my shorts with a smile and shook out my hair, playing it cool, so I didn't appear to care that my mascara had found its way around my eyes and down my face or that my foundation had been smeared off, revealing a face speckled with acne.

Anyway…I saw a classmate on the upper level of the porch. She was dressed in mostly denim and had a yellow flower crown and round sunglasses on her face. In October, she was one of the two that pulled me off the Breathalyzer Bro. We danced together, and over the music, she asked me why I was all wet. I simply pointed to the pool and said, "Riley." She nodded and rolled her eyes while someone we didn't know handed us two more beers. We clinked our cans together and then shotgunned the beer. Why so much chugging? I honestly don't know. A trash can was leaning against a wall a few yards behind us. My classmate tossed her can but missed by a long shot. I threw mine like a frisbee. The can bounced off the wall and into the can. Bank shot. My classmate high fived me, and we celebrated. Two other frat bros then came up to me and high fived me. I heard someone else yell, "Nice shot, Barbie." One told me he was going to buy me a drink later. Yeah, he said that. Didn't ask.

Many college kids drink and throw things, hoping they'll sink into whatever glass, cup, bucket, bin, or whatever the target of choice is that day or night. And that's an accomplishment, apparently. We celebrated a "made shot" every time as if our team had just won the World Series. Bonus points if you can make those shots while hammered. Triple bonus points if you're a girl. Apparently, drinking games were important, and winning them made you fit in. *Thank God I'm athletic.* The thing is, though, I looked like I fit in and acted like I fit in, but I never felt like I belonged. I felt mostly at home with Maren and Finn. They were fun, kind, and amazing humans—they still are.

I belonged on a soccer field, but I gave that up. I didn't know where I belonged anymore. I never felt worthy for winning a drinking game. Sure, it was kind of cool to be underage and drinking at times, but continuing this path was not going to win me an Emmy or become a best-selling author or save me enough money to be a dog mom.

Can someone honestly tell me they feel worthy and fulfilled by winning a game of Beer Pong or Quarters? Beer Pong professionals need not answer. I was supposed to be learning there, but the learning I was doing was all about my inner truth and very little about a topic of academic interest. *Maybe it'll get better if I stay here. Maybe I can focus more on my studies and still find a way. I am a determined person. I can do this. I can make this work.*

At some point at Woodstock, Riley, in the same manner that he'd entered, took off without saying a word. The Riley Effect, I used to call it. I let out a sigh and looked up to thank the heavens that he left. Then I burped and spun around with my arms open. Riley was the human equivalent to a puppy as far as cuteness goes, but his immaturity and lack of lesbianism, he was never much more than that to me. That distraction was nice, but once we departed for the night or go our separate ways, I was flooded with memories of Lauren and how I wished I was with her instead.

After a few more songs, I made my way back to Finn. He instantly took my hand and twirled me around. We were both drunk by now. Happy, silly drunk. *Why can't all my drunks be like this?* My feet moved fast, not because I was running this time, but because I was dancing. Finn almost fell, and my belly suddenly hurt, not from a queasy stomach but from laughter.

"You seem suddenly more fun," another friend says to me.

I smiled, knowing she was right. As soon as Riley left, I felt lighter. I felt like I was free to have a good time with just myself and some friends. I didn't want the pressure of knowing a potential male suitor was watching me.

Woodstock turned out to be an amazing day. Every day with Finn was. I loved day drinking. I wasn't out late, and the hangover wasn't ever nearly as bad as it was when I'd stay out drinking late. *Maybe I can just be a weekend day drinker. Is that my ticket to handling alcohol?*

By early evening, my clothes were mostly dry. I was still drunk, but not to the point where I was slurring my words, and I stayed put instead of running away like a mad woman. I wish I could've stayed there—in moments like those, in days like those.

Finn and I sat outside on the other side of some other frat house. I looked around and soaked in how college was supposed to feel. Fun. Safe drunk. Staying put and not running. Learning. The back patio had a basketball hoop, and a few guys played while Finn and I sat on a concrete ledge that framed a leg of the perimeter of the patio. My phone dinged. It was Jo, another gay softball player who lived up the hall from me. Jo was a beast on the field and just as outspoken off it as she was on it. She was unapologetically gay—and out and proud lesbian for as long as she could remember. Jo was team Ally and Lauren more than she was team Lauren and Cori.

She sent me a text about Lauren, saying she was sad that we weren't together anymore. As I crafted a text back, Finn said something and made me laugh for the millionth time, and he laid his head on my shoulder just long enough to see the text from Jo.

"Who's Lauren?"

My stomach suddenly hurt—this time, not from laughter. There was no running away from this now. Finn scrolled up to read the rest of the messages. I didn't stop him. He now knew about my relationship with Lauren. I let him because I was not about to lie to my friend, even though I hid my relationship from him. I didn't want to hide right now. I was sick of hiding. I was sick of running. I pulled my knees into my chest.

"Wait. You're dating...you dated a girl?!"

He wasn't mad. He was surprised, excited, and sad about the breakup but happy for me. I told him all about me and Lauren. I let go of my knees and swung them off the ledge, letting each heel lightly tap the concrete. He had no idea.

"Why didn't you tell me?"

I shrugged. Although I was drunk, I was so unbelievably calm because of Finn's reaction. He was kind, patient, and loving—the exact opposite of the reaction I feared from anyone. *Why was I so afraid to tell my gay friend that I fell in love with a woman this year?*

I learned how to perfect the following role: Straight Woman (age 18-30); knows how to flirt with men sober, drunk, and most things in between.

Passes for being straight.

I had been surrounded by straight women my entire life and had picked up on a few things, like how to be cute, as I sipped a drink with a straw. And how to make eye contact in a way that makes him wonder if you're actually looking at him or someone else. So many damn games I was playing. I remember thinking how exhausting it was, putting on a mask all the time, being someone I was not. No matter how drunk I got, I had a sense that I wanted to be in control of myself—the control serving as a tool to keep my outward identity in check, never revealing the true self that lay beneath.

On one Sunday afternoon, I was hanging out with a friend from back home in her dorm room. I was shocked when she told me she didn't remember the previous night. She'd blacked out. She thought it was hilarious as her other friends gave her a recount of her whereabouts and antics. I was appalled by my own actions that I did remember; I couldn't even imagine what I'd do if I blacked out completely or the shame I'd feel hearing those actions recounted to me.

I wished I were strong enough to be in a social setting and not drink. Why aren't coffee shops open until 1:00 a.m. in this town? Or any town? Or perhaps we could sip tea until 9:30, so I'd be back home and in bed by 11? I dreamed of performing a lot during this time. My dreams kept me going. My dreams of writing for television. My dreams of staring in a show or movie. My dreams of writing books. I would slay open mics. If only I were strong enough to seek something else out or start something on my own.

I craved another escape the way soccer let me escape. I wanted something to work toward that was bigger than me. I missed being a part of a team, and now that I was no longer part of a team, I dreamt of something similar.

I remember reading the label when I'd started antidepressants for the first time earlier that semester: *do not take with alcohol.* Finally! A concrete excuse not to drink. No one would think twice if I said I wasn't drinking because of a medical reason, right? HA. But I never rallied up the courage to use my medical excuse. I had even conducted my very own series of trials, slowly testing how my body reacted to drinking on the medication. As far as I could tell, I was a much better drunk, a safer drunk, while drinking on my new antidepressant. I ignored the warning on the label and also the warnings in my mind and body.

Figuring out antidepressants was a pain in the bum hole, with or without alcohol. *What's the right dosage? What's the right medication? Do I need to take this for a few months, a few years, forever?* Forever. The answer is forever.

At some point, though, between January 2011 and May 2011, I stopped taking the medication because I decided I didn't need it. I did not need to rely on a medication for my *happiness.* We create our own happiness, goddammit! I learned quickly that most people did not openly talk about a lot of things: depression included. I was trying to fit in at Ole Miss, so I was certainly not going to bring up something that's going to outcast me. A probably gay woman that is depressed and taking medication for it. That would be highly unwell of me if I spoke up. *Keep drinking. Keep playing straight. Don't act, talk about or mention depression. Got it!*

Getting mono, I admit, was my own damn fault. I climbed in bar windows to avoid paying the cover to get in. I stole drinks when patrons looked away or left their full drinks unattended. That was probably the most disgusting thing I ever did. Gross. I never took a drink that was less than 80% full. That would have been REALLY gross, right?!

On one particular evening out, I did one of several walks around the bar. I returned to Maren with a drink in my hand.

"Where'd you get that?" Maren asked.

"I stole it."

We both laughed. I offered her a sip, but she said: "I'm not drinking that!" And then we danced.

Over the course of my spring semester of freshmen year, I stole countless beers, several whiskey and cokes, and handfuls of vodka sodas. Yuck. I cannot stand vodka sodas. I'd prefer straight whiskey, but most people can't handle the taste like I can, so they choose to sweeten it with soda. Do they not know that alcohol already breaks down into sugar? Another reason I drank was for the taste. I loved the taste of whiskey chilled by ice. I loved the taste of beer and how the hops bounced in my mouth down my throat, and into my body. I loved how the drinks looked in my hand while I danced. Holding drinks felt like armor. It was as if my existence was an advertisement for the college experience or for the breweries and distilleries whose beverages I carried like gold, sweating in my palms.

I never acquire the taste for fruity drinks. The only sweet drinks I liked when I was nineteen were champagne and some white wines. Maren and I always loved Moscato and this wine called Polka Dot. It came in a gorgeous, dark, royal blue bottle with a large pink dot on the center of the label and a white cap. As we got ready for our night, we'd pour wine into large opaque plastic cups we'd collected from local restaurants. Those cups were Ole Miss' alternative to the solo cup. I poured mine into a Newk's cup, and Maren pours hers into a cup from Oby's. We blasted music in the bathroom as we sipped and showered. I loved being wine drunk. Wine drunk was my best drunk. I was always happy, fun, and light.

I was still a little over two years away from turning twenty-one. On the nights when my friends of age were not with us to buy us drinks, our routine was to drink as much as possible before going out and hoping that some guys would be stupid or nice enough to buy us drinks when we got to the bar. Fortunately for us, this was pretty typical of the regular bar goers in a college town during 2010-2014. I did not want to talk to guys. Maren, though, could talk to anyone. She was a spitfire who could get any guy she wanted. I cheered her on in her sexual adventures. Meanwhile, I was just trying to get through the night without throwing up and silently hoping no guys talked to me. I'd flirt with them when I was drunk, but I never wanted to. Getting drunk and flirting with guys was normal for college women, so I convinced myself I was just trying to be normal. What I didn't realize then is that I was trying so hard for normalcy when I was not born to be normal. I am not normal. I am not traditional. I am not like most people.

Having mono threw me in to a parallel universe. It was like a constant fever dream. My tonsils swelled up, and my fever was especially high the first week. My body ached, and I slept twenty hours a day. Between sleeping that much and eating only a handful of crackers and a can of soup daily, I started to lose weight. My tonsils were sharp, and so swollen by week two that they were practically touching.

I must admit, though, being sick with mono gave me another escape, granting me a wish that I didn't make. Mono gave me another mask to wear, too, but this mask wasn't a lie. I was relieved to have a valid reason to sleep all day.

Even though I started the summer off with this wicked illness, I was glad to finally have an excuse to rest. I looked forward to the time to reflect and relax. I still didn't feel at home in Oxford, but I was determined to give it one last try that summer. I listened to the voice that told me it would be okay to remain in the south. I wanted to be there so badly, so I decided to stay.

Convinced that staying in Oxford for a few more months would be good for me, I was hopeful for the summer. I thought that extending my time there would've been the magic trick for it to all work out. Even with my friends going home for the summer, I truly believed I would make it work there.

CHAPTER XIII

I tossed the last bag in the trunk of my car and slammed it shut. Maren took one final look at Hefly Hall and hopped in the passenger seat of the car. Our freshmen dorm saw a lot of tears, laughter, and growth. To my knowledge, neither of us would ever step foot in there again. That fall, Maren and I planned on moving into an apartment a mile or two from campus with our friend, Rachel. There was a lot to look forward to. Strangely enough, I felt little excitement in that moment. My primary feeling was sadness that I wouldn't see Maren for three months.

The drive from Oxford, Mississippi to Memphis was usually a long ride, but it went by too quickly that day. Despite her being still drunk and me being way too hungover to be in broad daylight, her open spirit carried mine through the adventure. I didn't want the car ride to end; the school year had already been one of the longest of my life, and this summer would be even longer. I so badly wanted to fast forward to some better life I hadn't yet conceived of. I didn't want to do the journey. I just wanted the destination. I wanted the rewards. Not the struggle to get the rewards. It's no wonder I hadn't reached that destination yet, however, as I couldn't even say what it looked like at that time. There was so much for me to learn and experience to get to where I eventually needed to go.

I pulled up to the terminal at Memphis International and parked in the first spot I saw. Maren scrolled through my music and played "Dancin' in September" for the last time before she headed home to California for the summer. Countless bottles of wine, sleepless nights, hundreds of workouts, and one matching tattoo later, Maren had become one of my best friends at Ole Miss. And over a decade later, when we do call each other up, it's like no time has passed between us.

"Ba de ya de ya de ya de ya!" We sang as loudly as our lungs allowed, loud enough to have gathered an audience looking on in confusion. I hesitantly turned the car off and went with Maren inside the airport. To keep me from crying, I started singing show tunes as Maren checked her bags. A well-dressed man walked up to us.

"Are either of you two trained singers?" he asked.

No.

"I'm not, but she is!" Maren said, pointing to me.

"Well, I'm a producer out in Nashville. Give me a call sometime." He took a business card out of his wallet and handed it to me. It was red, black, and gold with a guitar on the front.

I never called him, but I placed his card in my wallet to keep as a reminder that I do not suck. After tearful goodbyes, I watched Maren disappear through security. *There goes my last friend in Oxford.*

I walked as slowly as I could back to my car. I got in, and immediately started sobbing, my head in my hands against the steering wheel. I'd miss her, yes, but my tears came from the grand fear of not knowing. Fear of being alone with my thoughts. Fear of not having a friend around to hang out with and talk to every day.

What if someone finds out? That won't happen. I won't let them know how bad it is.

I'd be staying in Oxford over the summer. I did not admit it, but that summer would be incredibly different compared to the school year. Discovering myself beyond the friends and people I constantly had around me was scary to me. I wondered what was truly beneath my façade, if there was anything at all. I think that was what I was most afraid of: what if there wasn't anything deeper or bigger? Peeling away a truth that I know but won't tell myself.

Even with my hair longer, it felt like a wig. My hair didn't feel like my own. The longer it is, the more heterosexual it feels. It feels too girly, and I am definitely not a girly-girl.

In addition to denying my sexuality through my outer appearance, I also struggled relating to my straight friends and teammates in college when it came to dating. Conversations were difficult for me because I found myself lying to *fit in* and contribute to those conversations. I bragged about having a crush on so and so. I agreed that a dick pic an upperclassman showed me was, in fact, *nice.* I much later noticed a pattern with some of the guys I dated and had 'crushes' on: most of them looked like masc lesbians.

If I began taking off the masks of the lies in those conversations or thought about chopping off my hear, I feared I would have to answer questions I was not ready to answer. I also was afraid that I didn't have the answers to those questions. If I came out, I worried someone would ask me *what's your type?* or god forbid, *do you have a crush on ME?* I didn't want to have to answer to anybody. The inevitable comments and potential rumors were things I did not want face. My mental health was already a winding road. If I started telling and living my truth, deep down my body told me that I would be more depressed. I didn't focus on the positive impacts of releasing **my** truth and letting go of who I am not.

As hopeful as I was after the Woodstock party, I felt it start to fade after dropping off Maren. Doubt started to settle in on the ride back to Oxford from the airport. I sobbed, attempting to gather the courage to want to be in Mississippi. That was not the first time I'd attempted to convince myself of this; I just hoped this time would be different. I hoped this time that want would actually come true. *I want to be here. I want to be here. I will make this work.*

My mother drove down from St. Louis to help me move into a three-bedroom apartment for the summer, with a monthly rent of $420. The apartment was perfect, except that my bathroom did not connect to my room. That summer, when my roommate, Tiff, had people over, I sometimes would hold my bladder to avoid interaction. I was mostly quiet when meeting new people. It was awkward for me at nineteen, especially since soccer had always been my icebreaker—an icebreaker I no longer had. Who wanted to hear about the girl who used to play soccer for Ole Miss in the SEC? But get a beer or two in me, and my nerves would be settled enough to have an easy conversation—it was far from meaningful, but a conversation, nonetheless.

My room's window was small, and when the shades were down, it was almost completely dark. Almost. The window always provided the tiniest bit of light around the edges. Everything else inside the panes is completely black. If I hadn't had a job that summer or a class for the first month with somewhat of a consistent schedule, I would never have known what day it was.

I managed mostly in the early part of college, but I was bored and apathetic, except for my theatre classes. I would step in to class knowing it was a safe space to express my emotions—whether the emotions were from that day or pulled from a memory. I should have delved deeper into my academics in college or at least found something theatre related that summer when I needed another distraction.

After my mom left from helping me move in, I sat on my new bed, surrounded by organized clothes and personal items. I was grateful for the quiet, the time to rest. That summer, my room quickly became my escape. My closest friends had gone back home for the summer, and instead of venturing out more often to meet people, I retreated into myself, into my depressive state. The only thing holding me up most days was my bed. *I want to be here. I am supposed to be here. I will make this work.* I told myself that lie every day for a year until my grandpa was in hospice.

CHAPTER XIV

I blinked back to consciousness as I laid on the floor of my apartment bedroom. It was a Wednesday morning—a month into summer break. Plenty of sun poured into my room due to the drunken forgetfulness of closing my blinds before I passed out. The amount of sunlight led me to think that it was well past the hours of the early morning.

My hands pressed into the floor as I slowly eased myself to an upright position. My eyes squinted immediately as I faced the window, grunting at the disappointment of light. Perhaps I was not disappointed by the abundance of light so much, but rather the disappointment with myself for running away from my own light….and also not feeling any light within me. *Where did MY light go?*

It was hot and sunny that day, but I wished it were gray—gray like the fog that had entered my brain and didn't want to leave. *Is there a world cup game today? I hope I didn't miss it. Fuck. I don't even know what time it is.*

I turned away from the sunlight, although I still used it to find my phone. I crawled over to it, laying in the corner of the room. I pressed the home screen button and breathed a sigh of relief when it reminded me that today I was off from work and also class. I scanned the room for my keys next but couldn't find them. *How did I get home?*

My eyes followed the path of the clothes I wore last night. Tank top. One sandal. A bra. *My bra?* I picked it up. *Yes, my bra.* The other sandal. My shorts. I grabbed the shorts and flicked them over to find my keys resting halfway out of the righthand front pocket. I looped my finger in my blue and red Ole Miss keychain and tossed the keys into my hands. *Good. I have my keys AND phone.* I closed my eyes and rubbed my temples. Within seconds, my eyes shot open, and I jumped up to stand. *Fuck.* I squeezed my eyes shut again. *Ouch.* Then, the Wall started to come down.

I've told you all about The Wall was something that always came up when I drank too much, and these days, it had become more and more frequent. It was like a switch. I would be drinking and having a so-called great time, but I kept on drinking, throwing myself closer and closer to the Wall, not realizing I was approaching it until I hit it...hard. When the Wall hit, I ran. I ran away from people. From parties. I don't know if I realized I was trying to run away from myself, but that would never happen. Ha. This Wall coming down was the worst one yet. My breathing thickened as I remembered the night before...

Last night was just as hot as any other, and a friend of a friend from the theatre department at school had a group of people over to their apartment, not too far from mine. All I remembered drinking were shots. One after the other. I didn't feel like I had much to contribute to the conversation, but I could take a shot. That's what I brought to the party. My ability to tip it on back and entertain from silly dances and singing loudly to all the songs and my ability to sink nearly every beer pong cup because of my athletic competitiveness. I fit in when I drank. So, I drank.

I was at that apartment all of two hours, and I was fine drinking like I always am until Op!

Here it comes. The Wall. Then it's time to run. Most of the guests left one shortly after another. Then only a few of us remained, including my roommate, Tiff. Tiff and Mickey, the guy's apartment we were at, went on the balcony to smoke a cigarette. I learned here in Oxford that smoking locations are nuanced. Weed was for inside smoking. Cigarettes were for outside smoking. Maybe because one's legal? I didn't fucking know. I was just a 19-year-old who only had gotten high maybe twice.

"Wanna come smoke, Ally?" Tiff asked.

"No, I'm good." *I'll stick with the alcohol to ruin my body, but THANKS SO MUCH.*

Maybe cigarettes will be in my next life. Cheers though, for real.

"Okay, we'll be right back."

I was left alone. I looked around the apartment, and I already knew what I was going to do next.

This was my chance. My opening. My window. Once Mickey closed the door behind them, I grabbed my keys, phone, and wallet and headed for the door. It was time to leave. I didn't want to be there anymore.

I got in my car and recklessly drove back to my apartment. No one saw me. **The only witness my memory, never letting me forget.**

I tried blaming my age as an excuse for drunk driving. There's no one to blame but myself. I was the one who drank and continued to drink. I had only verbally spoken about driving drunk two or three times before writing it in this book. I am forever grateful no one was hurt. My stomach flips every time it crosses my mind. I'm so sorry.

The biggest repercussion from that was living with the memory of it, but even that wasn't grandiose enough for me to quit drinking. I was just getting started with my bad habit.

How the fuck did I get to this point?

I remembered swerving. Driving off of the road. Driving back on to the road. Zig. Zag. Swerve. *Was that me driving though?*

I quietly exited my room, successfully avoiding Tiff, my roommate. I walked outside, and there was my car, my midnight blue 2006 Mazda 3, double parked with the front right wheel up on the curb. *Fuck.* Now the Wall really started to crumbled, and I remembered the night completely. *Yeah, it was you driving, Al. What the fuck? Why can't you just sip on a drink or two? Why is it always one too many?*

I closed my eyes, trying to erase the memory, but I saw the ride home now as if I were in a movie. Swerve. Swerve. Swerve some more. *Drive straight ahead. Drive straight ahead.* The car hopped over the median and then back onto the street. Miraculously, the gate to the complex opened. I didn't have a gate opener yet. I squeezed my eyes harder. I drove over the median yet again and stepped on the gas to make it inside seconds before the gate crushed me, or worse—my car. I found my building and parked (double apparently), and then stumbled inside.

The only witness was my memory, not allowing me to forget.

It's a miracle I was alive. It's a miracle I didn't hurt or kill anyone else. It was nothing short of a miracle and luck that I got back to my apartment in one piece that night. And by the grace of God, the traffic stop that was set up earlier that night was gone by the time I headed back to my apartment.

In my regret, my decision flashed before. Just the year before, I'd graduated high school, ready to play Division One soccer for a team in the SEC, and now I was soccer-less and driving drunk on a weeknight. *What the fuck. Was quitting a mistake? No. No. It was NOT a mistake. That's what caused you to feel so awful, Ally.*

Right? Right. Soccer = depression.

I ate something the night before. The apartment was quiet when I got home. I opened the cupboard to find a dozen packs of Top Ramen noodles. *Did I buy Ramen noodles?* I rarely bought them, but the questioning in my drunken state didn't last long.

"Whoever did buy 'em won't miss one!" I loudly whispered even though I was in the apartment by myself. I reached for a chicken flavored pack and tore it open with my teeth after fumbling with it for what felt like ten minutes.

Despite drunk driving minutes before, I was extra careful not to burn myself while cooking the noodles. I grabbed oven mitts to handle the boiling pot. I unnecessarily turned the fan on above the stove. As soon as the noodles were cooled off enough, I ate them in the same amount of time it took to cook them: three minutes. I then chugged a glass of water, spilling most of it on my shirt. I did not clean up, leaving all evidence of stealing food and being a lousy roommate all over the kitchen. I took a step toward my room, but immediately turned around to the kitchen to turn off the fan.

I took my clothes off the second I closed my bedroom door. I just wanted my own bed, but that was not where I ultimately ended up. Whenever I was that drunk, I had to sleep on the floor. The floor was the only thing that settled the spins and could quickly rock me to sleep. It was even better if that floor was a cool surface. Many nights I passed out cradling the toilet, desperately asking how I'd done that to myself once again.

I breathed heavily as I settled on to the carpet, glad not to feel the need to throw up. I'd already forgotten my joy ride that ended just moments prior. It was forgotten at that moment, but I'll remember it forever and be haunted by it forever.

A sudden chill ran through me, and I sat up and pulled a blanket off my bed. As I laid back on the floor, I opened my text messages and searched for *Lauren*. I began to type "I miss you" but deleted it without hitting send. She was right up the street, and I missed her so much. I grunted again as I tossed my phone away from my body. I got as comfortable as I could with the blanket now draped around me, pillow-less and naked.

Lauren.

I'd seen her at the pool earlier that day. She was all smiles and laughter, the same laugh that pulled me in for the first time during preseason the previous August. I left the pool shortly after she got there to go back to the darkness of my bedroom. Her light, along with the sun, was too much for me to bear.

As my phone rested on the middle of the floor, my mind swirled me back to a happier moment when we kissed for the first time in the backseat of our teammate's car.

Her gentle hands, much smaller than mine, softened me as she laced her fingers in mine. It was cold out that night in January, but she made me warm. She always made me feel better and helped me forget the cold and all other things bad.

But just like soccer, I didn't have her anymore either. I had given both of them up. It was June in the dead of Mississippi, and somehow, I felt colder than ever.

I was punishing myself. I was embarrassed about how I left things with Lauren. I was ashamed that I hadn't given more thought to our relationship. I was ashamed that I gave in to societal norms and went against what really made me happy.

I could have reached out to Lauren, even if it was just as a friend. However, it was so much easier to run in the other direction than to admit I was in more pain than ever before. I didn't have the strength not to be a recluse. I didn't have the strength to let a wall down that I was working so hard to actively keep up. That work to hold up the wall took so much from me. It took my energy and time, but I was so afraid of being rejected by Lauren that I reached for a bottle instead of reaching out to her – or anyone.

A simple conversation with Lauren or a check-in with someone might have been enough to push me in a healthier direction. I wish I had held myself a little tighter like I held a bottle of whiskey, wine, or beer. I wish I had given someone I trusted the chance to hold me, even if that hold was in the form of a text message or a cup of coffee. I didn't necessarily need to cry in someone's arms, but I needed to be held in the words of someone else's encouragement and company. Shit. I needed therapy.

So, there I was the next morning after a night of drinking, which followed a day of misery pining after Lauren, and I had no concept of time. Other than a throbbing headache, I was in no other pain nor danger. I was grateful for the hangover, actually; it was the only proof that something lived inside of me, that I could feel something, even if it was pain. I drank to feel, I guess, even if that feeling was one hour or so of fake happiness followed by feeling like shit. I mistook this lightness that comes with drinking for being happy. I felt something other than numbness as soon as the alcohol buzzed in my blood, allowing my head to feel lighter for a few hours. I thought this was happiness, but damn did that *happiness* come with a price or what?! The Price? The Wall would hit, and then I would be filled with rage.

After checking on my car and crawling back into bed, it occurred to me that no one had called or texted me about last night, not even the 'friends' I had been drinking with. Hell, not even my roommate. *Do I have any friends left in this town?* I felt so alone. I was alone.

If my brain was chemically imbalanced, I did not know how to balance it by myself in Oxford. I didn't want to put that burden on my friends who deserve to have the time of their lives in college, and I was unsure of how to verbally communicate my insides to others in my life.

This was my issue, but I couldn't figure it out while in Oxford, I thought. Maybe I could spend just a little bit of time in St. Louis and then be on my way to Chicago or New York or LA, sooner than moving there after graduation like I had originally planned.

The good in Mississippi did not outweigh the bad. I tried my hardest, but my depression won this battle. It was time to make a change, but it was not really a change. It was simply going back to what was familiar to me. My comfort. My home. My dog. My family. My St. Louis. The thought stayed with me during the next few weeks. St. Louis would be a safe option for me. Anything felt better than Oxford, but I was too afraid to go anywhere unknown, if I went anywhere at all. Maybe I'd get a handle on my mind and drinking habits if I were to go home. Maybe the support of my family would have more of an impact if I were closer to them. Whether I made the decision to go back home or not, I was still running.

CHAPTER XV

My parents came to visit me that fourth of July weekend. The whole weekend was a blur. Prior to their arrival, I sat in the darkness of my bedroom for days. I became an expert at hiding my feelings when I was out in public. I didn't want to be called out. I didn't want anyone to ask me if I was okay. I barely had the energy to pretend outside of my bedroom walls. As soon as I returned from my shift at work or from class, I closed the door, turned off the lights and returned to sleeping with my eyes open. Dazed and detached, I would stare heavily at the ceiling, wishing for sleep to come quickly.

When sleep didn't come quickly or at all, TV kept me company. During sleepless nights, I either watched infomercials or the reruns of the TV show *Numbers*, a drama about a math guru who helps his FBI agent brother unscramble cases. In between daytime naps, I watched the U.S. Women's National Team play in the 2011 Women's World Cup. I didn't feel sad to watch soccer. I felt comforted in the familiarity. The strung-together passing, the penalty kick shootout, the announcers, the celebrations after scoring a goal. Watching the USWNT play was like a warm hug from another continent.

Their loss in the final to Japan was devastating, but I felt less alone knowing how they were feeling. I was numb and felt like shit. I know it feels like shit to lose, and I know the numbness that can come along with it. I thought briefly about how it felt to win and how it would feel for them to win the World Cup again. Victory is always sweeter after tasting vinegar of loss.

It felt weird to not be actively training or working on something. I was no longer part of a team, and I didn't count the 'team' at my part time job. That kind of team was a bit of a joke.

Other than my main goal of getting through the day, I did not have any goals at that time. I did, however, daydream about returning theatre classes—a positive escape from my day and from my mind. Mostly, though, I focused on getting through the day. As soon as I left my bed in the morning, I looked forward to getting back in it later that morning, afternoon, or night. I was uninterested in most things, including things I loved not too long ago: exercising, journaling, talking to friends, sitting by the pool. Going through the motions while being emotionally numb was exhausting, but those motions helped me keep going.

Despite recently being told my grandpa's health was declining, when my parents arrived, their presence took a burden off me. I felt more relaxed around my mother. She brought a comfort that helped me release the mask of a constant fake smile. I didn't have to pretend I was *okay* around her. However, I did not provide full transparency for how numb I felt that summer. My mom didn't realize how bad my mental health had gotten because I didn't keep her informed. She was under the impression I was having a decent time and relaxing by myself. I was by myself, but I was lonely. There's a massive difference between being by yourself and being lonely. I didn't want her to worry, especially with her father getting sicker.

Even though I didn't speak up about how I was really feeling, I was glad to have someone familiar to talk to for a few days. Someone that not only knew me, but someone that knew me for my entire life. I was absolutely devastated when they left, not wishing to return to the darkness. I was running out of hope that things would get better.

That Monday, I was opening the store. They came in to say goodbye, and as I contemplated the heaviness that came with the farewell, I realized that the only thing that would replace the hole where hope once lived would be either of them staying or me leaving. I had the next two and a half days off, so an hour after my shift, I decided to go home.

One speeding ticket and six hours later, I got to St. Louis. I opened the door to the garage and saw my mom first. She practically jumped off the couch and walked over to give me a hug. Her loving squeeze released the bags from my hands and filled some of that hole that had been open for too long. Just like the last weekend, these couple of days spent with my parents were a blur. I questioned why I had even come during the work week. Everyone had work to do, including my brother who was interning for my dad at the time.

However, one vivid memory stands out. It surprised me that I could remember my drunken memories from the nights prior, but when I was completely sober, I struggled to remember some things. My sober mind those days, though, was still clouded by the darkest clouds of depression. The morning of my last day there, my dad made me his famous scrambled eggs with a bagel and bacon on the side. I picked over my breakfast, wanting to speak up about what I'd been feeling, but instead, I ended up choking down my scrambled eggs so no one would ask "what's wrong?" prompted by my lack of appetite.

My dad and brother were about to head out to client meetings. I wanted to tell Dad about my ticket, but I bit my tongue and decided to do it over the phone when I got back to Oxford.

My mom didn't realize how bad my mental health had gotten because I didn't keep her updated. I behaved and spoke in ways that would not leave my mom worrying more than she probably already was. I left out key parts of that summer every time I spoke with her. Instead of saying I was lonely, I played it off like I was having alone time to recuperate from a long, busy school year.

Dad never yells. Just tell him.

I didn't think I could even talk about the ticket without puking up the bitter misery I had felt for the better part of the last ten months. I felt it would have been an inconvenience if I had spoken up, and I certainly did not want to be the one who made them miss an important meeting or sale. I offered to clean up the kitchen, and as they headed out the door, I followed.

I stood there in the center of the garage, feeling the heat from summer and the coldness of the concrete floor on which I stood. With it, I felt an atom of sunlight peeking through the cold darkness of my thoughts.

Maybe I <u>can</u> try.

I opened my mouth to speak but nothing came out.

"Be careful, Al. Okay? Love you!" Dad said.

I stared ahead as I watched him join my brother in his dark red Pathfinder parked but running on the driveway.

I opened my mouth once more.

All I cracked out in return was, "Okay. Love you."

They backed out of the driveway, and as the garage began to close, blocking the sun, the atom of sunlight I felt moments ago vanished. In its place: panic and fear.

This goodbye went too quickly. It seemed like all of my goodbyes were going too quickly. First Lauren. Then Maren. Now this. The moments I wanted to hold on to were always going by too quickly. I had a chance, and I missed it. *Why can't you just speak up? You can still call them. Follow them! Speak up.* **They don't want to hear you, that's why.** *Oh, right. Thanks for reminding me, Depression.*

I also felt that at the time big news had to be shared in person and said out loud. I thought that by saying it out loud, face-to-face that I'd be taken more seriously.

That's what I'm here for, Ally. I'll never leave you, depression told me. Funny how something will never leave you, but that same thing can also make you feel the loneliest in the world. Yes, funny. So funny. Absolutely hilarious.

The people around me couldn't see how much pain I was in because depression is an invisible illness. We are not mind readers. I can look sad, thin, tired, but you truly cannot physically show depression outwardly as it is inwardly, as it is: an imbalance. My life seemed pretty balanced. I thought I had my shit together. On paper, it looked like I did, but no. Again, it was all a façade.

I was working and going to summer school—look at me working hard! I was just going through the motions so I didn't burden anyone else except myself. I didn't want to hurt anyone by speaking up, even if it meant sacrificing my own healing and wellbeing.

The garage finally closed, but tears forbade me to see it. With the garage closed, the dampness and blackness of the space around me matched that of my body. The atom of sunlight was nowhere in sight. I did not want them to leave me, and I did not want to leave to go back to Oxford. There was nothing there for me except darkness.

But in that moment, for the first time in my life, I did not run from myself. I fell to the cold concrete floor and sobbed. Hysterical.

I was being crushed. I was suffocating. Something was still very wrong. Quitting soccer did not ease my pain. I screamed on the inside because I couldn't scream on the outside unless I was drunk.

But I wasn't screaming my truth when I was drunk. I was…well I was just screaming nonsense most of the time.

I could only tell the truth when I was sober. I just hadn't learned how to spit it out of my mouth. I hadn't gotten into that habit yet. It was unknown. I wasn't acting on it because I was afraid of feeling it. Afraid that I'd fall and not feel the weight of the pain lifted.

What if the pain doesn't ease up if I do speak out? Even if I do tell the truth, will it ever truly set me free? Will I ever be free? Will a closeted depressed possible lesbian with a drinking problem ever be free? This is my life's challenge. Guess I have to just deal with it. Alone, too, maybe.

But there I was. I may have been alone on that garage floor sans human beings, but I was feeling every wave of pain that was rushing through my body. I was feeling it and letting myself feel it.

I was there; I'm not sure how long when my dog Heidi trotted next to me and lifted my chin with her nose. Only then did I realize my purple hands were chilled instantly by the garage floor due to Raynaud's, a syndrome that heightens one's sensitivity to the cold. I was devastated, but I was relieved. I was feeling something and allowing myself to feel. I felt the icing of my hands along with the heaviness of every other surface inside and outside of my body. Not only did I feel the wetness of the tears on my cheeks, but I tasted their salt on my tongue, reminding me there was still life inside me. Maybe that atom of sunlight was still in there. Somewhere. It was up to me to dig it out.

I had not cried since dropping off my best girl, Maren, at the airport. I was no longer a vegetable of numbness. I was alive. I was not completely alone. I was not completely empty. I cared.

I thanked Heidi for seeing my pain without me even having to say a word. I thanked her for seeing my pain when the humans in my life could not. I thanked her for making me feel better and for not speaking up time and time again.

I laid on the garage floor with Heidi for a little while longer, my head eventually resting in my arms. I finally pressed my cold hands into the cold ground as a voice whispered from within me: "Get up, Ally. Rise up."

So, I got back up.

CHAPTER XVI

There was not a cloud in sight a month later on August 10, 2011. My family bared the heat only because a cool breeze countered it, and the humidity was at a minimum. The Cardinals lost 5-1 to the Brewers, but we lost more than a baseball game that day. We lost the life of one of the most genuine, hardest working, funniest people I would ever know: my grandpa. He was a diehard baseball fan. He loved everything about it and every second of it.

Sterile. Natural light from all angles. Absolutely zero dust particles slivering in the sun of the St. Anthony's Hospice House in Sappington, MO. My grandma, a neat freak, approved of this cleanliness.

Fifteen or so of his nine children and several of his grandkids, myself included, gathered around his bed, crying and praying together in the last breaths of his life. A six-foot four-inch teddy bear, my grandpa laid nearly lifeless on a hospice bed.

He showed early signs of Alzheimer's a few years earlier, but a heart attack was what sent him to his final demise.

My older brother sat at Busch stadium watching the Cardinals play. That was exactly where he was supposed to be. Everyone was where they were supposed to be. I wished I were at the game with my brother. I felt that would be a bigger way to honor my grandfather on his death day than to cry over him. But I was glad I could be there.

My grandpa is a huge reason that I am who I am. A huge part of why my childhood was filled with magic, laughter, and life at every corner of my small but big world. Our time together consisted of some of my earliest performances. Grandpa made everything fun, and everywhere was a stage: the car, the dinner table, on his boat, baseball games, fish fries in the backyard.

We made up stories. The songs we had sung together became the soundtrack of my childhood. We made up characters that had silly, ridiculous, but loving conversations. He brought out the best in me. My mother says that I am him but in drag.

His name was Ray, and just like his name, he lit up every room he entered like a ray of sunshine. He had the people in those rooms laughing or smiling in seconds. Grandpa worked three jobs. When he wasn't at the firehouse, he bagged groceries, and on the weekends, he drove a limousine for weddings. Along with his work ethic, my grandpa was a man of great faith, too. He went to church most Sundays and always carried a pocket prayer book.

Although his comedic routines didn't extend further than his home and church in the Oakville area of St. Louis and the firehouse in Kirkwood, MO, the laughs he got were impactful. He reminded me of Robin Williams. May they both rest in peace.

After what felt like hours, Grandpa stopped breathing. We cried harder. He breathed again. *Just go. Take him, please.* I prayed. He stopped breathing. *Thank you.* Grandpa breathed again, sending us all into a wet laughter. This went on for an incredibly long five minutes. True to himself in the final inhalations and exhalations, he made us all laugh.

Finally, Grandpa passed on. He was seventy-one, an age too young to leave earth and a number that would always resonate with me from that day forward. He was seventy-one, and I was nineteen. Our time together was much too short. I wish he could've stayed longer.

On the day we buried Grandpa, I ran eight miles. I'm sure you're not surprised by this. Just like when I'd run when feelings would come up that I didn't want to face, I ran because it took away my pain or at least gave me something to focus on. I was physically running from it instead of feeling it, instead of talking about what I felt. I ran until I couldn't feel it.

Instead of crying or talking about the cave of sadness inside of me, I ran, slept, studied, or drank about it. His death catapulted me into fitness and most of the time nutrition, aside from an unhealthy activity, I could not let go of drinking.

The week before, I had dinner with my parents at Sunset 44, a nice locally owned Kirkwood restaurant. As we walked to our table, I remembered a fun celebration at the same restaurant with them. It was a Friday night, and we gathered to celebrate after I made the Junior Varsity basketball team my freshman year of high school. It was a big deal for me because I hadn't played competitive basketball at all. Prior to high school, I had only played for my grade school's team. My spirits at dinner that night were not as high as they were five years earlier.

I sat across from my parents at a four-top table in Sunset's main dining room. As I smeared cheese on the house made Lavosh, I blurted out, "I'm not going back to Ole Miss."

I took a big bite of the Lavosh as my shoulders loosened with relief. My mom sipped from her wine glass as my dad chewed his own Lavosh. My mom set her glass down and asked, "Are you sure?"

"Yes," I said firmly.

"May I ask why?" she replied.

"I'm not happy there. I don't want to go back. Please don't make me go back." I said with my voice getting louder with each word that came out.

"Okay. Well, what are you going to do then?" Mom asked.

"Well, there's SLU or Wash-U or you could always go to St. Louis Community College for a semester," Dad said.

"I'm not going to STLCC," I said, knowing that if I were to go to a community college or take any time off, I'd feel like an ultimate failure. In hindsight, going to a community college would have been an incredibly logical and financially sound decision. There is absolutely nothing wrong with going to a community college if that is what's best for the student.

"You have to do something, Al," Mom said.

"I guess I'll go to Webster," I said.

"Okay. What about your stuff in Oxford?" She asked.

"Umm. I guess I could go down and get it."

"No. I'll take care of it. Don't you worry about it, kiddo," Dad said.

"Alright. Thank you."

"You'll need to withdraw from your classes and apply to Webster as soon as possible," she said as she typed something on her phone.

A couple of minutes pass and as she locks her phone and sets it down on the table, she said, "You have a meeting with Admissions tomorrow morning."

Mom exhaled and took a sip of wine.

"Was it really that bad?" She asked.

"Yeah. I spent most of the summer by myself."

"Why didn't you say something sooner?"

I shrugged and said, "I thought it'd go away."

The next morning, my dad drove with me to Webster's Administrative building on Lockwood Avenue. The Admissions Counselor was delightful. She was incredibly welcoming and answered any questions we had. I can't remember if we go a tour, but as the meeting ended, the woman asked if we had any last questions.

"Uh, yeah," my dad said and then looked at me. "What about soccer?"

I shrugged.

"I think it could be good for you."

"Yeah…okay. So, I, uh, played last year and in high school I played for St. Joe and St. Louis Scott Gallagher. Um…," I said.

Carrying on for me and Dad said, "Her club team won state multiple years, and she played soccer for the University of Mississippi her freshman year. She started a few games and saw ample playing time. She played defense for them mostly but prefers center-mid or forward. I believe you guys have a team here. Is there any way we can get in touch with the coach, or do you know if there's any room on the team?"

I was calm, not thinking this conversation would go anywhere. I was also tired. All I wanted to do was get this over with and go back home and take a nap.

The Admissions Counselor said, "Actually, the head coach of the Women's Soccer Team, Luigi's office is right up the hall. I'll go get him."

She stepped out of her office and walked down the hall. My dad looked at me, raising his eyebrows with a pat on the back for encouragement. A moment later, the Admissions Counselor reentered, this time with Luigi Scire, a short Italian man with a kind, soft demeanor and with, as I would soon learn, a passion for soccer second to none.

We all shook hands and introduced ourselves.

"What position do you play?" Luigi asked me.

"I can play anywhere, but I prefer center-mid," I replied.

"Center-mid? Okay."

With his hands lightly laced, he nodded. He looked up briefly as if thinking about his roster. "Yeah, I think we can find a spot for you. So, we play in the St. Louis Intercollegiate Athletic Conference. SLIAC for short. Fontbonne, Greenville, Spalding, just to name a few teams we play. Preseason starts in ten days."

Ten days. Ten days! I've barely done any exercising. I spent the summer feeling low as hell and hiding from my ex-girlfriend in a small southern town.

My face showed only gratitude, not including any traces of panic.

"Alright. Sounds good," I said as I shook his hand again. "Thank you."

"I'll get your contact information from your application and have our athletic trainer, Coach L send you the schedule and what you can expect," Luigi said as he stuck out his hand for us to shake again.

My dad and I left the office and headed back to the car. I walked in there that morning not expecting to walk out with a spot on another college soccer team. Mixed emotions started hammering me, includ-ing self-doubt. *Was I still good enough? I hadn't played in ten months. Would I remember how to play? Would it be like last year? Would it be better? I guess it would give me something to do to keep my mind busy.*

After my application was accepted, I met with my academic advisor. Although I was declared a theatre major the year before, I decided to change my major to Speech Communications. I did this for a few reasons: 1. Webster's theatre program requires a rigorous auditioning process, which I had totally missed the deadline; 2. Even if I had auditioned and been accepted, their course load would have made it nearly impossible to also play soccer; and 3. I was truly inter-ested in the classes Webster's Communications department had to offer, and this was many years before they offered Sports Commu-nication. The students have it better there now than when I did, and I'm so glad for them! My advisor enrolled me in a couple of English classes along with several Communications classes. Even though I had already been accepted, signing up for classes made it feel more official. I was officially a Gorlok at Webster University.

Now, I had to navigate depression on top of grieving and loss, in addition to transferring to a new school. I am not good with big changes. I can handle one big change at a time, but the more big changes that came, the more lost, anxious, and depressed I felt. The more change, the longer it takes for me to comb through the feelings. The longer it takes for me to adjust. The longer and harder it is for me to push off the pile of hurt lying on top of me.

The next time I saw my grandpa was in the middle of the night a few months after he died. I was sound asleep in my bed but wide awake in my dreams. In one particular dream, a parade had just finished. I did not know what the parade was for, but I could tell someone was being celebrated. It certainly was not me being celebrated in this dream from what I could see. I was my current self in this dream: lost, alone, with little direction as to where to go.

Standing in the middle of a crowd, I turned around to see where I was supposed to go, to run to, to be. *Where am I supposed to be? Who am I?* I was cold. I wore nothing but shorts and a T-shirt. My shoes and socks are both missing. The wind blew my hair all around my face. The sky was gray, as if rain would fall at any moment. No one seemed to mind me standing in the middle of whatever production ran wild and free all round me. People bumped into me without saying a word. They bumped into me, but only I felt these shoves. They did not feel their force against me. They might as well have just bumped into air…or simply nothing at all. I screamed at them: "I AM NOT INVISIBLE!"

Suddenly, the chaos of the parade disappeared. I was then in a field at some sort of carnival. The winds had gotten cooler. Leaves rolled around me. A small Ferris wheel, once filled with young, happy families came to a complete and empty halt like they were never even there. The freshly painted carts of the wheel were now covered in rust. Thunder rolled in the sky, and children shrieked as they found shelter in their guardians' arms and vehicles before the storm began. Stuffed animals hung on the sides of game booths now faded in color. The grass beneath my feet felt as though it had not been cut in months. Muddy puddles appeared, but no rain had fallen to create them. The field now resembled a rundown amusement park that no one bothered to clean up after it ran out of business - abandoned.

As the last of the crowd migrated to the shelter, I still stood there, not knowing where to go. A man approached me from a distance. I tried to move but couldn't. I told my feet to step, but they didn't listen. I don't know how I got there. I stared at the man, hoping he was a friend and not a foe. He wore a suit and tie and was drinking beer out of a tall, chilled glass. Through the howls of wind, I could hear him sing. I recognized his voice before I recognized him. He finished his tune just a few feet in front of me. Grandpa. Much younger, though. He donned a mustache like he did when I was a child. He finished his beer, looked me in the eye, and told me: "Go and leave."

Seriously, grandpa. That's it?!

Go and leave? But when? AND where? What the fuck, dude?!

He was gone before I could ask where I needed to go and what I needed to leave before I could even say hello. Everything was gone except that fucking gross Ferris wheel. It was just me in the empty field with an empty Ferris wheel with a sky that so desperately wanted to rain but still wouldn't. I frantically searched for grandpa. I was not finished talking with him. I would never be finished talking with him. I had things to say. I had things I needed to hear come from his mouth.

I jolted awake in the wetness of tears and sweat and immediately wrote in a journal so I would never forget this dream. The setting may not have been real, or maybe it was an alternate reality or realm. It was him in this dream, though. He was real. He was alive and well.

When I woke up, I checked the time: 3:42 a.m. I smiled, looked up, and said thank you. I needed to leave St. Louis, the only home I had ever known. My stay there would only be temporary. I wanted to leave right away, but I realized I'd have to stay until I figured out where it was that I needed to go. Where I needed to be. I held on to this dream. I did not want to forget it.

It was his total embodiment that visited me that night. I had faith for the first time in a while and decided to trust this little wink from the afterlife. It was enough to hold on to for me to keep going. No matter how powerful it was, though, it did not prevent me from slipping further into a depressive episode. That wink from the afterlife gave me a sliver of faith. Seeing and feeling that faith from another source outside of myself gave me accountability. I had a hard time keeping myself accountable and taking care of myself for me. However, knowing there was an angel or someone else looking out for me gave me more motivation than I could give myself. It wasn't a lot of motivation, but it was enough. Any time I felt like giving up, I just thought of that dream.

Even with that new sprinkle of motivation, though, I wrote a note to God around the same time:

"Dear God, I know you have to take some people, but why do you always take the best ones away?"

I am still trying to find an answer. I'm not sure if I ever will.

After my moment on the garage floor the month prior, I realized that I needed to make a change, a big change, if I wanted to ever find happiness or be my true authentic self. While I had some sense that I could make it through, I still felt powerless and stuck in a pit of despair and learned habits. Grief only came in to crush me down further into the safety of those habits, the safety of my sadness, which had become fully a part of me. That dream came at exactly the right moment—it was hope and reassurance from someone I loved, someone who loved me, that I could make a change, that I could leave that dark and abandoned place within me and come out into the light. Again, I held onto this hope but sunk deeper into despair, not being able to figure out what that next step would be. Where do I need to go? What do I need to leave?"

CHAPTER XVII

Early is on time. On time is late. I parked my car in front of Webster University's Administrative building. The women's soccer team's first preseason meeting was starting soon, and I was about to be late. Part of me wanted to be there. Part of me didn't, but it was the best option right now. Being on this team would allow me structure. It would be a distraction from my grief and my mind. Being on this team meant I would not fail at achieving my childhood dream of playing soccer in college. The reality of the dream looked drastically different from what I had planned for so many years.

Just over a year ago, I thought I would be playing for Mississippi for the last four years of my soccer career. Instead, I ended up packing my bags and moving back home to mom and dad. On one hand, I was relieved to no longer be in Mississippi. On the other hand, though, I felt like I failed.

As I shook my head in an attempt to rid my mind of those thoughts of failure, I opened the door to the main entrance and walked inside. Not a soul in sight. I looked around without a clue where to go. I probably should have read the email with instructions a little more clearly.

I peeked my head into a few rooms and an office, but all of them were empty. I reached for my cell phone in my pocket but paused as I heard something in the distance. A sign of life flickered in the form of muffled laughter. I followed it. I remember feeling as though I was not supposed to be there. I was supposed to be still playing for a Division One school in the SEC. The SEC. I gave up the SEC and now I was there. THERE. At a small school not too far from where I went to high school.

I found the source to the laughter in a medium sized conference room. I took a deep breath and then walked in. All eyes were immediately on me. I smiled and said hello to Luigi, who then introduced me to our assistant coach and athletic trainer.

I was the last one to show up at the meeting. All eyes were on me as I walked into the conference room. I was the last one to arrive. No school mascots were on the wall. No chairs with the school logo on them. No players' couch in the back corner of the room. No white board. This certainly was not Division One anymore.

I didn't want to waste an opportunity to finish what I started. Based off my experiences without soccer for the last ten months, my guy told me that playing again would keep me from sinking deeper than I had been that summer. I was willing to do something positive to keep me from sinking deeper into the depression that sometimes reminded me of the ocean floor. Still, a part of me asked: *what am I doing here?*

I needed a sign to know this was the right decision. Something to tell me that I could stay put for a while and not run away to another city or school or drop out completely and move to L.A. or Chicago or New York. However, I didn't really want to wander. I wanted to play the game, but I needed something else to give me full permission to do so. I suppose I needed that because I didn't fully trust myself to make that decision. *How could I trust this school and this team when my first college experience didn't work so well?*

I wasn't scared to start playing again. I was nervous, though, since I was not in the shape I was the previous year, and I hadn't touched a soccer ball in months. A tiny yet noticeable part of me worried my body forgot how to play. I hadn't gone that long without playing since I started playing the game as a child.

I found the only empty chair left that I assumed was mine. Resting on the back of the chair was a T-shirt. It said C9, meaning the next Conference championship would be the program's ninth win. That was always our goal at the start and end of each season. The players sat in numerical order. I grabbed my T-shirt and turned it over. I was given the #20—the same number I was given just over a year ago. Part of me giggled at the coincidence, but that giggle was cut short by the thought of it not being a coincidence at all. I was given this number not once but twice. That number was small sign that maybe

I was meant to be there. I googled the numerology of twenty later to see what it meant, and according to a couple of sources, the #20 meant that I was on the right path in life to success.

What struck me, besides the sign of receiving the same number, was the energy in that room, how different it was from where I'd been the previous year. The team wanted to be there and wanted to play with one another. There was none of the goddamn tension that stained the locker rooms and halls at Ole Miss. The division three athlete is grateful just to play a few more years outside of high school. No one I know plays a division three sport because they don't love it. Th ose that don't love it...they quit.

Number 19, Nora talked to me first after I was introduced to the rest of the coaching staff.

"I'm Nora."

"Ally."

Nora gave me a run-down of each player on the team in just two minutes. She was a senior at the time, and the next day, she physically skipped during our fitness tests because she was so ahead of everyone and still blew everyone out of the water on time. Being there was not the worst place to be. In fact, it was not even a bad place to be. *It'll do for now*, I told myself. I needed to give the team a chance.

The meeting concluded, and I awkwardly followed the rest of the team over to the athletic department, wondering why the meeting wasn't held there in the first place. I quickly learned things were done differently here. Instead of being gifted with fresh cleats, running shoes, bags, and clothes, the only new thing given to the team were the t-shirts from the meeting. I gratefully took what was given to me, feeling a lightness come over me. This was far less overwhelming than all of the gear I had received last year.

The major fitness test at Webster was the Fenton run. A one-and-a-half-mile run in a local park up the street from Soccer Park. Soccer Park houses dozens of soccer teams, including local professional teams, high school state championships, and Webster: *home of the Gorloks*. The Fenton run never made me nervous. I asked my grandpa to lend me his wings for that moment, anyways—I think I needed them more than he did. Without having ever ran the loop before, I let the majority of the team run in front of me. I did not know the route, where to turn, or what. I saw Nora fly ahead of the pack early on, skipping and jumping up to pull leaves off of trees as she got ahead far enough that no one would catch her anyway. She had all the time in the world.

After everyone finished the first fitness test of the day, we headed over to the fields for the remainder of the tests. I rolled down all the car windows. I knew the way this time, so I drove ahead of everyone else. I'd spent half of my childhood at Soccer Park, after all. I blasted Lady Gaga's "You and I" and pretended I was playing the piano and singing a cover of it at a bar. A glass of whiskey resting on the piano. A packed crowd captivated by my voice. The daydream ended just as the song did; I pulled into Soccer Park and parked my car in the shade for her to cool off.

I loved the heat, but my stomach turned as soon as I looked at the turf field. Heat rose off of the turf like oil frying in a pan. Cones had been placed accordingly for a timed back and forth run. Six-yard line and back. Eighteen-yard line and back. Twenty-five yards out and back. Half field and back. Rest thirty seconds. Repeat. I stepped up to the line next to my soon to be friend, Michelle. Despite drinking most of my summer away, I managed to sprint faster than I thought I was going to and finished first in my group. I crossed the finish line and pulled my shirt over my face in an attempt to cool off.

Fitness tests came to an end, and I was still alive. I felt like I could pass out or shit my pants or throw up or all of the above simultaneously. But none of that happened despite my heart pounding around my entire body. I drove home in my sports bra and shorts, barefoot, an old orange and yellow beach towel covering my seat. I pulled into my parents' garage and kept my stuff in the car. No reason to bring it inside.

I cooked scrambled eggs and whipped up a protein shake with a side of fruit. I chugged two glasses of water and passed out on the hearth room couch. Two hours later, I woke up from Heidi barking.

So far, it felt comforting being back in St. Louis. Going to soccer practice in the summer heat and then coming back to crash was familiar. I knew this routine. I loved this routine even though I was physically exhausted. My body remembered the tiredness that came from running sprints on hot turf in the middle of August in St. Louis.

My eyes weren't open yet, but I was wide awake. I could have lied there for the rest of the day, but I rose back up, cracked my neck and stretched my legs. I so badly wanted to sit on that couch, close the blinds, and watch TV. *Get up, Ally. Get up.* I didn't want to get up, but I did. I was already sore, and we hadn't even touched a ball yet. I turned around and saw Heidi at the back door, waiting to be let outside. I opened it for her, leaving it ajar for her to nudge when she was ready to come back in. I chugged two more glasses of water and took two gulps of lemon lime Gatorade. The clock told me I had just over under hour to replenish my fluids and get ready for practice. Heidi ran back in and went straight to her room: the laundry room. She banged her paw against her water bowl, demanding I refill it. I did and added some ice cubes to cool her off.

It came time for me to leave, and I kissed her goodbye and left. For the thousandth time, I looked in the dining room window in the front of the house as I backed out of the driveway. There she was again, my baby girl, Heidi, watching me like a guardian angel.

I got up and left because I needed soccer. I needed an outlet. I needed to run myself into the ground. I needed it to keep me away from a bad way to numb my feelings.

Soccer saved my life. More times than I could count. Being on a team again was oddly comfortable. I knew how to be a teammate. I knew the game. To my surprise, my competitiveness returned. I didn't even realize it had been missing.

I easily took on my role as a soccer player again, leading me to think that maybe I was wrong before. Maybe soccer wasn't why I was depressed. Instead of dwelling on the potential mistake of quitting the Ole Miss team, I reframed playing again as a good thing---a saving grace and a way to honor my grandpa. Above all else, soccer served as a welcoming distraction and an opportunity to finish what I started: playing soccer in college.

I was too physically trained from practice and pre-season scrimmages that I didn't have time or energy left to focus on my grief. I took my grief, and I freakin' ran with it.

CHAPTER XVIII

Liking therapy is kind of like reading. If you don't think you're a reader, then you just haven't found the right genre yet. And if you don't think therapy is for you, then you haven't found the right therapist yet. Time should not be wasted with a therapist you are not connecting with.

A month after I joined the new team, I tried therapy again. I spent two hours with my new therapist, Melissa, before I refused to step foot in her large and damp office ever again.

Melissa's office connected to a hospital. So, the waiting area was a beige, sticky room with other struggling strangers. My sunglasses stayed on my face underneath my hat until I was out of the waiting room. I did not want to be there, but I knew I needed to at least give therapy another try. I wanted to try to understand what my mind was doing to me. If I could understand it, then I could beat it.

I walked up to the window that separated the secretaries from the mentally imbalanced. I whispered my name. The secretary told me to speak up. After telling her my full name, I scanned the room for a seat. At first, one row of chairs was completely empty. *Hell yeah.* I jinxed myself, and within a few minutes, the waiting room and my row filled to half capacity. And, of course, one person sat on my left, and then shortly after, another sat on my right.

I look at the clock: 10:42 a.m. Only four hours and seventeen minutes left until practice. *I can make it.* My head remained down, but I could still see everyone. I studied the patients. I recognized two moms of people I went to grade school with, but everyone else I didn't know.

Melissa was the type of therapist who does not talk much, so most of our time together was spent with us staring at each other. Her long brown hair was thick and curly, and she wore a different floral dress each time I saw her. She sat in the middle of the couch opposite me with her hands neatly folded on top of the notepad on her lap.

"Is there anything particular you want to talk about," she said.

Yes.

"Nope," I said.

"Are you sure?"

No.

"Yes," I said.

"I understand your grandfather just passed and you recently transferred schools."

"I...,"

"Go on," she said.

I shook my head, and we then sat there in silence for the next 40 minutes. It was so painfully silent that I could barely stand it.

Besides the awkwardness and the sterile environment, the waiting room was freezing—a stark contrast to the intense heat that still lingered outside in early October. My first mistake with my new therapist was forgetting a sweatshirt or jacket. The second mistake was coming back—at least the second time I brought a jacket.

After that first session, I treated myself to a venti unsweetened green iced tea from Starbucks. This was my reward for showing up. I didn't put in the work, but I still showed up. It sucked, so I wanted to cheer myself up a bit. *Is this what they mean by self-care? Treating yourself to something after sitting through crap?* If I hadn't had practice later, I would've grabbed a beer.

I made up for my first mistake and brought a jacket with me next time, but as I zipped up my hoodie in her office for hour two, I realized it wasn't enough to keep me coming back. This second session was just somehow worse than the first. I didn't mind talking about what was on my mind, but I needed someone to help me open that can of worms. At least the counselor in Mississippi did that. This chick was SO quiet. Too quiet.

I later learned this is a style of therapy. Not for me. Not at all.

At first, my eyes easily avoided hers. The unnecessarily large office had plenty for my eyes to search, but halfway through the first session, I ran out of things to look at.

Just from looking around, I knew where she went to school, that her fiancé was not cute, and that she had a cat. Of course, she had a cat. I'm a dog person at heart. If the silence of this session didn't foreshadow the short term of this relationship, the cat certainly did. It should be noted that my love for cats has grown since that time as I have gotten older, but my memories of this therapist don't grow any fonder.

I decided this person would never know me. She did not deserve to hear my story. It was already treacherous for me to be there. My ass sat in the waiting room for almost thirty minutes only to sit on this couch and stare at her for another fifty minutes.

Her left thumb grazed her engagement ring dozens of times throughout our sessions. *She must be planning her wedding.* Right in front of a new client, thoughts of flowers, cake, and vows filled her mind, all to the tune of the song that she would walk down the aisle to.

Physically, she was there, but she was not present. I was more present than she was. I introduced myself before she did. She waited for me to begin. Silence broke after fifteen minutes when she mentioned the weather.

I never asked her enough questions because I did not plan to stay long enough to learn more about her than what her nonverbal method and office decor told me. Towards the end of our session, she threw some clichés at me. I learned later that this is a style of many therapists, but it is not for me. Not even a little. I needed someone to look alive across from me, not blankly stare at me for fifty minutes.

"You're going to be okay," she said when our time was up.

The word OKAY sent my brain over the edge.

OKAY! Okay? That's okay for you to say? You think that me, someone who has talents and gifts to give to the world, is going to be okay? How dare you tell me or anyone else that that's all you can see in me. I am broken, yes, but I am not striving to be okay. I do not want to be okay. Okay to me means not great. I should not have to settle for being okay. I want to be way the fuck above and beyond okay. I deserve to thrive. How dare you minimize my capabilities? Fuck you.

According to Dictionary.com, here is one of the definitions of the adjective OK: "satisfactory; adequate but unexceptional or unremarkable."

Satisfactory, my ASS! Ok is UNACCEPTABLE. I know that I had to take baby steps, which may be okay and would be a good step in the right direction, but still, I hated the prospect of it. I hated the word altogether. I hated that I couldn't skip over okay and go right to the good. I didn't want to put in the work to get there.

When someone asks, "how are you?" and the person responds with, "I'm Okay," there is a decent chance it means they are NOT okay, that they are actually something worse than okay. Being depressed is worse than being okay, but saying I'm okay usually means I am depressed. At this time in my life, I would say, "I'm okay," because I did not know how to tell anyone what I truly felt—that I was depressed, fighting every day just to go through the motions. Today, society is more accepting of mental illnesses, but not too long ago, this was not the case. Depression and anxiety may have been talked about, but they were talked about behind closed doors. Not mentioned on social media. Not mentioned at family gatherings. It was pretty hush hush. Society did not accept depression, but it did accept a woman playing the role of a heterosexual who enjoys whiskey and beer. Bonus if she's a tall blonde with well-maintained abs and gorgeous thigh muscles but somehow still manages to leave a gap between those muscular thighs.

After that second therapy session, I went directly home and slept four hours before my dad woke me for dinner. Therapy was draining, even if I didn't say much at all. I stopped seeing that therapist shortly after that and didn't see another one until two years later. I didn't feel that all therapy was bad, but these few sessions left a bad taste in my mouth. Plus, I wasn't mature enough to move my ego aside and suck it up.

I felt that retail therapy was more my speed. I searched for a quicker fix and found it in a new pair of cleats. My best soccer shoes were the ones that cost less than $50. In sixth grade, my dad bought me these insane Nike cleats for $120 or somewhere around there. They were blue ombre with a smaller white Nike swoosh in the center of the boot and dark blue laces. I for sure had the coolest shoes on the team…and the most blisters. Even after breaking them in with a few days' worth of wearing them in the shower, the shoes ripped up my feet. Not cool. The white and blue Nike's I found years later cost me $29, purchased with my very own money. I found them on a sale rack at Dick's Sporting Goods. A lone pair on the row, they sat there waiting for me to buy them. The only pair in my size was an American men's 8.5, a Euro size forty-two. I slipped them on, and they fit with perfection. I scored many goals with those shoes and literally ran them into the ground. I wore them until electric tape could no longer hold the soles together.

A few months after Grandpa passed away, I was sitting on the sidelines during a game. I was just subbed out right before half time. I wore one of my favorite pairs of cleats I'd ever owned: a pair of Nike white and a darker shade of light blue with a black swoosh. I took off the left shoe that was filled with far too many rubber turf pellets. As I was shaking it out, I noticed the line of numbers assigned to the shoe. I blinked several times and wiped my thumb over it. Sure enough, I saw what I saw. The shoe's tongue read: 413022-940. Here's what these numbers mean: 4/13 is my birthday, and 02/29/40 was my grandpa's birthday.

Seeing those numbers on my shoe, I couldn't help but think about the dream I had where Grandpa visited me. He was singing, and he told me to leave. *Leave what exactly?* I still held Chicago in my heart. Maybe it meant for me to leave eventually, but not right then. Maybe it meant for me to leave my troubles behind. To let them go. Maybe it meant to leave Oxford even though I already had. Maybe it meant nothing at all.

Just like wearing the number twenty, the numbers on my shoes held great significance. Those shoes were meant for me and only me. Numerology is not accidental. The universe communicates with us in so many ways. Numbers are just one of the types of patterns and ways the universe sends us messages. This message from the universe was and still is such a gift. It reminded me that I was okay and solidified my place on that team. It was no accident.

The universe was sending me a vibe that was strong enough to help lift my spirits and change the course of my thoughts. After reading and rereading those numbers, I couldn't help but feel a stronger connection to where I was in my life. My original plan for college hadn't worked out. It wasn't supposed to work out my way. The universe's and God's timeline will always surpass my own.

One Communications Seminar quickly became my favorite class. It incorporated somewhat of the performance aspect of theatre, and I had the opportunity to prepare my own written material. The Professor allowed us to choose our own topics to discuss within certain guidelines each week. Parts of him reminded me a little bit of my recently deceased Grandfather, like his simple habit of telling many stories wrapped up in one. His cynical demeanor came across as intelligent humor. His feedback was honest, and he could tell one hell of a story. So, a lot of our classes were just him going off topic about his life story or someone he used to know. He was not as old as my grandpa was. He looked like he was in his late fifties or early sixties, but I wouldn't be surprised if his actual age was younger than he appeared. I'll refer to him as The Professor from here.

The Professor never failed to include me in conversations. We would banter back and forth, talking about relevant and not-so-relevant topics. I quickly became The Professor's favorite student.

I showed up to most classes in college wearing soccer clothes, either because I was on my way to practice or coming from practice. Only on a few occasions did I look more put together. The Professor took a liking to me instantly, though I never thought anything of it. I enjoyed his classes because it became another distraction. One that I thought was positive. I looked forward to presenting in that class and hearing my fellow classmates, as well.

Along with soccer and enjoying some of my classes, the Cardinals helped me rally my grief into something more positive. In late October, the Cardinals were in the 2011 World Series against the Texas Rangers: game six, the odds were not looking good for the Cards.

I couldn't bring myself to watch the rest of that game. The Rangers led the series three to two and had bottles of champagne on deck ready to pop. After the eighth inning, the Cardinals were down, and I retreated to my bedroom. I couldn't bear to witness the Rangers celebrating on my home turf. I couldn't bear another loss. I did not want to watch my team lose. It would hurt too much after I had already lost.

I sat in the dark on my bed waiting for a blanket of silence to fall on the city of St. Louis while I hoped I'd be able to fall asleep sooner than 2 a.m. I closed my eyes and pretended I was tired, hoping to lure my body into sleep with my eye lids shut.

Then, my phone rang. It was Sammie, a teammate who I believed loved partying more than soccer. She was also never afraid to say what was on her mind, whether it was nice or not. I picked up the phone, and before I even had a chance to say hello, she said, "Ole Miss, we fucking won."

For a split second, I thought she was joking, but I skyrocketed out of bed ran into my parents' bedroom. My mom's eyes were closed but the TV showed a replay of one of the single greatest sports moments in history, the walk-off by David Freese. Angels were in the outfield that October night at Busch Stadium.

I sat on the floor in front of their bed with my mouth wide open. I whispered to myself, "Holy shit. We're going to win." Then I said louder, "Mom. We fucking won." And then quieter again, "We're going to win the whole fucking thing."

For student athletes, those of us who were of legal drinking age were not allowed to drink alcohol within forty-eight hours of a league game. The next night, I broke that rule, but it *was* a special occasion. I was at game seven of the World Series. Without beer at this game, it would be an insult to baseball. However, I wasn't twenty-one yet, so I was breaking more rules than I'd like to admit. Trying to be on my best behavior, though, I only let myself have three beers.

That series gave so many people hope that things were not only going to be *okay*, but were going to be amazing. You may wonder why a sports game or series on television mattered to me so much and impacted me so much. Well, I'll tell you: I will almost always watch a championship sports game. One of the top reasons I love baseball and sporting events is because, in each one, someone's dreams are coming true.

When I'm sad, I sometimes pull up highlights from that entire series. Okay…I'll watch highlights from multiple sporting championships, including the USWNT 1999 World Cup final. Those moments remind me that hardships can lead to wins. And those incredible moments are worth every second of grief. You gotta have bad times to feel better in the good times. We can appreciate them more that way. When I watch professional athletes step out on the field, I just know that most of them are living their wildest dreams. I cry at college football national championships, and I don't even like football. I cried on Molina, Pujols, and Wainwright's last opening day. I cried when the Blues won their first ever Stanley Cup championship in 2019. I cried when the USWNT won their third and fourth World Cups.

I inherited my love for baseball from my grandpa. You can't tell me that the Cardinals winning the 2011 World Series months after my grandpa's passing was just a mere a coincidence.

What I love about baseball is that it mimics life. Anything can happen. Many people think baseball is boring due to its pace, but something amazing can happen at any moment. Something amazing is happening at all moments if we are aware of our surroundings.

Baseball is slow. Baseball is fast.

Every time I watch a game, I know that at any moment, I may witness history or someone's best game or a no-hitter or a cat running onto the field, or a person running onto the field; or if I'm there, I may catch a foul ball or a homer. One day, that'll happen. One day.

Anything can happen. And if it does during a game, none of that happens; it's only a matter of time before something amazing does. At the very least, when I witness professional sports, I witness a bunch of adults who were once kids who went on to become exactly who they wanted to be: professional athletes.

During this time in my life, watching sports was one of my only sources of inspiration. They reminded me that it only takes one pitch to hit a home run. It's only a matter of time before I step up to the plate, patient for my pitch, but when that moment comes, I need to be ready, I need to dare to step up. I need to have put hours in at batting practice. I can't hit anything if I don't show up to the plate to begin with. You gotta at least show up. Could you imagine if David Freese didn't step up to the plate on that October night? Magic wouldn't have happened.

Even when I was depressed, I tried (although I sometimes didn't succeed) to live every day like that: knowing at any time, something amazing can and will happen, if not to me, then to someone I know, or someone by me.

Showing up is most of the battle. Because for someone living with depression, it takes the last bits of our hope to get our asses out the door in the morning to school or to work or do anything.

Keep going. Keep stepping up to the plate. Remember, just as I needed to remember: it only takes one pitch to hit a homerun.

Our team had a good, solid, and united season that year. Reflecting on that season, I feel that I was able to bring an energy to the field that they didn't know they were missing. I hadn't realized it back then, but looking back, it's clear as day. I saw ample playing time and got the team on the scoreboard here and there. Being part of a team again helped me more than I thought it would or ever could. Playing in my hometown again could have been a factor. Playing on some of the same fields as I did while growing up could have also been a factor. It was also the kindness of my teammates and their love for the game.

We were favored to win against Greenville in the semi-finals of the conference tournament that year. It was a chilly, rainy early November day. Greenville always played a little on the dirty side. Arm grabbing there. An elbow here. And even a punch and head-butt over there. This isn't tackle football, ladies. C'mon!

A Greenville defender punched and head-butted Sammie, taking her out of the game and to the hospital for a broken nose and lost tooth. Sammie and I were in the same class and played together for a couple of years when we were younger. I thought the Greenville player knocked Sammie out completely. Sammie was a tough, consistent player and someone you'd rather have on your team than the opposing one. The ref called a foul, but the Greenville did not receive a card—not even a yellow. She should have been thrown out of the game.

Sammie's injury ramped the team up, and we scored shortly after she left the game. However, after that goal, we slowed our aggression, which cost us. On a low shot, the ball skidded passed our goalie. The game was tied 1-1.

Soon after they tied, Greenville had a corner kick. I watched the ball as it floated into the box like it was in slow motion. The ball found the ground and then found the foot of a Greenville player. She kicked it toward the goal, and I reached my long legs for it, a perfect opportunity to save it. But it wasn't enough. I lost my footing slightly, and the ball rolled into the back of the net. Greenville won the game 2-1.

I, along with two other seniors were named to the SLIAC All-Conference first team. Several other teammates received honors, including our freshman goalie who was named Newcomer of the Year.

Even with the right mindset, not every game can be won. We ended the season 12-6-1, finishing second in the SLIAC regular season with a record of 7-1. Our only SLIAC loss that year was against our rivals, Principia College. However, after losing to Greenville, we absolutely had another target to hit back next fall.

The day after our season ended, I found myself deep in thought about the last few months. Chicago was still on my mind, but I wasn't quite done with Webster yet. Webster was, perhaps, the exact place I was supposed to be at that time. At that school. On that field. With these people.

CHAPTER XIX

The first couple of weeks post-season were busy even without soccer: the entire team studied for finals and prepared end-of-semester presentations and projects. We also had many late nights and early mornings helping one another with our work or just hanging out in general, enjoying the break from practice and games.

By the time Thanksgiving break of 2011 rolled around, there was plenty to celebrate: the end of the season. The end of the semester. The Cardinals winning the World Series. Being 19. Most memorably, an announcement was made by our head coach for next season's captains, effective immediately. The two captains that year were graduating seniors, and the lone junior on the team suffered an injury mid-season and ended up not playing the next year. I definitely wanted to be named captain, but I hadn't fully expected it. While I showed up each game and practiced that season with energy, heart, and determination, I didn't want anyone to be upset if I was named as a captain. I quite literally just showed up days before preseason started without warning. My intentions were not to waltz in and take over anything. I just needed a healthy outlet to mourn the loss of my grandfather and be alone with my thoughts as little as possible.

By the end of that season, all I wanted was to keep competing and win the conference tournament the following year, especially after losing in the semi-finals the month before. Coach had announced me as captain along with two other rising juniors, Timmy and Sammie. Being named captained made me feel like I made an impact in a short amount of time, too. I was proud of myself, although I didn't admit it. The good news kept me going with a good attitude and positive outlook on the spring semester ahead.

Tsuki, my closest friend since arriving at Webster, was the first to send me a congratulatory text. We went to get much needed post-season mani-pedis as a treat to honor the announcement. Getting manicures together became a bi-monthly get-together, but it had been a while since we had last gone. I always looked forward to them. I didn't know it then, but I needed that time with a friend more than I recognized. It was so important to have a friend to do things outside of soccer and school. Tsuki was a beautiful reminder to me that self-care is essential in life. Tsuki is someone you absolutely want on your team, too, but only a few of us are lucky enough to be. She was and still is one of the hardest workers and players in life I know.

With my freshly painted nails, I went into Thanksgiving Break with good vibes and an eagerness to party. A few teammates and I called that week 'the best week of our lives,' though we really should have called it 'the drunkest week of our lives.'

After acing my last presentation for the semester, I celebrated first by taking a fat nap. After that nap, I opted out of studying for the next day's final. I made plans with another teammate, Blair, earlier in the day to hit the gym after she got off work, but I ended up doing something much more appealing.

She got home and walked into the basement to see a lively game of beer pong. I was kicking Alyssa's ass and told Blair I'd work out with her after the game.

Monica was there, a senior biology major who would later become an anesthesiologist. She chimed in, "Well, it is going to be counterproductive now that you have alcohol in your system. You can technically still workout, but you're better off waiting until you sober up again."

Well, there you have it, an easy excuse to not work out and to absolutely continue slamming beers. "I suppose we are getting some cardio in this game," I said. "Want to play?"

I woke up the next morning on the living room couch of the Heege house to the sound of pots and pans clanging in the kitchen and to the smell of coffee about to burn. The couch at that house belonged to another teammate, and it felt like somewhat soft sandpaper with a few unidentifiable crusty spots here and there. I considered looking under the couch to see if any Jell-O shots remained from Labor Day, but I was too scared of what I might find after a semester's worth of parties.

I quietly yelled, "Yei!" and heard Alyssa reciprocate it from the kitchen. Yei was our team's way of communicating the following: heck yeah! Hello, or let's go!

I pushed myself from the couch and grabbed a cup of coffee. I drank it black because I liked the taste. It reminded me of a freshly lit cigarette, and since cigarettes are a death sentence and the fact that I was just announced captain of the women's soccer team, I wouldn't dare be caught smoking a cigarette.

I was feeling alright that morning. I had been drunk the previous night but was far from sloppy. So that day's hangover felt like a distant annoyance that'd be sure to go away in a couple of hours. As we drank our coffee, Alyssa crushed me in a game of '94 Nintendo Mario Kart.

We hung out most of the morning until I headed to campus to take my last final. I passed it, but only just barely. By the time I got home mid-afternoon, I felt a nap coming on. I took a shower and napped with my hair wet, knowing that by the time I woke up, it would dry in perfect waves. After dinner, I headed back to the soccer house, over-dressed for a Tuesday night out.

Two hours into a decent party at one of the guys' soccer houses, we headed back to the women's soccer house to hang out with some of Nora's friends from high school. I thought it was cool because they were all two years older than me. They appeared to have more life experience, and them giving me attention felt nice, kind of like when you're a kid and you look up to the eighth graders solely because they're older. That is, until you get to eighth grade yourself and realize you still don't know shit yet.

I hit it off with this guy named Tanner. I can't recall if he was actually attractive or if he just had a nice tan and was in amazing shape. We started flirting immediately, and he told me I was like a breath of fresh air as I sat on his lap in the corner of the basement.

This wasn't just *any* corner, either. The landlord had once upon a time rented it out to a beautician. So, there was a full working salon in this unfinished basement operational with used equipment. I vaguely remember the beautician occasionally coming in to do someone's hair. That night, though, I was sitting on a stranger's lap who happened to be sitting in the salon chair. He swiveled it around, making me dizzier than I would've liked, but still, I said nothing. All I did was laugh and breathe to keep me from throwing up all over the makeshift salon. The last thing I wanted was to be helping this guy clean out my puke from his follicles.

On the opposite side of the basement was an extra mattress far from brand new. A few hours later, I found myself naked on top of him. I was drunk enough to hook up but not drunk enough to enjoy the miserable penetration from a twenty-one-year-old cis-gendered male.

As soon as it started, I wanted it to be over. It was easier to go through with it than to open my mouth to say 'no.' I "powered" through physically while keeping my mind occupied with other things. I longed to go back to a bed where Lauren was if she were to welcome me.

As Tanner touched me and as I touched him, my mind drifted. I thought about Lauren. I thought about what I'd tell people about this interaction or if I'd tell anyone. I wished I had more alcohol in my system. I wished for it to be over as soon as possible. I thought about my to-do list. I thought about a few sentences I could have added to my last paper I turned in for a communications class. I thought about soccer. I even found myself wanting the approval of my peers while simultaneously wondering how I could possibly tolerate straight sex.

The physical act of straight sex was impersonal. It wasn't awkward. I knew exactly what to do, but it was robotic. Hand here. Lips there. Other things in…there. I was acting in a performance where I felt zero connection to myself or my counterpart.

What could I do to tolerate sex next time with a cis-man? The answer came immediately and with an intense clarity. *Drink more alcohol beforehand.* I hadn't considered the alternative to my question, which was never to have sex with a guy again. I didn't feel that was an option for me.

We were naked, and so was the mattress we slept on. The next morning, I woke up early, cold from a night without a blanket. I got dressed as quickly as I could without waking Tanner. And of course, I left immediately. I ran out of that house as fast and as quiet as my hangover would let me. The rest of the house was still asleep when I left.

I tossed my stuff in the trunk of my Mazda and drove barefoot to the fourth Walgreens away from my house so I wouldn't be spotted in any of our neighborhood corner drug stores by a neighbor or worse, my own mother.

I didn't care if he had a condom on or not. I didn't trust him. I didn't trust condoms, but I did trust my anxiety, and spending $60 for a little pill in a box felt like the only sure way not to get pregnant...other than not having a heterosexual.

The pharmacy drive thru line first thing on a Wednesday morning was pretty empty, so I didn't have to wait. My heart skipped ten beats when the technician told me I had to come INSIDE the store to purchase Plan B. I told her that I didn't have any shoes. By the grace of God, she let that go and gave me what I needed. I dry swallowed it right after I ripped the box open and then I headed home.

Nervous for what off-season would bring, I applied to a couple part-time jobs to occupy my time outside of soccer. Only one called me back for an interview, and I scheduled it the day before Thanksgiving. It was up the street from my High School at a restaurant called Brio.

I only had forty-five minutes to get ready, and I used thirty-five of those in the shower, hosing off every crevice of my body. I made it to the interview on time, but I was flustered as a duck that lost all of its feathers and anxious beyond belief.

I was supposed to meet my friend Paula for coffee after the interview, but we both ended up cancelling on each other. I bombed the interview but simply laughed it off and told myself that I'd find another job to occupy my time that winter. I went home, took another shower, and slept the afternoon away.

I returned to the girls' soccer house shortly after I woke up. Hours later, I was on the floor in the hallway, sipping on a beer and talking to Nora and Alyssa, when Claire walked into the house. At the time, Claire lived there, and we just happened to be sitting outside her bedroom. Claire was loud and not the most welcoming person I had met since I got to Webster. The second she saw me after turning the corner, she looked me in the eye and yelled in a condescending and angry tone: "Hey, slut!"

Since then, I have taken power back in the word slut, but the way she called me that was with bullying intentions. My heart sank, and the heat left my body when she stared at me with her head tilted, waiting for me to reply or deny that I slept with a guy I barely even knew.

I wasn't reprimanded by society, but I was still slut shamed by my own peers. Sleep with a guy you just meet? A total whore. Make love to a woman you fall in love with? A weird gay girl. Sleeping with that guy felt like the opposite of truth and desires. Why had this felt so icky and not like how it felt with Lauren? I didn't delve deeper into answering that question because I gave myself an open and shut answer: it would feel better with the "right" guy. I simply needed to wait until he came along, and then sex would be good again.

I believe my subconscious wanted me to compare the two. To see how sleeping with a male would compare to sleeping with a female. Except I wasn't aware of my subconscious.

The bubbling water started to move up. The fizz slowing bubbling toward the answer of why I was different. I knew I was, but I still did not think that I was gay. I sure as hell wasn't calling myself that, either, in my inner monologue.

I didn't deny sleeping with Tanner. I didn't even try because I didn't want to. I was going to own it even though I ran from him. I feared the next time a sexual encounter with a guy would present itself. It was humiliating. All of it. The act. What it took from me. What it buried. The response from my peers. The only positive that came out of it was that I felt like I bonded with them.

You couldn't tell from my exterior composure and ability to pretend to laugh along with the others, but I was humiliated. Mostly by the betrayal of myself. Instead of trusting myself here, I found myself craving Claire's approval despite wanting to shrivel up and crawl into a hole and hide.

I asked myself again how I could tolerate having sex with men. And again, the answer came loud and clear: *with alcohol.*

Although I was humiliated, I thought of one good outcome from that week: I thought I had the answer to my sexuality. *I didn't like doing 'it,' but I did it, so that must mean I'm not gay.*

The only thing I could think of as Claire stared at me was…*they can never find out about my ex-girlfriend.*

Part TWO

JANUARY 2012 – MAY 2014

CHAPTER XX

With the shame and guilt I carried into the new year after my post-season debauchery, I refocused myself on fitness. I didn't have to deal with Claire anymore. She was off to study abroad and would be graduating that spring.

Timmy, Sammie, and I all committed to run the St. Louis GO! Half marathon together in April. I wanted to run it for four reasons:

1. Bragging rights,
2. To see if I could actually do it,
3. It would keep me in great shape during the off season, and
4. I'd have a valid excuse not to drink as much or not to drink at all

A few weeks into training, Timmy and Sammi tapered off, and subsequently I would be the only one of us three to finish the half marathon three months later.

I ran over 13.1 miles one day during training. Nora, who was an avid long-distance runner herself, told me that I was not supposed to do that before the actual race. If I followed my training guide correctly, I would not run longer than ten miles prior to race day. The thing Nora didn't realize was that sticking to the training guide to a T was not my main focus. Along with my love for running, my main focus was the distraction that came along with it.

When I set out for the ten, I felt I could keep going, but just because I could didn't mean I should. It wasn't healthy to keep pushing myself like that. There is healthy training, and then there is unhealthy training. I was tiptoeing just over the unhealthy threshold.

Rules kept me in line for the most part during the season, and I tried my hardest to apply them to my off-season training schedule.

If I had planned on going for a run early the next morning or late evening, drinking was at a minimum or not on the table at all.

While the first several minutes sucked a lot of days, running made me feel like I was flying. Running became my greatest escape. At times I felt freer on a long run than I did on a soccer field. It was only me and the pavement. I got lost in the music, which let me escape from my depression. I didn't have to worry about anyone chasing me, nor did I have to pay attention to dozens of other components that came during a soccer game. On the soccer field, I had to know where my mark was at all times, along with my teammates' marks. I played center midfield. Even though I couldn't physically see the players behind me, I could feel them, and I was constantly looking over my shoulder to see who was around and who wasn't.

I relied heavily on instinct when I played. I could see my right-winged forward in my peripheral, and I could feel my defensive center mid six yards behind me. Ten yards behind her, our sweeper, who I could always hear yelling at the back line to push up.

I knew my left-winged midfielder liked to hang back on an angle, but she was ready to take off the second I sent the ball down the line. I couldn't see all my teammates, but I trusted that they would show up if a ball was played into the right space.

Like I said before, it was just me and the pavement while training for the half marathon. My only teammate and my only opponent were me. I built a significant yet different kind of mental and physical stamina. Yet, I was doing a disservice to my mind by continuing to push away my feelings. I thought I ran them out of my body, but the running acted as a wave that washed away those feelings temporarily. And the thing about the tide is that it always comes back.

I got stronger mentally when I ran long distances because I was only fighting with myself and who I was yesterday. I immediately replaced any negative thought that came into my mind with motivation and ran that much harder—too much harder some days.

One Saturday night, half of my team was in the soccer house preparing for a baseball party. I had moved into one of the rooms for the semester. One of the reasons I signed up for a half marathon in the first place was to get out of a spring semester of drinking, which was always so much more than fall semester drinking because it was off season.

The race was barely a month away. I was dressed to go out, too, but only because I had just returned from dinner with my parents. I sat in my desk chair as the giddiness of the house grew in anticipation of a drunken night of college antics.

A few chugged beers later, it was time to go to the party. Except I hadn't drank any of those beers. I didn't have a single sip. I had nine miles waiting for me in the morning, and I wanted to be as fresh as possible for it.

As everyone headed out, I told them all to have fun, be safe and to call me if they needed a ride. At least three of them stopped and turned around, looking at me with disappointment.

"You're not coming?" one of them asked.

"Nope."

"What do you mean you're not coming?!"

"I have an early run tomorrow."

After a few boos and being called a Party Pooper and Grandma, they all left, and to my delight, I had an entire house to myself. I laid out my running outfit for the next day, put on pajamas, and turned on a movie.

If I didn't have the marathon excuse, I think I would have followed all of them out the door and took as many shots and drank as many beers as they did that night—maybe even more. Saying no wasn't enough. There was always backlash. Although the intent behind the backlash was rarely malicious, it still pricked me many times.

Running became the Wall I could hide behind. Rarely did I ever say something like, "Why do I need an excuse to not drink? Why can't I simply just be?"

It was nice to have an excuse to hide behind, a way to have some semblance of belonging while avoiding the self-destructive behaviors that I was so prone to overusing.

The last place I recalled being free, safe, and unafraid was in Lauren's arms. She allowed me to be me and only me. It was the unhiding that was uncomfortable.

It was one thing to be seen by Lauren, especially in the bubble we created in Oxford. It was easy to let my guard down with her. She encouraged me and allowed me the time and space to do so. However, unhiding myself in front of my peers and society freaked me out. The pot of water was starting to simmer, but being yelled at by Claire in November for doing something *straight* felt like the pot had cooled. Claire made me feel like I took one step forward and then thirteen steps back. I didn't like that. I knew if the pot kept getting hotter, it would eventually boil over. I wanted it to boil over. Only then I felt I could fully unhide.

During that interaction in the hallway, I wanted to mention that I dated Lauren earlier that year. I was afraid of the what-ifs, though, and I clenched on to horror stories about homophobic families and workplaces. Still, all the while, not saying or thinking the words "I'm gay." There was never a label on my sexuality…not yet, at least. I didn't necessarily want my queerness to go away, but I did want to be heterosexual. I thought it would eventually work out with one if I dated more guys. One that I could settle down with. Not only was I constantly trying to prove to others of my straightness, but I was also constantly trying to prove it to myself, too.

If I unhid from the heterosexual wall I stood behind, what would the consequences be? I didn't feel brave enough yet to find out.

The next morning, I woke up around 7 a.m., fully rested. The house remained quiet except for the creaks that my feet made on the decades-old floorboards. I ran through campus and parts of Affton, always making sure I passed the cemetery to say hello to Grandpa. I forgot the pain in my knees as the sun kept me warm. I made it up one last hill to the front of the house and checked my phone. I had been running for almost two hours straight.

I plopped my ass in the grass and stretched. Grateful. I would not have been able to run that if I was hungover. I would have most likely felt sluggish, and negative thoughts would have stayed in my head instead of being sweat out of my pours.

Why did you drink so much, Ally?

Why couldn't you just have ONE beer?

Why didn't you just stay home and watch a movie like you wanted to?

And if these thoughts had entered my head while running hungover, I would've punished myself by running even more. Even harder. To burn off the booze. To make up for the wrong I had done, but as I'm sure you know, two wrongs rarely ever make a right.

I spent the rest of that Sunday with my family. We went to the zoo with my aunt, uncle, and eight-year-old cousin and had a lovely lunch afterwards. It was a great day. Any day I woke up not hungover was a great day, though I don't think I realized how great that exact day was until I reflected on it years later.

I felt my feet on the pavement.

I felt the sweat all over my body.

I felt my heart beating hard.

However, I did not take the time to feel after I had finished running. I did not thank God and my body for taking me on that run on that gorgeous day. The moment was over.

I seemed to remember the darker moments much more vividly; those felt like they'd last forever as they were so much more frequent and consistent. The bad memories are familiar. And familiar, a lot of times, means comfort. Comfort and knowing trumped being uncomfortable and not knowing.

I ran that day not to run off the alcohol I drank the night before. I ran for me, but like I just said, I didn't let myself be proud and sit in that feeling long enough after my run. I was constantly running to the next thing on my to-do list. Always wanting to arrive at the next thing and the next thing and the next. I didn't want to stay in one place for long.

My one and only goal for the half marathon was to complete it, and I guess I technically already had because I ran 13.1 miles just a few weeks before the race. I did not focus on a specific time for the race because I didn't have much to compare it too. Although I played soccer for most of my life, running long distance was never on the table. I remember when I was twelve, and our warmup was a ten-minute jog around a track, I was annoyed each time. Ten minutes felt like forever, running in a circle with nowhere to go at the same pace as my team. So uncomfortable.

It had never once crossed my mind at that point that I'd survived each uncomfortable moment, no matter how shitty or annoying or scary it may have been.

On a Sunday, two days after my 20th birthday, my parents dropped me off in downtown St. Louis on Market Street for the race, and I told them to meet me in two-and-a-half or three hours. My nerves began to set in as I approached the start line. I squeezed into a sea of runners, barely having warmed up. I stretched my quads and calves before the gun snapped, and everyone took off. By the first quarter mile, my nerves disappeared.

Nearing mile ten, there was an opening to take you on the rest of the route for the full 26.2 miles. I considered continuing on to add another 13.1 miles to this race, but I didn't want my parents to worry if and when I crossed the finish line many hours after originally planned. I was comfortable finishing the 13.1: I knew what that looked like, but the unknown and the uncomfortable awaited if I had entered that opening. *Another time*, I thought.

Just under an hour and forty-eight minutes in, I crossed the finish line. I never stopped once, only slowing down to grab a cup of water or Gatorade.

Immediately after crossing the finish line, I knew I wanted to run a full marathon. I always wanted more running, always assumed my body would be capable.

I felt I had to prove I was capable, though I didn't know to whom. All the pressure was put on me by a story I made up in my head based on a few comments and some societal norms. I was in denial about so many things, including a feeling deep down that my body was running out of time to run—physically and emotionally.

I put a picture of the Bank of Chicago Marathon on my vision board and made plans to run it within a year or two after graduation, but I never did.

As soon as the race was over, I found a reason to begin drinking again: I'd completed a half marathon! And it was also my birthday weekend. And three other soccer players also had birthdays in April. April was a constant party three years in a row.

After a long shower and a huge breakfast with Timmy and Sammi, we headed over to the soccer house. I wore an oversized red frat t-shirt from Mississippi with jean shorts so light pink they almost looked white. My hair was in a bun with my wavy bangs perfectly swooped across my forehead, and on my feet were brown slip-on sandals. I looked pretty gay. Looking back on photos, I sometimes wonder how on earth I denied it!

Two beers and two shots in, I noticed a beautiful woman on the other side of the basement. She was not an athlete, and I didn't recognize her. I chugged the rest of my beer to drown out the thoughts of talking to her and maybe kissing her. I was three beers in now. Before I could even find I stop for my empty can, someone put another beer in my hand. I looked over at the woman again. She was breathtaking—a confident smile, long, dark, wavy hair with a backward baseball cap.

I opened the beer and took a large gulp. This one stung for some reason, so my eyes shut as I winced. When I came up for air, the woman was talking with a baseball player.

I turned my attention back to the beer pong table, failing to flick away a thought of ache: *I wonder how Lauren is…*

I pulled out my phone and opened my text messages. My fingers fluttered with the temptation to text Lauren. I could easily blame the message on the beer I've been drinking all afternoon. I hadn't thought that much about Lauren in months. I hadn't messaged her much since I told her about joining the team at Webster.

I wondered how she was doing. Was she dating anyone? Was she happy? What were her plans for after graduation? Did she think about me? Did she miss me at all?

I closed my phone and looked up again, hoping my eyes would land on that woman I just saw. My eyes scanned the room in seconds. She was gone. *Was she even here? Is she an angel?*

I didn't see her the rest of the day or night.

CHAPTER XXI

After that party, I threw my energy and attention even more into my schoolwork and off-season training. Timmy and I got into a training routine first thing in the morning, grabbing breakfast and then hitting the library before practice.

My favorite spot on campus was the Emerson Library. It was always clean, and I was rarely interrupted there. I find solace in most bookstores and libraries—there's something about being around hundreds and thousands of books that gives me hope. Something about being surrounded by millions of possibilities all in one place. However, I never stepped into the interest of the possibilities from books beyond those of my major. *One day, I'll make up for lost time.*

The Cyber Cafe within the library was the only place on campus to get a decent cup of coffee, and there were not many options. One cup of coffee from that shop, and we were set to conquer the goddamn world.

To save money on textbooks, I would scope out which ones I could use from the library for a couple of hours to study and complete homework, instead of spending hundreds of dollars on a book I wouldn't need after eight weeks of usage. There were some items I couldn't justify spending money on back then. Booze: take all my money. Books: nah.

At the end of the semester, I found myself in the best shape I had ever been. However, much like my relationship with alcohol, the relationship I had with fitness was becoming unhealthier, too.

As disciplined as I was about training, I was just as lazy when it came to recovery. Recovery was not in my vocabulary. I didn't want to take a day off, and for a lot of weeks, I didn't. My "days off" would look like long swims at the pool or a quick thirty-minute run or a hot yoga class. From a young age, I loathed stretching before and after games. I rolled my eyes at anyone who suggested foam rolling. I cringed at ice and ice baths because I didn't want cold anywhere near my still sweating body. I refused to stretch out of laziness but mostly because of impatience. Plus, it made me physically uncomfortable—it's no wonder I avoided it.

By the time the summer of 2012 came, I felt like I was in a decent place. A place where I was not drinking as much and was focused on soccer more than I was two summers ago, preparing for Ole Miss. I had been catching up on lost time and didn't want to stop until my final whistle blew. I was racing against an invisible clock. St. Louis is hotter than hell in June, July, and most of all in August. It's humid. The kind of humid where you step outside for a few seconds, and it feels like you're in a shower.

Even though the temperature might say eighty-five, the turf will always be significantly hotter. So, most days, I trained during the hottest window of the day, so I'd be ready to play in any heat August and September threw my way on the field. Training sessions were followed by protein shakes and smoothies, yet stretching and recovery were nearly non-existent.

The pain in my left knee was always ignored. Fear of missing any part of my season quickly shut me up from saying anything about my pain. The pain of missing any more time felt like it would be harder than the near-constant pain in my left knee. I did the same thing during high school when I sprained my ankle during my senior year. Only then had I spoken up sooner, I wouldn't have missed any training at all and would've gotten back on the field two weeks faster.

I either biked or ran the 2.3 miles to the local track as my warmup. On days when I needed to time runs more efficiently, I drove to the track or gym in lieu of running or biking. A lot of days, I trained twice a day, spending in between sessions at the pool or taking a summer class or two, and always playing in a summer league with my teammates at Soccer Park.

After the school year ended, I decided to continue using training as my excuse for not drinking. As a result, I ended up not drinking much that summer. More training replaced more drinking. But on the nights I did drink, I binged like I normally did.

The most dangerous form of running wasn't the Cooper test. It wasn't running hills. It wasn't running the entire campus of John Burrough's High School at 7:30 in the morning. And it wasn't running miles with a 10-pound weighted vest.

Nope.

The most dangerous form of running for me was drinking alcohol.

Running. Drinking. Running while drunk. Two activities and hobbies that were equally as hard on my body as they were on my soul.

That was proven yet again one night that summer at a concert.

Hours before the concert, Timmy and I met with Logan at his friend's house to hang out at their pool. Logan played on Webster's men's soccer team and was a year ahead of us in school. He was silly and outgoing, and he always looked out for us. Whether he'd admit it or not, I always felt safe around him, and he brought a lightness to any situation that effortlessly eased the tension. He was handsome, but not in a mainstream conventional way. He was handsome in the nice boy-next-door kind of way. Logan's friend's house was barely a mile from my parents, so we stopped there first to pick up beer that was leftover in the basement from various events.

Soon after we arrived, a game of pool volleyball commenced. Beers were placed on the side of the pool while we split into teams of two. Just before the last game, the friend of a friend's sister walked outside. I recognized her immediately. I knew her from growing up through mutual friends, but we were never close. It had been a good eight years or so since I'd seen her last.

From the time of her arrival, someone from one of the teams left, so the sister stepped in for the last round.

My team won, and I scored the last few points. The boys complained while the sister told me, "You've always been so athletic. That's how I remember you."

I couldn't brush off what she said. Those words stuck to me like sweat on my eyebrows. I have always been accepted for my athletic body and what I can do. Just like in the murky water at the frat house my freshman year, I was tossed another beer, cracked it open, and chugged it entirely, celebrating my victory in a Pool. Volleyball.

Match. Pool volleyball! My trophy: another beer followed by a depressed hangover in the days to come. *What a fucking PRIZE!*

As I got out of the pool, our friend Logan handed both me and Timmy yet another beer. Logan played on Webster's men's soccer team and was a year ahead of us in school. He was silly and outgoing, and he always looked out for us. Whether he'd admit it or not, I always felt safe around him, and he brought a lightness to any situation that eased the tension. He was handsome, but not in a mainstream conventional way. He was handsome in the nice boy-next-door kind of way.

I don't know if Timmy opened her beer yet or even finished one. I opened mine right away and awkwardly took a big gulp of the fresh suds, wondering if anyone would remember me for anything more than being the sportiest of Spices.

I assumed that was how most perceived me; growing up, most people associated me with being a great athlete. That was true, and it was a label I wore proudly more often than not. However, it made me sad that *athletic* was what most people mostly described me as when I was and still am so much more than that. Of course, this was when these descriptions were said to my face. I rarely was told what people said about me when I wasn't around.

When I wasn't hiding behind a bottle, my next best hiding spot was in sports. When the two were combined, I looked like I was flourishing. I was, or at least I felt that I was, as I was doubly accepted for two societal gold stars: alcohol and sports. It was a win-win for the spectators, but I was losing the game on the inside.

Maybe I'm making more of it than it was, but early on, I'd internalized that my self-worth came from how fast I could run, how many goals I could score, how many games I could win, how many times I could beat the boys and how good I was while doing it.

While I am proud of my athletic career, it ached that it was my body others put before my mind and spirit. Maybe I just didn't hear it often or enough to think otherwise. What would my worth be when or if I finally stopped running?

I put off answering that question for years until ignoring it became harder and scarier than facing the answers.

Perhaps they were saying, "yes, your body is capable, but what we really mean is that you mentally pushed through to achieve that level of greatness. You're the one that consistently showed up and put in the work."

If only they saw the work athletes put in to being *great.* Maybe then they'd see me more than a machine and instead say, "Ally has grit."

"Ally's persistent."

"Ally pushes through the hard stuff and brings others to the other side along with her."

"She's a leader, a good teammate, an even better friend."

Perhaps that's unfair, though. How could I expect so much from others when I was the one hiding more of me than they could see. It wasn't their responsibility to say the things I needed or wanted to hear. Particularly so since I never asked in the first place. It was much easier to hit the ball of a small part of me that was widely accepted, much easier to drink a beer than to dig any deeper.

Between the beers and volleyball and the early summer heat, Timmy and I lost track of time. We were an hour away from the concert venue without traffic, but there was always traffic. Plus, we still had to get ready. We hustled back to the soccer house. I opted out of washing my hair. I wore it longer those days, and after a day at the pool and in the sun, my hair dried into imperfectly perfect beachy waves. I rinsed off to freshen my skin and quickly changed into a coral tutu skirt that I bought from Kinnucan's, a cream-colored cropped tank top, and copper cowboy boots.

We couldn't bring booze into the venue, nor were any of us old enough to buy some there, so we pre-gamed on the way to the concert. Hard. Well, I was pre-gaming hard, assuming that everyone else was drinking just as much as I was. Assuming, never bothering to find out if that was the case. Again, not speaking up.

Britt was our DD. Upon arrival, I was drunk. I drank enough that I should have stopped. No more alcohol needed to be consumed by me. BUT...give me music that I love mixed with the love of the taste of whiskey and beer. Good luck trying to get twenty-year-old Ally to stop. I always wanted more, even though more never ended well.

I did not know when enough was enough until it was too late. Enough was impossible for me, but I always knew when I had too much, and by then, I had already hit and surpassed the Wall. If only I had a warning sign on my person: "You are now approaching Wall.

Slow down and come to a complete stop. Enjoy the rest of the night without any more drinks. You don't need them. Dance for a while, get some cold water and a greasy snack, and get your ass in bed."

When I woke up the next morning, the warning sign would tell me, "You need more water and healthy food. Do not sulk and dwell in your sorrow. Be kind to yourself."

Honestly, even if those warning signs came—and sometimes they did—would I even listen to them? Probably not. I usually ignored the nice hangover voice within me. While I did believe I deserved her, the volume of self-punishment was much, much louder.

At the concert, I ran into a family friend that I'd known for years. I hadn't hit the Wall just yet, but I was approaching it at a rapid pace. She bought me two beers in the three or four songs I had been with her. I drank the first one quickly and consciously, noting to drink the second slower, wishing I had a stomach and tongue that loathed the taste of this drug. But I loved it. I loved the burn. I loved the warmth. The tang. I loved the buzz in my body. I loved the refreshment of the first few sips.

When half of the second beer was gone, I departed to go find my friends, but before I knew it, I was running again. I ran from them. I ran from my ride home, and I was suddenly crying uncontrollably in the parking lot. That wasn't the first time, either; the first time, I was sixteen, crying in that same parking lot, but I was stone-cold sober, and my friends had ditched me. I was drunk this time, and I was the one who ditched my friends, who were worriedly annoyed, trying to get my drunk ass home.

While standing in the parking lot among hundreds of strangers, not one person came up to me. Not that I was anyone else's responsibility, but there was zero kindness of strangers that night. As I stood there alone underneath the parking lot lights, I cried harder. I stumbled towards a group of people and asked for help. They ignored me, which caused me to keep crying and not ask anyone again.

No one around me wanted to help the drunk hot mess crying in a parking lot after a concert. But who was I to blame them? I had put myself here. I wasn't their responsibility. I didn't deserve their help, especially if I couldn't/wouldn't/didn't help myself.

My friends finally found me, and I got in the car. They asked me why I kept crying, and I said I didn't know why, which made me cry even harder. Sometimes, when I cry, it's hard for me to stop.

Once we got back to the house, I started throwing shit and yelling. Shoes came off and were thrown down a hallway. I woke up to see pictures on the wall were tilted the next day. A few areas had chipped paint, too. Other than that, I was careful and cautious only to throw my own belongings and eyed open spaces to throw my stuff so I wouldn't break anyone else's.

I knew why I was so angry. I was angry for letting myself get so drunk again. I was angry that someone else's words triggered me to drink more. She complimented my athleticism, but I internalized it as if that was all anyone would ever see me as. When I got that drunk,

I was angry at myself for letting myself fall down the well again. This was the angriest drunk I had ever been and one of the loneliest, too. No one was coming to my rescue.

But would I have let them help me? I guess I'll never know. I remember a voice or two yelling behind a closed door for me to shut up and be quiet. I do not remember anyone coming out to help me or someone coming to calm me down. Maybe someone did, but that could be one of the few memories that are gone. I'll never know for sure.

Three of my teammates were home and probably ignored my tantrum because they didn't want to deal with it. Although they may have heard me, I am glad they did not see me after the concert, especially after how much of a shit show I was all evening. I'm glad they didn't see me throwing my shoes in the house and having a toddler-like meltdown in our living room. They must have all heard me, though. The house wasn't big, and I was screaming long and loud enough to keep people up for a while. Still, I do not remember anyone coming out of their rooms to sit with me or talk to me.

I entered the kitchen at some point and opened the fridge. A large Brita water container was filled to the brim. I starred at it, my mouth sweating for a taste. I closed the door without taking it out. At some point, I grabbed a thin pillow from the couch and then passed out on the floor.

Timmy asked how I was the next morning. I lied and said I was fine. After I apologized for my behavior the previous night, I left the house in haste because I didn't want her to see me cry again. I was so glad, though, that she asked me how I was. It felt nice to be asked that genuinely. I didn't think at that moment about how it would feel to have answered just as genuinely back, but she made a difference. Thanks, Tims.

I wanted someone else to pull me out of being drunk. I wanted someone to see how much I hated drinking and how it made me feel. I needed to be that person for myself, but I couldn't see that yet. I didn't want to do the work it would take to get better. I didn't want to do the work it would take to stop for good.

A month or so after this concert, I saw the same family friend who bought me those two beers. She pulled me aside and whispered, "I saw how you were after the concert." I looked at her quizzically. "In the parking lot…" Her tone was harsh, and the look she gave me was that of a 1950s nun reprimanding schoolboys for talking during service. My heart sank so far, I swear if it were audible, you could hear it hit the bottom of my torso.

Oh, crap. I've been found out. I clutched my water bottle as tight as I could without it caving in. I bit my tongue as my body temperature rose. I was mortified on the inside, but other than to touch, my outer appearance was cool, calm, and collected. All I could say in return was,

"Yeah, it was a bad night for me."

I avoided her for the rest of the evening but still stared at her from across the room and yelled silently: *Why the fuck didn't you come to help me? I was standing alone in the middle of dozens of strangers. Yeah, I put myself here, but no one came up to me to see if I needed help. No one offered to phone a friend. You were the one older adult I knew at the concert, and you just left me there? How dare you judge me? Why aren't you asking if there's something wrong?*

She wasn't to blame, but it hurt that she saw me like that and didn't come get me. No one was coming. I had put myself there, so I guess pulling myself out was up to me. It was up to me to ask for help, but like hell, that was going to happen. At least not anytime soon. I was more ashamed and even more afraid now to speak up.

I wouldn't drink for months or would drink very little, but then, when my excuses ran out, the alcohol ran in. I did this a lot over the years. Fortunately, that was the only night I saw the Wall in the summer of 2012. I knew if I kept that crap up, my soccer season would be ruined. I needed and wanted to play soccer more than anything by then. I was on a very fine line that I was gratefully unwilling to cross. Just like many times before, soccer saved me that summer.

I didn't even want to think about what would save me after soccer ended.

Time was running out. I only had two seasons and a little over a year left.

We lost in the semifinals of the conference tournament the year before, and that was not something I would let happen again in my last two seasons. With each step, with each kick of the ball, I was stomping my real feelings further into the ground. On the other hand, I was also teaching myself things that still proved who I am at my core. I was showing myself my higher self and didn't even know it.

I was distracted from my pain, yes, but I was also making a choice to be a champion. I still showed myself that I can win. I still showed up in my talents and was proud that they weren't wasted. I am so glad I stepped back on the pitch after that ten-month hiatus just the year before. Playing soccer proved to me that I could rise up after being kicked down. It also proved to me that I could do great things if I showed up consistently and kept going even when things got hard. It's a fine line though; it also proved that I could get so deeply lost in something that I can forget about the world around me. So, I must choose wisely the things in which I get lost.

I need to remember to come up for air. To have an off season. To make sure I'm putting in the work outside of the escape of being hyper-focused on my goals, my talents, and my work. To make sure I am not utterly consumed by something that will keep me running and running and running. Escapism is good, but not when you're constantly in search of it. Not when escape consumes most of your reality. Not when one pain is swapped out with another, even though healing may occur.

Balance is attainable and required, but I must not only be aware of unbalance, but I also must acknowledge it and then take action to make the changes needed.

CHAPTER XXII

After the concert, I refocused yet again on training. My drunkenness at the concert was a temporary wake up call. Temporary because that's all my non-drinking stints were for years. I never thought about quitting alcohol completely. It didn't feel like an option because that's what most people I knew were doing back then. Plus, of course, the whole 'I don't want to deal with my feelings' aspect of being sober.

However, I knew if I continued binge drinking that summer, I could kiss my junior season goodbye. I wasn't about to let that happen to my second to last soccer season, but more importantly, I wasn't about to let that happen to my team. I couldn't let them down.

Just like last summer, pre-season started two weeks before classes. Most of us showed up stronger, and our efforts of training together during the off season started to show. I was in the best shape I've ever been, despite my left knee pain increasing daily.

That September, the team attended a party at a house that several of the baseball players rented. Later that night, a baseball player named Tyler texted one of my teammates, asking about me and making sure I got home okay that night, which I did because I was sober. All the women's soccer players weren't drinking. We had a game the next day. So, none of us were drinking. Even though those of us who were not twenty-one should never have been underage drinking anywhere, but hey, this was college in America: the world's capital of underage drinking.

Up until that point, Tyler was a random guy to me. *Who was this random guy seeing if I got home okay?* Turned out he was an opportunity. I didn't see him as that at the time, but reflecting on it, it's clear that he was something else for me to hide behind. I thought it was sweet but also weird that he asked my teammate about me. I had my teammate text me a picture of Tyler after she told me. I couldn't remember which baseball player he was.

A couple of weeks later, we went on our first date: burgers at Red Robin, followed by a movie. We occasionally smoked weed, and each time I was in his presence, except for mornings, we were drinking beer. We didn't have a lot in common other than we loved beer and were both student athletes at the same school. He did look out for me, mostly, but it felt like a façade. Like he was just half-ass playing the role of boyfriend to the captain of the women's soccer team.

I should've held myself to a higher standard even when dating guys. However, we all learn from our past relationships, whether they were straight, gay, or anything in between and beyond. I didn't care for Tyler as a girlfriend should, but I saw an opportunity to appear as though I fit into this heteronormative society by pairing myself with a 'man'.

I wish I could have thrown myself in to *The L Word;* like literally diving into my screen to ask them how to live my life, or at the very least, observe them more closely. During my time at Webster, my college team lacked diversity in both sexuality and race. There may have been people in the media who looked like me and felt what I was feeling, but those role models were not around my circles. They were not around for me to confide in.

In retrospect, Tyler was an immature college baseball player who just wanted to play ball, drink beer, and get laid. I don't even know if I would have considered him a boyfriend. He was more of a person I occasionally smoked weed with, drank with, and fornicated with for a few months. He was hardly even a friend. There were no deep conversations. There was hardly any hugging or hand holding, either.

A few weeks after I'd established whatever this thing was with Tyler, I found myself on a stupid party bus for Timmy's 21st birthday. I loathed party buses. Since I was a runner when I drank, it was harder for me to enjoy myself on a bus when its destination is twelve different bars across the Gateway to the West. Lyft and Uber weren't around too much yet, and the majority of my go-to designated drivers were either with me that night or at another party. I felt stuck until I finally found a DD, a sophomore teammate.

She came and picked me up and took me to a party Tyler was at. It was at the baseball house. The same house in which we met.

I left the party to go meet him because he wanted me to come. I thought going there would make me look like a good girlfriend. So, I went. I was drinking a beer in the kitchen, chatting with a few other student athletes and some girls on the basketball team. I had on some pretty pinkish-purple high heels and a tight black mini-dress. Tyler walked over and joined the conversation. For whatever reason while we held hands, he kissed my fingers. It was cute at first, but then he bit one of them.

"Tyler, that really hurts," I said calmly but firmly.

He didn't reply because my whole finger was in his mouth. He pressed down harder.

"Seriously, stop," I said a little firmer while my head grew lighter.

"Tyler, I am going to pass out. For real. Let go!"

My ankle twisted as I failed to reach the countertop on my way down to the floor. I landed hard on the dirty kitchen floor. Several seconds or minutes later, my vision came back to me. The two female basketball players held either of my arms and leaned me against the cabinets on the floor. One got me water while the other asked if I was alright. "I think so," I replied. Followed by, "fuck that hurt."

And Tyler. What did he do?

He went and grabbed me another beer.

And me. What did I do? I cracked it right open and chugged it.

"Atta girl," he said as I stood up fully, even without my heels, I was a few inches taller than him. I stood up a little taller, so I could look down at him even more.

Every ounce of my being told me to dump his ass right then and there, but I didn't. I saw everyone's eyes when I walked in. Those eyes were on me: the tall, beautiful captain of the women's soccer team walking to her boyfriend. People talked to me like we were actual friends.

I felt like I fit in. In this mini dress. With this longer hair. With these high heels.

But I wore all of this out of fear. Fear from the uncomfortable feelings inside me. I never named those feelings. I just knew they were there. I was fake happy—fake happy enough to believe I was truly happy, but I'd do nearly anything to keep the real feelings, keep my truth from coming up. Got a boyfriend? Check. Can drink beer and whiskey? Double check. Fuck, make it a triple while we're at it.

The two girls were really nice and sympathetic but also seemed afraid to stand up to Tyler. No one stood up to him for me. Not even myself. Tyler was not a scary guy, but he was a baseball player, and a lot of them walked around like they owned the fucking world. Tyler was one of those who walked around like that.

About twenty minutes and two beers later, the sophomore who drove me there took me to my car at the soccer house. I drove home—buzzed and by myself. Tyler didn't even make sure I had the help getting home.

I just blacked out and rocked my entire body on a dirty kitchen floor, and you don't offer to take me home or find someone capable of driving me home. Who the fuck do you think you are? No one at that party who saw what happened made sure I was okay getting home. I didn't want to complain or be a burden, and I didn't want to be seen as weak, so I didn't say anything.

I was way too nice to Tyler and shocked that I could be so strong on the soccer field yet so weak off it. What I didn't realize was that I wasn't weak at all. I was scared, and being scared doesn't necessarily mean you're weak.

Being scared means you're human.

In addition to finger biting and not listening to me, Tyler and my four-month relationship consisted of a lack of communication and lame sex. It was sooooo lame. I roll my eyes just thinking about it. Usually, I could look at straight sex as exercise, at the very least, but in that case, I might as well have been a blow-up doll when we did have intercourse.

Tyler may have used me for sex, but I got what I wanted out of it, and that was to blend in with my surroundings. A month after Timmy's birthday, we were all on another party bus for Sammi's twenty-first birthday. Tyler tagged along that night.

Like most of my nights out in college, I did not bring a coat or jacket. It was way too hot in the bars and not worth holding it, and Tyler wasn't the type to hold his girlfriend's items. I didn't drink as much that night, and the whole time, I really just wanted to be in my bed alone with Heidi nearby on the floor, being the best dog she was. I'd read a book or maybe actually return to watching *The L Word*, but I was there on another party bus on my way to another bar, wishing for peace and quiet instead of sticky floors and crappy loud music.

In late January, Tyler and I exchanged Christmas gifts. I got him a nice sweatshirt of his favorite football team, and he got me a lousy gray GOLF pullover. A few years after I graduated, he popped on my Facebook feed…still wearing the same hoodie.

A couple of weeks after our gift exchange, we broke up. It was mutual. He is the only male ex of mine that ended a relationship in person. Kudos to you, Ty, for doing one thing right. I felt relieved when it ended. I was bored and tired. Relief came mostly from this breakup because it would give me something to bond over with my straight friends and teammates. I was excited, too, a little bit because that bondedness meant I could relate more. With that, though, I also felt confused.

Since I was not drinking much during that time, I felt that I wasn't pretending as much. Alcohol was something I could hide behind, right? So, when I started having more sober sex with Tyler, at times, it felt more tolerable. So, with that, I drifted away from how incredible it felt to be with Lauren. I confused tolerance with being heterosexual.

Looking back now, though, I believe that I was starting to become too good at suppressing my feelings without ample amounts of alcohol. I hadn't reflected much on how painful it was emotionally to have sex with another male. It was difficult to tolerate but not admit that was suppression at its deepest.

Before I left, I hung out for a bit in his room. We shopped online together, and I helped him pick out a new couch. What the hell was that about, Ally?

CHAPTER XXIII

Coming off the half marathon earlier that year, I kept hitting the ground running. Too fast and too long. While I was glad to have not been drinking that much to prepare for pre-season, I was still hurting myself. I didn't give myself the rest I needed, and it backfired, but not until after the best season of my college career.

During my junior season, I had ten assists and sixty-three shots, and I was named conference tournament MVP, United Soccer Coaches Scholar All-Region first team, and United Soccer Coaches All-Region third team.

I was named the two latter the year prior and would be named the following year, too, along with being named to the All-Tournament Team. I also had several game-winning goals that season, including the game-winner that named us champions of the conference tournament. The local news came by to interview me one day, too.

We played Greenville that year in the 2012 SLIAC conference tournament finals. Last time I played a championship game on that field was when my high school lost in the state finals to our rivals when I was a sophomore. Except I didn't play in that game. I was brought up from the Junior Varsity team as an extra player in the state tournament. So, to play on that same field four and a half years later felt amazing, like I was given a second chance.

The field was lit with Friday night lights. The crowd bundled up on a chilly November evening. It was the perfect setting aside from a light mist in the air and on the turf. I was ready. My focus was different from that game. It was more of a laser, more hyper, more aware. I wanted to give it my all, and I told my team that no matter what happened, I wanted them to leave that game knowing that we did our absolute best. That each of them did their absolute best.

At halftime, we were tied 0-0. The defense on both sides was strong. We played Greenville just a couple of weeks earlier and won 2-0, but the stakes were higher tonight, and the crowd was the largest of the season—just shy of 400 friends, family, and fans.

Everyone stepped up their game. Everyone wanted to win. There weren't many scoring opportunities in the first half. I knew going into the second half that it would come down to one chance…two if we were lucky. And I did not want to go into overtime. I was tired, and the knee pain that I'd been ignoring started to ache even more. Still, I pushed that out of my head and played on.

A third of the way into the second half, a teammate crossed the ball, and dumb defenders left me open. ME OPEN?! Big mistake. Huge. I saw my chance and knew that was it. I took two steps forward and kicked the ball so hard that no one would've been able to stop it. Toes down. Laces up. The ball found my foot and then the back of the net, giving me my most favorite goal I've ever scored.

Did I have to kick it that hard? No, of course not, but I wasn't going to take any chances with tapping it lightly.

Everything was great in that moment. Everything was more than okay. It was a moment of pure bliss, relief, and excitement. A moment that showed that all that hard work is worth it, even if it's just for that one unforgettable moment. The crowd was the loudest it would ever be during my college games.

After scoring, I kept running, hugging, and high-fiving each teammate as I ran back to mid-field. We all hung off each other, a perfect balance, keeping one another from falling to the ground. We held each other up like teammates do.

For part of the summer's training, Timmy and I flipped tires in a field. So, when I found her after that goal, I grabbed her face and yelled, "Flipping tires! Fucking flipping tires!" several times as the team gathered in a celebration huddle. The picture printed in the school's newspaper had me holding on to Timmy's face surrounded by several teammates, including Frankie, whose hand was mid-slap to my ass—a picture to capture the victory of a job well done.

I felt like I was flying. My legs turned into wings and my head became so light like a weight lifted off it. The adrenaline was from not just a goal scored but a long-term goal achieved, a manifestation granted from pursing what was on this season's team t-shirts: C10 - Committed to Excellence. The C10 meant that the next conference win would be the tenth for the team.

I was right when I said there would only be one chance to score that game. The next thirty minutes were a defensive battle. One that our team won.

Two hours later, most of the team gathered at the soccer house for an afterparty. We took shots, shot gunned beers, and cheered for hours until we all passed out.

There was no way I'd hit the Wall that night. I was distracted. I was on a high. I was happy, though not realizing that happiness was fueled by the boost to my self-worth, all of my worthiness tied to my ability to win. I did my job and did it so well that only then I could be happier. Only then could I be accepted. Only then would I be worthy. Oh, Al. I wish I could go back in time to tell her: You are so much more than the goals you score. You are not this game. Being a great athlete only has partly to do with your physical ability. Your grit. Your heart. Your mind is where your strengths truly lie. Your worth has nothing to do with how productive you are.

The only pain I felt the next morning was a slight headache and an extremely stiff left knee.

Something was not right. The outside of my left knee, where my iliotibial band met the joint, was throbbing. It felt like a wound, a tangled cord, and pressed against my bone with each and every step.

After losing in the first round of the NCAA tournament, my body and spirit were ready for the winter break. All I wanted to do was rest, and for once, I actually listened to my body even though the pain in my knee kept getting worse as the days grew colder.

Shortly after Christmas, I went to see an Orthopedic Doctor about my knee. I was diagnosed with Iliotibial band syndrome, aka ITBS. The medical definition reads that ITBS is "a painful condition in which the connective tissue rubs against the thighbone." It basically becomes so tight that it rubs against the bone. ITBS also occurs when you repeatedly bend your knee. So, basically, it happens when an athlete overuses their knee and doesn't stretch or rest. I could've been the poster athlete for this injury. I had no one to blame but myself.

The doctor put me on a resting plan that included very little exercise. Which, I suppose, is the definition of *rest*. I was allowed to use a stationary bike but only on a low resistance level, and I was allowed to use light weights for upper body exercises only. Other than that and rest, I was on a strict stretching, icing, and ultrasound massage regimen.

I rang in the 2013 New Year with some fresh equipment, too. I was put in a straight leg brace for eight weeks that prevented me from bending my knee at all. The goal for the brace was to allow my IT band to loosen up. Fortunately, I had schoolwork to distract me from not being able to train to the level how I'm accustomed to. My teammates and mom both separately kept me company and kept me distracted, too. For my mom's 50th birthday that February, we rented a limo with her closest girlfriends and two sisters. I opted out of wearing my leg brace that night.

I wore a black minidress with tights and my favorite shoes at the time, a pair of Steve Madden booties with small spikes on top of the toes. After a delicious dinner, we went to 360, a rooftop bar in downtown St. Louis near Busch Stadium. I wasn't twenty-one yet, but when you're out with your mom and several of her close middle-aged friends, no one questions if you're of drinking age.

After we ordered drinks, one of my mom's friends told me to take a lap around the bar. A little experiment, I supposed. She wanted to see how many men looked at me. I protested at first, thinking it was a bit of an odd request. She continued to 'encourage' me to do it, and after the third or fourth time, I obliged. I hopped careful off my bar stool and took a lap around the bar.

I felt like prey or a piece of fresh meat thrown into a lion's den. I felt like an object for the taking. Like I was on display at an auction, and this was my shot at getting the highest bidder. I don't recall her comments after my stroll, but I always thought it was such an odd thing putting a young woman on display like that.

We wrapped up the night at a dueling piano bar on Washington Avenue. Back then, Wash Ave. was somewhat safer after dark and bustling, with a mix of young and middle-aged folks having a good time and holding on to what was left of their youth. Much like our youth now, most of those bars are now closed, leaving dusty memoirs of what it was once upon a time.

Two months after my mom's birthday, it was my turn to celebrate a milestone year. As the semester went on, Logan and I got closer. We started hanging out more, and in between rounds of Beer Pong and Quarters, we'd kiss frequently and laugh even more. It felt like there was always something holding us back from dating. I think we were both comfortable with how things were. He wanted to have a good time, and that made me want to have a good time together. Nothing more.

I really thought that once I turned twenty-one, things would change for me when it came to my relationship with alcohol. *Now that I'm approaching legal age, maybe I'll be more responsible.* I thought a magic switch would turn on once the clock struck midnight on April 13th, 2013.

Logan texted me to wish me a happy birthday and to say that he was looking forward to meeting me later that night.

Remember when I said I can count on one hand the number of times I had fun and was okay while drinking alcohol? Well, my twenty-first birthday was one of those times.

For four years in a row, I spent my birthday at Busch Stadium watching the Cardinals. My twenty-first was no exception. My birthday that year fell on a Saturday. I had a nice breakfast at home with my mom and dad, and then we got ready to head downtown for the Cardinals game. I was eager to get down there but didn't want to rush my parents, so I turned on the TV after I was ready an hour before we left. I went straight to ABC Family (currently known as Freeform) and audibly yelled YES! And did a fist pump.

One of my favorite movies of all time movies was playing: *The Goonies*! The nostalgia!

The Adventure! The yearning for something better in these kids' lives! I was here for it.

I don't own a copy of it, so anytime it's on TV, I make a point to watch as much of it as possible. So, I sat and watched the rest, a perfect start to a birthday celebration.

By the time the credits rolled, my parents were still not ready to go, and my friends had sent me several messages asking where I was. They had already been at the hotel for thirty minutes.

They can wait. It's my day.

I knew I'd be drinking all day, and I didn't want to spend my birthday running away or in tears because of drinking too much. So, I drank slowly...for twelve hours straight. My avoidance of the Wall was possible this day because I showed up to drink with a consistently full stomach. All shots I took were chased with a glass of water, and a full glass of water was sipped between the other alcoholic beverages.

Had the avoidance of the Wall also been because I was in a better state of mind going into drinking? More aware? Maybe. Maybe not. There were plenty of other times I went into a night or day of drinking with good intentions and still ran into the Wall, full speed ahead.

We had a damn good time that Saturday, though. The weather was nice. It was a little chilly, but it was plenty warm to not worry about being cold. The sun was shining, and clouds were sparse. I was at one of my favorite places, drinking my favorite drinks with some of my favorite people at the time.

After an afternoon of drinking beer and a couple of shots of whiskey that Alyssa found, of course she did, we headed over to 360. Aside from the weird prey-like stroll on my mom's birthday, I've always had a good time there, and my 21st birthday was no exception. Some appetizers, a gummy bear shot, a lemon drop, and a split bucket of beer later, we then headed to our hotel rooms that were conjoined.

I spent months planning the perfect night outfit for my twenty-first birthday. I envisioned a lavender high-waisted mini skirt with white chunky heels and a white crop top of some sort. I had my heart set on this outfit for a very long time, but I could not find the exact miniskirt that I wanted to wear. So, instead, I landed on a royal blue badass high-waisted skirt and a fitted leather crop top. It fit so perfectly that my audience got a glimpse of my toned stomach (without me having to take a lap around the bar by myself). To top it off, I wore relatively comfortable five-inch wedges with this colorful pattern of royal blue, white, light blue, and orange with a sparkly golden trim.

After a quick birthday call from my brother, I re-straightened my hair after freshening up from the game and slid on bright orange dangly earrings to match the orange in my shoes. I opted for a bright light blue eye shadow. It was a little too much, but I wanted to wear it, so I wore it.

I was never going to wear a crown or tiara on that birthday or any other, but my mom got me a custom sash that was gorgeous and complimented my outfit. It was hot pink and had jewels trimmed on the edges. On the back was my birthdate, and on the front, which was written in jewels, was "legal and blonde." I hope it's in a box somewhere at my parents' house.

Logan and a few other guys from the men's soccer team met us at our first bar of the night. Not too long after that, a couple of other friends that I had from other areas of my life showed up. Logan kept close to me that night, and I knew he was doing so because it was my birthday, and he was a nice guy. At the same dueling piano bar from my mom's birthday, I stepped outside for some fresh air. Logan was already outside, along with one of his friends. I walked up to him, and he grabbed my hand and pulled me in for a kiss. I was drunk at this point, but I was not stumbling. I wasn't slurring any words that came out of my mouth. I wasn't even dizzy.

I pulled away from the kiss first. I started to pull away from him, too. He held on and tried to pull me closer. We locked eyes for several seconds before he goofily said, "What?"

I gave him a kind, gracious side-eye. "You still have feelings for your ex."

He gave my hand a light squeeze and let himself smile softly. He sighed, not admitting and not denying that he does. I stepped away, about to head back inside.

"I'm sorry," he said louder than I had expected. "I have feelings for both of you."

I stopped, but not for him. I stopped at the suppressed thought trying to claw its way out of the oceanic depths of my soul. From far away, like an echo deep within a sweaty cave, she said to me, *you can never be her.*

I stomped on that thought immediately as I turned around. I waved Logan over to me. He pushed himself off the concrete wall of the building and walked over. I reached out my hand, and he took it. I looked him in the eye, smiled, and said, "Let's just have the night."

We walked back into the bar holding hands and picked up where we left off: drinking and dancing. I had strong affection for him, too, but those feelings could never and would never develop into anything deeper than what it was. He would never be more than a close friend. I would always want him to be someone else.

I headed back to the hotel with Logan and a co-worker turned friend. When we got back to the rooms, each one was locked, and no one was coming to the door. They were all passed out. So, we sat in the hallway and chatted for a solid hour before someone finally opened the door. I suppose I could have just gone down to the lobby to ask for another key, but we were drunk, and that logical solution hadn't crossed anyone's mind.

I ended up sleeping on the floor in between two of the beds next to Logan while some of his friends and mine crashed on the beds. Honestly, I would've made it there anyway, to the floor, because, as you know, sleeping on beds while I'm drunk doesn't work out too well for me. The harder the surface of a floor, the better. It was the only thing that would calm the seas within me. Another calming presence was Logan's arms around me as we fell asleep.

The next morning, I woke up still drunk. I was proud of myself for not running or hitting any Walls. I didn't want to sit at home all day. I wanted the celebrations to continue. So, after a large breakfast with the girlies and a long nap, I quickly showered and headed up the street from my parents' house to one of Logan's friends' houses. I didn't want to be alone. I wanted to keep drinking.

I continued to drink beer the rest of the afternoon, and I'm glad I didn't hit the Wall. That's two days in a row! I wish that it was my birthday each time I drank so I could drink like I drank those days. Minus the one stupid thing I did later.

I justified driving home because the house I was at was only a few minutes away from mine. Honestly, I could've walked home, but didn't want to leave my car anywhere, especially when I had an early class the next morning.

I walked into the house extra carefully so my mom wouldn't suspect my level of intoxication. She didn't. As she entered the laundry room, I grabbed a beer from the fridge, went upstairs, drank it, and then fell asleep on the floor.

I was on time for my class the next morning and went straight to my designated seat: far back right of the room. On my way there, the hangover came into full effect. I did something different, though. Instead of punishing myself, I allowed myself some more grace and promised myself never to drive under the influence ever again. And I kept that promise.

With my hood up and head against the wall, my teacher asked me if I was okay, and through the cobwebs of what used to be liquor, I slowly said, "My twenty-first birthday was this weekend."

"Say no more," he said while the class laughed. "Happy birthday! Everyone, respect Ally's hangover."

I gave a thumbs up and kept my head rested on the wall for the rest of the class.

I think I knew Logan, and if I had dated him, it would've absolutely ruined the friendship. Plus, he still had feelings for his ex-girlfriend. So, that's what was holding him back. I, on the other hand, didn't want to make Logan the next guy I hid behind. I cared about him too much as a friend.

I don't regret sleeping with Logan, but I wish I had the courage to approach him. I think he would've been really supportive and understanding and maybe even try to set me up with chicks. God, he would've made the best wingman! Our fling barely lasted six months, and we never went on an actual date, but we hung out a lot. He would've been a great friend, but protecting my image was more important to my subconscious. I also wasn't really questioning my sexuality at that time. I was suppressing it with every drink I took.

I wanted to live how other heterosexuals lived. I wanted to live openly without questioning myself and without being questioned by others. I wanted to drink like a lot of others could drink— safely and responsibly. I wanted to not have to cover up my identity. *How long would I be able to keep my cover?*

I was glad, of course, to have tea to spill again to the girlies regarding any updates with Logan. Which soon became a ton of tea because a few weeks after my birthday, I met a guy named Chris while my involvement with Logan wasn't fully over. It was still lingering.

CHAPTER XXIV

One of St. Louis' biggest sporting events of the year took place at Busch Stadium in May of 2013, but it wasn't a baseball game. Two international soccer teams traveled there for an exhibition match: Manchester City vs. Chelsea. I knew a lot of people at this game: current teammates, past teammates, friends, and coaches. I went with my brother and parents even though we were sitting in different sections.

My dad conveniently needed to gas up, and we pulled into a Circle K gas station in Soulard just up the street from the stadium. My brother ran in and filled a large Polar Pop with Coke.

Before we left our driveway, he stuck a flask in the back pocket of the passenger side seat.

By half time, I was drunk. It was and still is the only soccer game where I'd be wasted. After the game, my brother and I met my parents at Mike Shannon's restaurant for what should've been a night cap. Instead of going home like I should, I followed my brother to a bar to meet up with some of his friends. I always should've just gone home.

Nick's Pub, an Irish bar in Dogtown, was packed again on a Thursday night for Dollar Beer night. Several of my friends were there, too. I found this amusing since we went there to meet up with my brother's friends. It was rare when my social circle collided with his because mine had never been consistent, whereas my brother's friend group always had.

I had recently told Logan that we should stop our physical relationship. He could not shake lingering feelings for his ex, and although she had clearly moved on, he kept holding out for her. However, that night, when I saw Logan, drunk Ally felt she needed to make him jealous. So, that became my night's purpose, along with getting more loaded. I had completely forgotten about those five little words I said to myself on my birthday: *you can never be her.*

Nick's Pub was split into two rooms. One with the main bar and the other with a small stage. A cover band played there that night. I liked it there. I danced by myself to make myself known, but mainly because I was bored of drunk conversations and dancing by myself was far better than dancing with anyone else. I scanned the room and my eyes fell on a guy that I would find out later looked much younger than his actual age. His eyes met mine, and I winked. A few minutes later, I looked back at him and pointed. Before I knew it, my right hand grabbed my beer, and my feet walked me right over to this guy. He was with friends, but I did not pay them any attention.

"You're cute," I slurred.

"So are you," he replied.

"What's your name?"

"Chris."

"Hi, Chris. I'm Ally."

He was cute. Not sexy. Not handsome. He was simply cute. I ignored his slightly yellow teeth. His smile outshone any flaws in them anyway. The next thing I knew, one of my hands held his hand while the other held my beer, and he guided me to the bar in the main room. He bought me a beer, which shouldn't have impressed me: it was dollar beer night. But then he bought each of us a shot of tequila. This guy had a thing for tequila. I cringed, wishing it was water instead, but how dare I be rude and reject an offer so many women are quick to accept? Some friends in college made a game of how many different guys could buy them drinks in a night out. I understood this from a frugal point of view, but this game seemed foreign to the real me. But also, most people could get pretty drunk with not that much of their own money. Too much alcohol is far too cheap.

Between the shot and the bite of lime, Logan cozied up to the bar stool next to me. He is now on my right, and Chris is on my left. I was in the middle of both of them.

After another beer and another shot drunker, I pulled Chris in, and we made out. I put my number in his phone with a kissing face emoji next to it and told him to text me. Logan scoffed. It looked like my plan to make him jealous had worked. I could blame Logan for getting me into a relationship with Chris. If Logan hadn't sat down next to me, I probably would not have made out with Chris. However, I take full responsibility for my actions then and now.

Drunken dating games with the opposite sex exhausted me. Sober me would never partake in this foolishness. Sober me would've been at home by now watching TV with my dog.

As I finished entering my number in Chris' phone, my brother called me from the bar's entrance. Time to go. *Thank God.* One of my brother's friends gave us a ride home. I waved to the rest of my friends as I left, tripping over the exit on my way out. In the car, I reached for my phone in my pocket to entertain myself on the way home by sending drunk texts. But my phone had died sometime during the night.

About a mile from home, my brother's friend pulled into a Phillip's 66 gas station near my parents' house. I wasn't sure why. They both went inside, and I crawled to the other side of the car, opened the door, and threw up half a dozen times. It could have been a half dozen more, but they returned to the car before I could return any alcohol to the surface. I held the rest of it in until I was home.

I woke up on my bedroom floor with chunks of puke in my hair and around my pillow, wearing nothing but a T-shirt. I rolled over to find my phone with a dead battery. I threw my arm around until my hand landed on my charger. I plugged it in and fluttered my eyes open. I had no idea what time it was, and as for the day, I thought it was Friday but was unsure. I exhaled heavily, ignoring the headache and dry mouth. I pulled myself up with the assistance of my bed and nightstand and slowly walked to the bathroom, showered, and brushed my teeth. My phone buzzed as I set down my toothbrush. A handful of text messages appeared on the screen, but I was only interested in the one that came from a number not saved.

I opened the text. It was sent around 1 a.m. It was Chris saying how nice it was to meet me. I grinned. Not because I had a cute boy texting me but because I had a new opportunity to fit in. As I was about to text him back, reciprocating such a lovely meet cute, he sent another text asking if I'd like to go out for drinks that night. He didn't meet me, though; he met drunk me. I was gross last night. Hammered. The thought of drinking again so soon after being that drunk made me want to throw up all over again. But I had rallied many times before and would rally many times again. I set my phone down, headed downstairs, and was able to stomach enough to keep down a breakfast sandwich.

I had learned from society it was good to make a man wait a bit before responding. I chugged two glasses of water and took the third back up to my room. Then, I texted Chris back and said how lovely it would be to see him that night. I spent most of the day nursing my hangover until my mom and I went to Target. I realized I was out of perfume and so worried that something wouldn't go right if I didn't have perfume on. I sniffed a few bottles and tossed one in the cart. Mom immediately questioned it, and I simply told her (without making eye contact) that I was totally out of perfume. As we left the parking lot, I caved and told her that I had a date that night. I was only excited because going on this date gave me something to bond with straight people, especially straight women, aka the majority of my teammates. All of my friends talked about dating and sex and hooking up and having *things* with so and so. All of them talked about things like this, and now I finally had something again to potentially contribute to the conversations.

The weather that May evening was warming up, so I wore a dress on our date with a denim jacket accompanied with my favorite turquoise and black wristlet. He picked me up and drove me in to the Delmar Loop. We parked and rode the elevator up to the rooftop of the Moonrise hotel. He ordered a margarita, and I played it "safe" and ordered a beer. If a drink accompanied my hand, flirting with guys came easily. I was nonchalant and charming and said all the right things at the right time, pausing perfectly to take a sip of my beverage.

Watching romantic comedies and dramas during my middle school and high school days sure paid off in my early twenties. At least I learned how to act like I was interested. That's what I was supposed to do, right? I am a tall, blonde woman; therefore, I must flirt and be with the opposite sex. Got it. Thank you, society and media, for showing me the way, even though I need to be far from sober in order to do so. A drink was the secret weapon for getting me through most physical and romantic interactions with men. Without it, it was completely unbearable.

Chris probed me about my family and school. Later, mentioning wanting a white picket fence life like he's Ward fucking Cleaver. I kept drinking to tolerate this and to prove to myself that this was what I wanted. I told him how sweet that vision was and that he deserved to have that happiness someday. I meant that, but my gut told me that it wouldn't and couldn't be with me. A minute or so after the *Leave It To Beaver* moment, he kissed me, and just like most of the actresses in the movies I've watched, I kissed him right back, convincing myself that Chris was my light at the end of my crappy spring semester hobbling around campus in that damn brace.

Eight weeks later, I went to visit Maren in California. Prior to this trip, I hadn't seen Maren in almost a year. We did what we do best, drank some drinks, shopped, hung out at the beach, worked out, dreamed, laughed, and were the two smart bitches we are with our witty banter and fierce bond. After Maren and I got our first tattoo in Oxford, we immediately discussed and promised getting another together. At a wine and cheese bar just outside Laguna Niguel, we decided that our second tattoo would be that week. Well, several bites of cheese and one glass of wine later, I called for the check. We headed to the tattoo parlor after the bill was paid.

The tattoo shop had exactly one chair near the back wall. The place was no larger than a studio apartment. A giant window in the front allowed bystanders to see in the person in the chair about to get inked, like the reptile room at the zoo.

As our fresh ink sunk further in, we celebrated with more wine and dessert at a different

Laguna bar. There was no reason for me to drink an entire bottle of red wine, but I did anyway.

Couldn't stop. Wouldn't stop. I looked like I was young, wild, and free. I was not as free as I'd like to be because truth was so far away. Instead of leaning into the constant feeling of something missing from my life and something holding me back, I had a reason not to go looking for it. Whatever that something was that I was missing would either come later in life or I could pretend to blend in with society and my surroundings that it would eventually fill the void. But much like the gravitational pull toward Lauren, I found that the further I ran away from my truest self, the more she wanted to be set free.

My excuse for drinking that night was celebration, for a new tattoo, a new boyfriend, and the last three months of soccer right around the corner.

Where there is celebration, alcohol is served. I'd never seen a celebration of any kind without alcohol. I assumed this would be part of the rest of my life.

Maren did not drink because she was driving. The bartender's name was Cameron, and I gave him my number. I didn't think he was cute. I was not attracted to him. Plus, I was dating Chris, but I was drunk, and I thought I was being *fun*. When we got back to Maren's house, I threw all that wine back up half a dozen times. I was a guest in that house, so I threw up quietly in a trashcan and then cleaned it out before passing out on the floor.

Hours later, Maren quietly woke me up, asking me if I would be joining her at the gym. I reluctantly said no. Still a little drunk, I was on the verge of a hangover. I was angry with myself for not getting up to train. Pre-season was a short two weeks away. It was my senior year. *What the fuck am I doing?*

I needed to go work out. Believe it or not, lying on that floor was more of a punishment than to get up and go workout. Working out that morning hungover would have sucked, but I would've been proud of myself for getting my ass up and out the door.

I didn't feel like I deserved to feel proud of myself. I thought I deserved to be punished. So, I laid in bed, drifting in and out of sleep until Maren got back.

I loved working out, especially at different gyms when I was out of town. Later in the day, I'd be mad at myself even more after not only drinking a lot the night before but also skipping the workout to compensate for my bad behavior the previous night. That anger with myself was something I felt I deserved.

By afternoon, I was feeling better, though. Maren and I spent the rest of the day on the beach, and I annoyed the piss out of her by repeatedly declaring my love for Chris. *If I can convince people, then it's true, right? Right.*

The more I convinced the people around me, the more I convinced myself. If I successfully persuaded people to believe that I was in love with him, then this must be the person I was supposed to be with to cater to him, to share my body and "thoughts" with, right? Right.

Lie to yourself, and it eventually becomes the truth, or more so, lie to yourself to keep suppressing the truth so it never comes out.

When I returned from California, Chris picked me up from the airport. He had just returned from a trip to Paris with his family. At baggage claim, Chris told me he had something for me.

He pulled out a gorgeous small French painting of a bridge.

"Will you be my girlfriend?" He asked.

"Yes," I said, not realizing the smile across my face was forced.

He smiled back and picked me up and literally spun me around. I finally had my very own scene from a rom-com. Lucky me…

Finally, I met a guy in college, and we could get married, but I was ignoring my twelve-year-old self when I promised her never to let anyone get in the way of her dreams, especially if that person was a man.

On paper, though, I was on the right track: rock star senior season, a nice boyfriend with a nice family, graduating college in the spring.

This was the life I was meant to live.

What could possibly go wrong?

CHAPTER XXV

To no one's shock, hobbling around for eight weeks in a straight-leg brace did not reverse my IT band. Just before I started dating Chris, the brace came off, and I met with a well-known doctor that was rumored to be the best orthopedic in St. Louis. The wait took hours. His daughter was playing in the State Championship soccer game the next day, so he moved all of his appointments to the day before. Oddly enough, his daughter played soccer for the same high school I played for. I waited three hours just to be told, "You probably won't play your senior season."

A thought entered my mind that would repeat itself throughout the course of my twenties: *Fuck your opinion and your medical school degree. I trust my opinion.* While depression may feed me lies, I knew by then how to differentiate when it was the depression talking and when it was the truest version of myself talking.

Most of the time, thought, I didn't listen to myself. Anxious and depressive thoughts sounded stronger and louder than my own. It was harder to listen to myself because I knew it would take longer to get used to that, and I was impatient. Even though my impatience and procrastination in speaking up resulted in a boulder-like incasing around my skin, it didn't compare to the heavyweight champ that depression can be.

I was David up against Goliath armed with just a slingshot and stone. I was Dobby up against Lucius Malfoy, waiting for a sock to set me free. I was the Pittsburgh Pirates up against the New York Yankees in the 1960 World Series, hoping for a walk-off in the bottom of the ninth.

I still knew my truest self was in there. She never even left. My inner badass. I refused to let someone else dictate my very last few months of playing competitive soccer. I was in more control than I thought.

I made a choice that day. I chose to listen to myself and not the mood disorder that is depression. I chose to play my senior year. Not only would I play, but I would go out with a bang. BIG. HUGE.

The rest of that summer was spent training and rehabbing my knee to make it stronger. I spent time driving back and forth between St. Louis and Columbia, MO where Chris was studying to get his PhD at Mizzou. A few months after we met, we had sex for the first time.

I didn't really want to have sex, but I forced myself to think I wanted to, and I did really want to keep him. So, we had sex. I still think it's weird he didn't have any condoms at the time, and he had to run out and get some. What guy doesn't have condoms on them or somewhere in their home? Whenever there wasn't booze in my system, and I slept with him or with any other man, I would think about anything and everything else. I thought about having sex with a woman instead. I thought about what I needed to do that week. I thought about how long before it would be over. I thought about Lauren. There was only one time I tried to go down on him, but he refused. *You don't want a BJ, babe? SAY. NO. MORE.*

I worked a few different jobs that summer. One was as a waitress at a local restaurant, but I ended up quitting weeks before soccer started because my bosses wanted me to either leave practice early to work the dinner shift or go to practice late.

Absolutely not. It should also be noted that I was a hostess before working as a waitress. I lasted barely three weeks as a waitress and barely three months at that restaurant. That's a shit show for another day.

While I was working a temp gig at the bookstore on campus, I called my boss at the restaurant and told him I wouldn't be coming in for my shift that afternoon, nor would I ever be coming in again. I'll spare you all the drama, but it's worth saying—that restaurant is no longer there today.

I had many jobs that year. My mom called me the Queen of the W2, and that continued into the following year when I was working at three different gyms while still working at a nursing home.

Was I avoiding my feelings and the change coming my way? Yes and no. First of all, I enjoyed working. I liked the feeling of work. You work, and you get rewarded. I liked that. I was just working for the wrong reasons. I didn't *need* the money. I didn't *need* to spend my weekends in an old folk's home. I was avoiding my feelings at that job but also avoiding something else. And that something else was a negative way to avoid my feelings...you know where I'm going with this, right?

Drinking.

I still drank that summer. A lot. A Fourth of July party that lasted nearly three days. Drinks out with Chris. Drinks with his family. Beer by the pool. Drinking wine with Maren when I visited her in California. A float trip that included resurfaced feelings or something for Logan ended with us sharing several kisses and with someone stealing the keys to my dad's Pathfinder. Still, those kisses with Logan came after a day of consuming beer.

The "feelings" for Logan I had were confusing, and at the end of the day, they weren't real. I liked being around him. He was funny and comforting. He was a great friend to so many. I wasn't attracted to him physically, but I was attracted to him in some way. Because I was attracted to him in other ways, I thought that meant I was attracted to him physically.

A slight annoyance looking back on this time: there were so many guys around to explore my sexuality, but not enough women and queer folks. I rarely considered turning to the internet to explore more. Sure, there was a plethora of gay anything online, but I craved in person connection and intimacy. If I had gone to the queer corners of the internet, I feared that it would feel too secretive and sneaky. I also knew I couldn't fully trust who was on the other side of my computer or phone. I wanted it to feel real, like it was with Lauren. Physical, real dates, and face-to-face conversations. Hand holding and snuggling. The energy that we shared from a look across a room. You can't get that same energy from a screen. I didn't want to cop out and settle for a screen when I had already experienced what a queer relationship felt like in real life. Instead of doing the 'sneaky' thing, I did what I felt society told me to do.

During my senior year of college, I was determined to keep my life looking good on paper. My relationship with Chris looked good on paper. He looked good on paper. My future ahead looked good on paper. My past looked good on paper. My resume looked good on paper.

On paper.

On paper.

On paper.

On paper.

The thing about having your life looking good on paper though… paper can burn, only leaving behind useless evidence of black soot.

Outside of soccer and classes the fall semester of my senior year, my free time was aplenty. I even signed up for a class to meet the minimum credits knowing that I would never attend the class. It was Intro to Italian. I did this on purpose. I withdrew from it weeks before the semester ended.

I was looking forward to my carefree senior season, and it started off with a strong, solid start…until an ovarian cyst ruptured just a few weeks into season. That was followed by an abscess that formed on a sensitive area of my body that quickly got infected. These two hiccups forced me to miss about a third of my season. Suddenly, it was not so carefree.

Time was running out…and fast.

I even showed up to the bus for an away game but was sent home by my coaches and athletic trainers. I didn't want to miss any of my senior year. I wanted to extend my time and be able to be there. I felt awful for Sammi who missed so much more than I did due to a torn ACL at the end of last season.

I noticed pain in the lower right quadrant of my abdomen during practice earlier in the week. Of course, I ignored it, thinking it would just simply go away on its own. I really gotta stop ignoring things that I assume will go away on their own. The pain gradually got worse, and I ended up in the ER at 10 p.m. the night before an away game. After several scans, it was determined that I had an ovarian cyst rupture. Once I was told the diagnosis, I had an immediate flashback to the same pain when I was a freshman at Mississippi. I was trying so hard during a drill at practice but had to stop every few seconds. I was trying my best, but my body was creating obstacles that I couldn't see.

Instead of asking if I was okay, my coaches yelled at me, "What're you doing?" "Don't dive in." "Don't just stop!"

Dear cis-male coaches, females have very painful experiences you will never ever come to know. I'm not saying I needed any slack cut, but a little empathy would've gone a long way. I suppose I wanted to be treated more as a human than solely as an athletic machine.

I quietly walked off the field to speak with the trainer. I didn't practice for the rest of the week; instead, I spent my time on a stationary bike while the rest of the team practiced. After finding out about the cyst senior year, I realized I had definitely been dealing with one freshman year, too, that I had never acknowledged or gotten checked.

Less than two weeks after the cyst rupture during my senior year, another more intense pain started growing in a highly sensitive area: my ass crack. Monday, the pain was manageable, but it got worse as the week progressed. Naturally, I followed my instinct to ignore the hell out of it, and I concluded, brought from past experiences, that it was one hell of a hemorrhoid I was now dealing with.

I was sure that it was *just a hemorrhoid.* However, the cream I applied did not help like it had in the past. Again, I ignored the pain because I didn't want to miss any more games. I was determined to play in the next game that Saturday, even if it meant sacrificing my physical wellbeing. I decided to push through.

The pain was burning like an open flesh wound that was bruised with fiery glass swimming within it.

Part of our warm-up included stretches while sitting on the ground. I opted out of the seated exercises because it hurt too bad to sit, and there I was, feeling all high and mighty, still about to go play ninety minutes of soccer in the late summer heat. I did not last the full ninety. I powered through the first thirty or so, but once my opponent ran into my backside and then I fell on my ass, it was game over for Ally.

Shortly into the second half, my coach looked at me and said, "Ally, you ready?"

"Absolutely not. I will not be playing anymore today." Later, he apologized, telling me he didn't realize I was in that much pain.

The rest of the day, my mom tried to get a hold of my doctor, but he never returned any of her calls. I should've gone straight to the hospital, but I was incredibly resistant. By Sunday night, I was dry heaving, sweating, and breathless, keeled over the couch downstairs with a fever of 104. If it wasn't for the constant dry heaving keeping me awake, I'm pretty sure I would've passed out.

Finally, on Monday morning, my doctor called back and had me go see a gastroenterologist immediately. This was the first of many visits I would have over the next eight years.

The car ride was excruciating. Even the slightest uneven piece of pavement made me squeal in pain. I just wanted it to be over.

The doctor came in and looked *down there*. I was diagnosed immediately with an infected abscess. I knew it was bad, but I didn't want to look at it. So, I didn't.

It needed to be drained ASAP, so I was scheduled for an outpatient procedure an hour later. I was still incredibly sore but gracious for the immediate relief and my body returning to its regular temperature.

The worst pain out of the entire experience came when I took my first bowel movement a few days after the procedure.

I laid on the floor, sweaty and gracious for the coolness of the tile. I'd been there before, but it felt different that time since I wasn't drunk or hungover. Either way, it was still not fun. Still in pain. Still wondering why now my body is betraying me. I thought I'd only ever have to deal with my mind doing that. That was the first of many, many times my body would betray me over the next decade. Which then has me questioning, *why you so abcess-ed with me, body?*

I asked the doctor what would cause something like that. He replied, "Bad luck, mostly." I guess I had a ton of bad luck then.

A week gone from an ovarian cyst. Another week gone from that literal asshole abscess. Both robbing me. I was robbed of time and last games that were so precious and taken away by things outside of my control.

The thing about my setbacks, though—is they are merely an elastic band pulling me back, preparing me to be launched into my greatness...closer to my higher being, which is the absolute best part of a forced break. One that gives you no choice but to take it.

The best part about any set back is that I always come back and make up for lost time. By the time I got back on the field, I was ready to fight and win.

I had made up for lost time and was named offensive player of the week after I returned from nursing my ailments.

The final whistle of the conference finals finally blew. My team was so exhausted that we slowly celebrated. There were no dog piles. There were no overjoyed celebrations. They were joyous hugs, high-fives, and laughter, but they were filled with fatigue while we slowly fell to the ground. We were all so tired but glad to have won one last home game.

Making the pain, the waiting, and the time lost worth it, one thing I wasn't robbed of that year was receiving the highest award: Conference Player of the Year. My dad came down from the stands and gave me a hug on the field after my name was announced. Regardless, I was happy to be receiving something I deserved and gladly proved that I'd quickly made up for lost time.

CHAPTER XXVI

By the time my very last college game came, I had never embraced the unknown because I never had to. Every Labor Day, I knew I'd be playing soccer. I knew what my summers looked like growing up: soccer camps, training, the beach, the pool, and hanging out with friends. My life had been amazing, safe, fun, and there was nothing I wanted to change. That's why it was so easy for me to fall back into playing soccer after Ole Miss. Soccer was something I know very well. Although I spent most of my time thinking about what I'd be doing if soccer was not my thing, it was safer to return to the field than to whatever is next, to the unknown. Plus, I wasn't done playing quite yet.

At nineteen, at twenty-two, and even at twenty-six, when I started writing this book, I was still scared of the unknown. I had no idea what I was doing. I had no idea where I was going. I was so fixated on finding out where I should be and where I should go that I neglected the entire grieving process of a nearly 20-year relationship.

My knees may have been ready to move on from soccer come November of 2013, but my heart certainly wasn't. I didn't even ask my heart if she was ready. To what's next. Whatever that was. I wanted to know as soon as possible because now I had a huge gaping hole left to fill. The sooner I knew, the sooner I could be more comfortable or at least less uncomfortable.

As the end of my soccer career approached, I found myself scrambling for my next chapter. I didn't know what was next, although I thought I was ready for it. I wanted to know what was next, so I had something to say to anyone who asked me about my post-college plans. *Uhhhh. Most people don't know their plans until way after college, so please leave us alone, and we will figure it out when we get there, okay?*

I played my last college soccer game in Wheaton, IL, against Wheaton College in the first round of the Division III NCAA tournament. We were not favored to win. Everyone knew it—even the other team—but no one dared say a thing. We still went in with a winning mentality.

On a Friday morning, everything remained the same, but the atmosphere of today's game was different. The air was light, yet heavy. I didn't feel sad necessarily, but something was different. That something different was change. Change was right around the corner, waiting for not only me but my fellow seniors to turn it.

It was a bitter, damp fall day. I was exactly where I needed to be. I deserved to be here. I wanted to finish what I started. A goal coming to an end.

One of my goals for my last season was to score a goal with my ass. The closest I got was a legendary ass-pass to a teammate in this last game. Popped my booty right on the ball as it came down from a free kick.

My only goal for that last game was to not stop. I would not stop running. I think I believed if I kept running, then it wouldn't really be over 90 minutes later. Maybe I still thought running in other ways meant it wasn't over.

While we kept the other team at a distance for most of the first half, we ended up losing 4-0.

When the final whistle blew, I didn't realize I kept running until I saw a few of my teammates drop to the ground, devastated. Not only was it the end of our season, but it was the end of our careers. It was the end of life as we've known it for so many years. For most of us, it was the end of life as we knew it for most of our whole lives.

I finally let myself lay on the ground, turf digging into my skin for what may be the very last time. My hand slapped the ground two times. I tapped out. Almost 20 years playing soccer. I have crunchy knees, awards, and memories to prove it was a long, successful ride. If I did cry after that final whistle, there weren't many tears. I swallowed them instead of letting them fall, unlike when I was 11, and I played my last soccer game with my Pittsburgh team before I moved back to St. Louis. I lied and said I was upset because I hadn't scored a goal in that last game, the finals for a tournament, which we ended up winning. I was sad to leave my team and friends all over again. My unknown about the move two years prior had now been known. Then, I found myself back in the unknown again.

The final whistle echoed, and my teammates came and comforted me and each other. Many with tears, all with long faces. I actively chose not to grieve this loss. Not the loss of this game. The loss of my life as a great soccer player. I wanted to run from the grief, so that's exactly what I did. I ran from the blow to the stomach. I ran from the heartache of losing a game I loved. A game that defined a large part of me and my life. I ran from the loss of the relationships that were bound to change, with teammates all moving on to lead different but amazing lives. I ran from feeling the pain of wandering, wondering, and worrying.

I suppressed the feelings. I didn't talk about them. I didn't even think about talking about them. I didn't even realize what I was doing. I didn't realize I was running away at the time. I didn't have the tools, the time, or the strength to process loss. I fucking loathe losing.

My body allowed me to play a game at a competitive level for nearly two decades. The game saved me from feeling and thinking about the uncomfortable feelings that lay doormat in my mind and body. Well, the game at least gave me the chance to not face them for many, many years. The game acted as many things for me. Near the top of that list, it acted as a distraction and stress reliever.

Without that distraction, I was left with time, and that scared the crap out of me. Time that I had no idea what to do with. I knew for sure it wouldn't be spent feeling the feelings from this major loss and processing them. I didn't want to feel any more pain. I've won more games than I've lost. I've won more battles than I've lost. But rarely did I spend time and give myself space to process the uncomfortable emotions of the grieving process.

I was mostly numbing those feelings and delaying the process with distraction after distraction. Soccer and alcohol being the main two for the last 4 years. I couldn't help but wonder (and sometimes fear) that alcohol would take over my life now that there was so much room to fill without soccer. I was tired and relieved. I was sad, and

I was also scared. The two latter weren't shown externally though. I did my best to hide them – among other things.

Timmy's Dad asked me this after final our game: "So, what's next, then?" With a smile and nervous laugh, I said, "I have no idea."

Then my Dad chimed in, "Well, we're about to head into the city to look at grad schools." Chicago was only an hour away.

We may have lost my very last college soccer game, but I didn't lose that day. Statistically, most collegiate athletes lose their last college game. Statistically, my games won outnumbered my games lost. As I grew as a player, I learned that most of the time, if I gave my all and still didn't win, then that's just how it was supposed to be.

I still love the game so much. It's too beautiful not to love, but most days, I do not miss it.

When I do miss it, it's the road trips and the camaraderie. I miss being part of a large team with a common goal. I miss the feeling when I score a goal. I miss seeing the hard work in off season pay off every single time during the season. I miss the way my body used to move.

The hard work and discipline soccer taught me is one of the things that keeps me going in pursuit of my life's purpose as I entered the "real world." If I work hard, discipline myself, and be kind, it will pay off. I trust that because I have seen it happen time and time again in my own life as well as in others. The harder part at that time was figuring out where I was supposed to be.

I was all for going to grad school, anything to avoid the real-world work force for a few more years.

A few months before graduation, The Professor took the time to give me a personal tour of Lindenwood and its facilities. The gray skies looked cold but allowed me to get away with just a sweater. I was there because I had been told I needed a plan. College graduates needed a plan, apparently. I saw one of three options:

1. Find a job.
2. Grad school.
3. Travel.

Option one looks gross. Not that I didn't want to start working, but I was not about to sell out at a desk job. And a desk job, in my mind, was my only option. I was so scared of being stuck in an office and never being able to leave my hometown. Option three was my favorite, and I did get to travel a little after graduation. Just not internationally.

I was also broke, so traveling a lot or far was not in the cards for me, at least not at that time. I also didn't feel that I deserved a three-month European vacation. However, I was more than grateful for two domestic trips to two major cities: L.A. and New York.

Ever since I was a child, I was always worried about money. For a long time, I didn't understand where it came from, how much of it there was, how much things cost, etc. Money was a mystery to me. My dad worked full time, and when my brother and I reached middle school age, my mom started working again. She was a part-time college professor at first and then full-time as a trainer for a bank once we were both in high school.

My parents have always been good with money. They worked hard for my brother and I to have a flourishing and abundant childhood. There was never anything for me to worry about money-wise, but still, I found myself asking nearly every time we'd go out to eat: "do we have enough money?" I guess I had this irrational fear of us not being able to pay our bill, and then we'd be summoned to the kitchen to wash dishes, causing me to miss soccer practice.

Similarly, I also have a chronic worry about car keys. It's gotten better with time, but I still can't fully shake it. I lived in Pittsburgh for a couple of years when I was a kid. During a soccer tournament, my friend, Gina, locked her mom's keys in her car on accident. To this day, I will almost always ask if the driver has the keys, especially if it's my mom driving. Not once does the driver not have the keys.

When I returned home from that Chicago trip, I quickly digested how much I disliked my newfound, what seemed like permanent free time. The free time seemed endless. *Will I ever find something to occupy my time? What am I to do without soccer? Who am I without it? Where am I to be? Where am I to run to now?*

What else do I know just as much as soccer? School.

Now that soccer was over, I had time to focus on writing. I felt I need direction, though, so I started thinking and looking at graduate programs. While I still wanted to pursue acting, a graduate program in theatre was out of the question. Most, if not all, graduate theatre and acting programs required a bachelors in the same.

But before more school came, though, I still had time to spare.

After my soccer career came to an end, all I wanted to do was fill up my free time. I wanted to work. I wanted to hang out with people. I wanted to do anything but sit in the silence of my thoughts and feelings. My surroundings were silent, but my mind was so loud. I didn't want to face the big change again: life without soccer, for real this time, followed by life without school shortly after that.

So, that winter, I got a job at a local assisted living facility where one of my teammates worked. She put in a good word for me. Soon, that gig filled up most of my weekends. I worked Saturday from 3-11 p.m. and again on Sunday. I told myself and others that this was great because I still had Friday night open and could enjoy most of my weekend. When I wasn't working part-time or hanging out with friends, I spent time researching and making lists of graduate programs I wanted to attend.

I shared this desire of wanting to continue my education with The Professor who taught several of my communications classes. He offered to help, immediately suggesting I check out a program at another St. Louis area university, Lindenwood University. He was a student there then, pursuing his M.F.A. in writing. He also taught classes there.

I was drawn to Lindenwood's Digital Cinema program (now called Cinema and Media Arts) because it incorporated writing with opportunities to perform in front of the camera. It also would give me a chance to learn a lot more about film and television production. This program opened my eyes and fueled my desire to both act and write.

The first week of December, barely a month after soccer ended, The Professor invited me to take a private tour of the school. I felt good about visiting Lindenwood's campus on that week because it was my brother's birthday, and there was also a full ride scholarship on the table. So, LU was at the top of my list for grad school.

Good things happen on birthdays, I convinced myself. Plus, a couple of days ago, Chris told me he loved me for the first time.

The digital cinema program caught my eye immediately. Sure, I'd create great content with their state-of-the-art equipment and facilities. Sure, I'd make a name for myself on this campus, and the location put me an hour closer to Chris. And sure, deciding about going to school here would give me an answer to the question: what are your plans after graduation?

During my personal tour from The Professor, we met with the head of the cinema department. Before we arrived at the cinema professor's office, The Professor warned me that he'd probably make a comment about my appearance and tell me I should be on TV or something. Sure enough, within ninety seconds of sitting with two grown ass men in a mahogany-soaked office, the professor said, "You'd look good on TV. You have a face for it." I could only offer a tight smile, and at the time, I thought the tight smile was rude of me. Never mind the stories I'd tell on screen. And totally forgo the feelings I would do my best to convey! It was my face, apparently, for why the people would tune in.

I thought to myself, *why can't I be on TV simply because I'm talented enough? And yeah, I may not be great at talking about my feelings in my day-to-day life, but I like to think I'd be great at it on screen. Looks shouldn't have anything to do with it.*

These two men were and probably still are big fish in a small pond. The Professor looked at the other professor and told him about Chris and said that he, "thinks we have a good chance of keeping her here." Here as in the St. Louis area. The Professor knew about Chris only because our relationship was a topic I chose to speak about in our storytelling class earlier that semester.

What the fuck?

My smile tightened, and I let out a laugh, which outwardly sounded normal, but I knew it was an evil laugh. *How dare he keep me anywhere? How dare anyone keep me anywhere when I am only twenty-one years old, and I have yet to see the world?!* There was so much more for me out there whether I ended up going to Lindenwood or not, and deep down, I knew all of this to be true.

But I was still more interested in a quick fix rather than navigating unfamiliar dark caves to search for better lighting at another end.

So, there I was at Lindenwood with my whole two feet already in the door, with a face made for other people to look at on a screen, and I hadn't even applied yet. I left unsure, but I did have one thing: an update for others about my plans after college.

I left their St. Charles, MO campus around 5 p.m. and drove to meet my family for my brother's birthday dinner. I arrived first at the restaurant and immediately ordered a glass of whiskey. Straight up.

The glass was empty by the time my family arrived less than fifteen minutes later. I ordered another upon their arrival.

My mom was eager to know how my afternoon went. I didn't want to take focus away from my brother's night, nor did I want to worry my mom. So, I told her, "It feels right to go there. It's the right choice. I feel at home on that campus. I can see myself going to school there." Blah. Blah. Blah. I just wanted to make her happy and calm her nerves about where her multi-interested, multi-passionate, and talented daughter would end up.

As I said, Lindenwood is a great school, but it was not my dream. My heart belonged elsewhere. I left my heart in Chicago when I was sixteen, and I've been trying to get it back ever since. I didn't know then that I ever would.

New Year's 2008, just a few months before my sixteenth birthday, my family drove to Chicago for a little getaway before my brother and I started school again. I had been to Chicago a couple of times before to visit family. A few of my soccer tournaments as a kid were in Naperville, but never in the city. So, that weekend in 2008 was the first time I had to truly explore Chicago and all the gems it has to offer.

I had heard of The Second City theatre, but I had never been. In a nutshell, it's a comedy theatre dedicated to using improvisation to create sketches. Comedic legends like Tim Meadows, Steve Carrell, E.R. Fightmaster, and Catherine O'Hara, all studied and performed there. I was intrigued by the legacy of that place, and I wanted to know more.

We had tickets to see a Main Stage show one night while we were in town. One of the actors did an interactive improvised bit with the audience. She walked on stage wearing a backwards baseball cap and tossing a football in her hands. When she spoke, her voice transformed into a child's voice – that of a young boy.

The boy went into a monologue about how his parents were going through a rough patch. He asked the audience, "What do you think my parents were arguing about?"

As he finished the question, he threw the football to an audience member to answer. A middle-aged gentleman caught the ball and said, "Uh…um…dad was having an affair."

The gentleman tossed the ball back poorly, and it bounced on the stage. Hilariously, making the actor fumble along with it until it rolled to a stop. He bent down and picked up the ball again, and said, "Gosh. An affair? I wonder what my mom thought about that. You know, I think she even caught them in the act. Mom? Are you there?"

The character looked into the audience and landed right on me.

"Oh, mom! There you are! What did you do when you found out?"

The ball was thrown to me, and I caught it mid-air.

Without missing a beat, I said, "I joined them!"

I tossed the ball in a perfect spiral back to the stage. The audience exploded with laughter. My dad put a hand to his forehead, not with embarrassment but more so to say, *well, what else could I expect from my hilarious kid?* My mom and brother laughed, too, while I just smiled, trying to act calm and cool even though I was thrilled on the inside.

"Wow. Wow. Wow," the character said while scratching his head.

He continued to walk around the stage in disbelief. He opened his mouth a couple of times to say something, but eventually shrugged and walked of the stage nodding his head. End scene.

The room of laughter from what I said was intoxicating. In that moment, I knew that I wanted to live and perform there some day in some capacity.

I held on to that memory, using it as a driving force to get me to Chicago.

Since deciding to go to Lindenwood, I was relieved to buy myself some time until or if I figured out any other next moves. Knowing I had somewhat of a plan was nice, but that plan didn't replace the utmost dread of life without soccer. There was still way too much time on my hands.

A week later, during my storytelling final in The Professor's class, he kept going on and on about Chris and our relationship. Okay maybe not on and on, but it was long enough to raise some eyebrows—mine specifically, accompanied by a few knots beginning to tie in my stomach.

The Professor announced to the entire class that I was going to be sticking around town after graduation because of a **boy**. *Why are you talking about my relationship?*

I was mortified not only by the perception of my classmates but also because I was betraying my inner child. It was a slap to my fourteen-year-old self who promised I would never let a man dictate my future or get in the way of fulfilling my dreams. It was a slap to my sixteen-year-old self, who longed to be in Chicago.

The Professor should have acknowledged my sticking around town to cultivate and nurture my education further and start and expand my art, work, and career in my hometown. While it was nice that I would've been closer to him, my decision had nothing to do with Chris.

I was scared to stay, yes, but I was more afraid to leave and speak up for what I wanted. I didn't want to stay in St. Louis. If Chris said he'd love me no matter what, maybe, just maybe I could still go to Chicago and keep him, too.

Despite the anger swimming in my blood, I only smiled. Smiling was so much easier than saying what was on my mind.

CHAPTER XXVII

Even though I had a plan for after graduation, life without soccer made me feel lost, but at least I had Chris and a plan for what's next. I kept telling myself Chicago could wait.

January 22, 2014, I wrote a journal entry:

I'm not so sure about grad school. I just want to get away from STL... Chris says he'll love me no matter what I decide, and I know he will. The energy and drive I used to feel before my heart was broken at Ole Miss and with grandpa leaving, that's starting to come back to me. Maybe it never even left. I missed it so much. Feeling my dreams again. I cannot ignore this. I must chase.

In other words...I must run.

Not long after that I wrote this on February 2, 2014:

Truth be told, I really don't know what I'm doing. I did buy a plane ticket to L.A. to visit

Blair after graduation. It is NOT 1-way.

On Valentine's Day weekend, I visited Chris at Mizzou. I found a copy of his favorite movie, *Cool Runnings* and gifted it to him for the day designed for capitalism more so than for lovers celebrating, like most holidays that have been commercialized.

He wrote me a lovely note accompanied with a Starbucks gift card. It said: "I don't want to contribute to your addiction, but I know how much you love coffee." Followed some Xs or Os or maybe a few little hearts.

Anytime we'd get a cup of coffee, which was often, he'd mention being a bad influence on my coffee addiction. We had an ongoing joke about my coffee consuming habits. More so him, I just went along with how funny and charming he thought this was. I was accommodating, which was so much easier than digging up the truth, so much easier than standing up for anyone else, including myself. I happily accepted his gift. Duh. Free coffee was my sober equivalent of free beer. However, part of me still wished he had made a comment on my drinking habits. By then, I felt that if someone called me out on it, then I'd be more open to talking about it. I wanted someone to notice how I drank and why without having to be the one to bring it up.

Before heading out for the evening he planned for us, we each had a beer. On the walk from the car to the restaurant, Chris pulled me into an empty bar before I could even protest.

Normally, it would be packed with local college students, but it was freezing this Valentine's Day. So, the only people out were those who could not only afford a nice dinner but were also willing to step out into the icy weather.

As a toast to my love affair with coffee, Chris ordered two espresso liquor shots. It had a delicious hint of chocolate that somehow balanced out the strong taste of coffee. Before I could protest again, he told the bartender "Another one!" *Um... dude, one of us must drive.* After the second shot, we were warm enough to not feel the sting of the cold as we left the bar. And I was warm enough to not feel the disappointment of who I was in those moments: a compliant girlfriend to her boyfriend, perfecting the role of heterosexual female.

We arrived at the restaurant, which had a prefixed meal for lovers celebrating. Chris ordered a bottle of red wine to go along with our meat and potatoes, and it somehow also paired nicely with our chocolate cake at the end of the meal. That's right. A whole bottle.

Beer — check.

Shots — check.

Wine — check.

The beer and shots were one thing, but I knew adding wine into the mix, I was really pushing my limits. But of course, I didn't acknowledge this. Wine drunk was my best drunk but only good for me when it was only wine that I consumed. I was being who he needed me to be, or at least I thought I was. By the time we got back to his apartment, I was pretty drunk, tiptoeing closer and closer to The Wall.

Stepping out of our evening attire and into sweats, we snuggled up in his bed and put on

Cool Runnings. Within the first ten minutes, he asked: "Wanna smoke?"

Despite knowing how terribly I handled myself when I mixed different types of alcohol and also when I'm crossfaded, I said, "yes," remembering months earlier how shocked I was to find out that he smoked weed. His conservative, preppy demeanor had zero flags of him ever smoking weed in his life, let alone buying it regularly. I was wrong. My boyfriend was a pothead.

Beer — check.

Shots — check.

Wine — check.

Weed — check.

I took my first hit, exhaled and said, "I dated a girl once."

His eyes remained fixated on the pipe and lighter. He fidgeted.

"Oh," he said as he squirmed in his seat.

"How do you feel about that?" I inquired.

"Well, it was just a fling, right?"

"No. I was in love with her."

"Oh. Are you sure? So, does this mean you're bisexual?"

"I'm not sure, but maybe."

"Well, as long as you don't leave me for a woman or cheat on me with one."

"K."

I did not like this response. I took another hit, and then I was high. Officially crossing the faded street and into the Wall, an official dead end. *I need to leave. I need to run. I do not want to be here anymore.* The Wall always meant I needed to run. Except something different happened when I hit the Wall this time. For the first time since I started hitting the Wall, someone was there to stop me. Crossfaded Ally, aka CFA, did not like that. I knew I could kick his ass, but in my current state, he was stronger than me.

Beer — check.

Shots — check.

Wine — check.

Weed — check.

Wall — check.

I packed my bag, put my coat and boots on, and held my keys in my hand. I tried to push through him, but he stopped me and held me tight, trying to calm me down. I didn't want to be touched. I stepped back as I ripped myself from his brace and sat on the corner of his bed, distant. He stood between me and the door.

"I should not have mentioned smoking. We should have not smoked. I'm sorry," he said. "Yeah. A little late for that now, isn't it? You can make it up to me by letting me fucking leave."

"Why are you doing this?"

"You're the almost psychologist, you figure it out."

He now stood closer in front of me with his arms crossed, his right foot kicked out in front.

In a rough whisper I said, "I don't even want to have kids!"

I screamed it again. I knew it would hurt him. I wanted him to feel pain like I had felt since my final whistle blew three months earlier. It felt good to see him defeated for once. It was totally unfair and hurtful, but I wanted someone to feel the pain with me. I didn't want to be alone in my feelings anymore. If I was going to feel pain, I wanted to bring him down with me. *Cool Runnings* still played on the TV. W*here the fuck am I? How did I get here? Why do I keep running?*

I turned and looked at the TV and watched for a few seconds before the light started to make me uncomfortable.

Chris took my keys away from me and begged me to stay there until the morning. He said he'd allow me to leave as soon as I slept off the concoction inside of me. I obliged. I knew I was sinking into a deep depression again since soccer had ended, but I didn't acknowledge it yet. If only I could sleep off depression like I'd be able to sleep off my soon to be hangover. But that would be too easy, and depression is a heartless bitch. It's never easy. It's not supposed to be.

Morning came too slow. As soon as I used the bathroom and chugged a glass of water, I picked up my belongings. It took less time since I packed everything the night before. Again, I sat on the edge of the bed, and he sat next to me.

"Do you want to talk about it?" I asked.

"Do you?"

I shook my head.

"Did you mean what you said?"

"Which part?"

"Do you really not want to have kids?"

Writing this next line makes me nauseous.

I responded, "I would have your kids…for you."

He briefly accepted this but soon realized his mistake, which was the exact moment he started to phase me out. I just didn't realize it until it was too late. This was the last time I visited him at school.

Within a couple of hours of returning home from my weekend, I bit the bullet and stopped avoiding my mom. I knew she was curious about my romance filled weekend with my *perfect* boyfriend. I sat down next to her in the hearth room, and she asked me how my weekend with Chris was. I told her about the fight, or more so my drunken stupor.

My arm rested on the side of the couch and Heidi trotted over and lifted my hand with her nose. She told me my behavior resembled that of how I was at Ole Miss. She then asked if I was depressed, and I whispered back, "yes."

I finally admitted it. It was finally real. It was real all along sure, but hearing it come out of my mouth made it magically become truly, fully real—undeniable. Maybe hearing it out loud is part of the self-acceptance.

This current depression started when the final whistle blew in Wheaton, and I did not know when this episode would end. *Right now, it feels like never, but I've been here before. I got through it last time, so I can get through it this time, too….I have a boyfriend to live for*, I reminded myself. Even though it was far from the truth, it was enough for me to keep going. For that part, I am thankful.

Heidi stayed by my side while my mom held me as I cried. Even when I finally got up and stopped crying, Heidi followed me upstairs. I texted Chris and told him I was depressed. He replied that he would help me find help. I thanked him and told him I loved him. Then, with Heidi guarding my door, I crawled into bed and slept without a clue as to what time it was, what day it was, or when and where I needed to be next.

I was stuck, and no matter how much sleep I got, I would always be tired until that episode of depression passed. I slept to escape. Sleep was the only safe way for me to escape my mind without harming myself further with thoughts or booze, or any other thing that I had yet to try.

Chris sent me a handful of contacts of mental health professionals. I thanked him again, but my mom had found a psychiatrist, and they also had therapists at the same location. Which, I was all for because I did not want to be galivanting around town for hours at a time. It was already exhausting going to one location. I was put on antidepressants and started seeing a therapist once a week. I liked my new therapist, Joe. However, I still had a dangerously hard time opening up to him at first.

I wanted it to work with Chris, so I saw Joe on a weekly basis for several weeks. While my reasons for going to therapy and taking antidepressants were mainly to appease and keep my boyfriend, they showed me what routine therapy and medication can do. I needed to show up consistently to see how beneficial the routine could be. What I didn't love, though, was that I needed an external reason to tend to my mental health. Despite not doing it for myself, it still had an intense, constructive impact on my life. The routine therapy and taking medications regularly gave me skills and shined a teeny bit of light on the fact that therapy and medication are not inherently bad.

Joe was a big guy with a small office. Any time I sat across from him, I found myself missing Melissa's spacious office. There was more to observe. That would've been ideal if I could kick Melissa out and plop Joe in there. No such luck. So, every Tuesday afternoon at 12:00 pm on the dot, I drove from campus or home to Creve Coeur. It was forty-ish minutes from my house and twenty-ish from campus. Further than I preferred, but with my mom's and Chris's support, I was more willing to put in the miles. Plus, it allowed extra time to think about potential topics of conversation with Joe.

Slowly, I started opening up to him. First, I said all the cliché things I could think of to say. You know, the things one may think a therapist *wants* to hear, even though they probably prefer honesty above all else. Essentially, what it came down to was that I was lying.

"I'm fine."

"I think I'm doing just fine."

Pretty much any phrase I said with the word *fine* was not true. They weren't cliches. They were deflections and something for me to say to pass the time. However, those words gave me time and space to test the waters with Joe. I was curious how he would reply to certain comments and suggestions.

The way the chairs were in Joe's office, I had no choice but to make eye contact more often than I preferred. The chairs were close together, and if I leaned a little to my left and reached out my arm, I could touch his desk. If I reached to the right, I could open the door and run. I never ran out of Joe's office, but I felt comforted by the fact that I could at any time.

CHAPTER XXIX

I barely said a word throughout dinner one Friday night in March. It was just eight weeks shy of graduation and a few weeks after Valentine's Day. I had been taking antidepressants regularly for two weeks, but they hadn't kicked in yet. Around that time, I was a few sessions in with Joe. Sessions with him were much more tolerable than with my former therapist, Melissa. So, I felt like that was a win. Classes at school were pretty breezy, too. Senioritis had fully kicked in, and I was excited to start working on my capstone project, a research paper about the differences between male and female comedians. While I struggled at first to narrow down my topic, after spring break, I felt I had a good grasp to start researching.

Prior to spring break, Chris and I went to the Cheesecake Factory for dinner at the St. Louis Galleria. I let Chris talk about school and his work. I indulged in potstickers and ordered a skinny mojito, a skinny one, because it's *healthier* and would look better next to my potstickers as opposed to a heavier beverage.

Chris talked about school and his career trajectory for the entire meal. I nodded between bites, adding bland, broad, but supportive statements. "You're so smart!" Other than that, I was quiet as hell, giving off a sour vibe, unable to hide it like I preferred…like I'm used to.

Despite my excitement for my capstone project and my desire to go to Florida for spring break soon, something still felt *off* inside me. A lot of me still felt empty. Chris finally picked up on my vibe in his car on the way back to his house. I wanted to tell him how empty and lost I felt. How I so desperately wanted this to work, for him and me to work. I tried, but I couldn't. He was not my rock. He was not MY person. He asked me what was wrong. I started to speak but stopped.

He raised his voice in frustration—why couldn't I be open with him, he pleaded. We were going to go see a movie after dinner, but he started driving toward his house instead. By the time he parked, he asked me again nicely what was wrong. I broke. Tears and bargaining. I had found myself again in a place where I so badly wanted to want to be but had no business being there. We have no business being in places that are not meant for us. Those places acting as roundabouts, going in a circle until we finally choose another direction. The right direction. *Why do I keep staying in places I don't want to be?*

He suggested we spend the rest of the evening apart. I frantically tried to convince him not to part ways, desperate not to be alone, and I was also pissed about the fact that he was about to send me home when I was clearly so upset.

If I let that happen, then we would break up, I thought. I wiped the tears away, and by the time we stepped inside the house, you couldn't tell I had been crying at all. If any of his family members were home, I would not let them know I'd been crying. When we got in the basement, I was back to being the girlfriend he needed and wanted me to be.

I massaged the spot on his back that'd been giving him trouble. I told him how proud I was to know him. I thanked him again for paying for dinner. I apologized for not being able to open up to him but said that with time, I thought I'd be able to. I told him how much I loved being his girlfriend and how much I wanted to be there.

With every word that came out of my mouth, I was lying to myself more than anyone else.

Things were never that hard with Lauren.

Chris and I finished watching most of whatever NBA game was on TV and then watched the highlights. I understood sports, but I did not understand why he needed to watch the highlights directly after a game. You literally just watched it, bro. Not to mention, that was the most boring basketball game I had ever watched. Although my mind did preoccupy itself with everything I could do to make this relationship work in the long haul.

2:48 p.m. time for me to go. He walked me to my car and kissed me again. We hugged tight, and I told him to let me know when he got back to school. He promised he would, and I got in my car and drove the five minutes to work.

My 3-11 p.m. shift was splendid. My afternoon with Chris was great. Everything felt great, I lied to myself. It had been an amazing day, meaning that I had found things to soften the fear of the unknown.

I had a plan after graduation. Things were falling into place!

I was unaware that ever since Valentine's Day, though, we had been seeing less and less of each other, only spending time together when Chris came home.

A little after 9 p.m., a visitor walked through the door. To my surprise, it was Chris. I ran around from behind the desk and threw my arms around him, and kissed him…like any heterosexual white bitch would. I've seen the movies! He stopped by and brought me some hot tea and a sweater.

I am chronically chilly, so any time someone brings me a sweater or a hot tea when I am without, I *really* notice it and don't ever forget that simple act of kindness.

It was slightly warmer outside that night, so I stepped outside with him to warm up. As sad as I was about the last few months with soccer officially ending, I started to feel the tiniest sliver of hope restored within me, and that was enough to push through. Maybe it was the tea. Maybe it was the spring. Maybe it was because graduation was close, and I was ready to be done with undergrad. I was ready to move on to the next thing, the next, and the next.

I had a plan and a kind boyfriend who not only brought me comfort but also showed up at my place of work so I could be seen with a dude. It didn't matter to me that I was lying to myself about that plan. It mattered to me that I had a plan at all because that meant I could keep hiding.

Chris and I had a deep conversation in those few minutes outside. He told me how much he loved me and gave me a pep talk. He told me that my future was bright. He told me that I'd be okay. And he was right. My future was bright, and I would be okay. But something in his tone made me panic a bit. In that slight unnerving moment, I made my decision about grad school. I told him that I was going to Lindenwood. I thought that being geographically closer to him would prolong or save whatever it was that we had. I thought that it would save me from dealing with myself. It was my Hail Mary in the fourth quarter with only seconds on the clock, and I was down by a lot, but not enough to make me not try. At least not yet.

Although I was glad that my future was a little less unknown, my heart broke a bit as I told him I'd be staying. The pressure of lying to myself was starting to crack my soul. Only the truth—the immense amount of pressure from speaking my truth—would form diamonds.

After Chris drove off and I ignored the crack in my soul, I was feeling the best I felt in months. I felt things turning around. I felt that if I could keep pretending and living a lie that eventually it would come true despite sacrificing my soul's wishes. I failed to recall my last biggest wish that didn't come true: wanting it to work out in Mississippi. I believed the lie of wanting my attraction to him to be true. My 'attraction' to ANY man to be true. If I had referenced recent history, I could've foreseen that those wants would **never** come true.

The next day, I proudly and excitedly called The Professor who connected me to the cinema department at Lindenwood and told him that, yes, I accept. I called Chris immediately after. He did not answer, so I texted him with the news. He congratulated me and told me he would call me later that night.

Several hours later, I was getting ready for bed. I had just gotten out of the shower and eagerly tapped my phone for any notifications, hoping to see his name on my screen. There were two missed calls, a voicemail, and a text saying he wanted me to call him back right away because he had plans to meet a friend.

I threw on some sweatpants and a T-shirt, my hair dripping wet and unbrushed. Two pieces of dark chocolate sat on my nightstand next to a glass of water. I unlocked my phone and tapped his name. He picked up immediately.

"Hey," he said.

"Hey, how was your day?"

"Good. What're you up to?"

"I just got out of the shower, and…"

"Eating some dark chocolate?"

I laughed, "Yes."

"So, listen, Ally. This isn't working out for me anymore. I'm breaking up with you." Damn, right to the fucking point, man. I tried to laugh again, but instant tears choked back any laughter.

"Are you serious?" I squeaked. "Yeah. I –"

"What did I do? I don't understand. You just told me last night that you loved me. Do you not love me anymore?"

"It's just not working for me anymore. It's over."

"I mean if that's what you want."

"Yeah. It's what I want. Good luck."

The call lasted just five minutes, but there was prolonged bargaining, all of which was on my part. He hung up, and I wept as I frantically texted friends. Sammi called me, and through tears, I tried to tell her what happened. I was not okay. "I need my mom. I'll call you later," I said. I let the phone fall to the floor and ran down the hall to my parents' bedroom. I buried my face into my mom's shoulder. Heidi jumped up on the bed and nuzzled her head near my lap. I hysterically sobbed for an hour, devastated at the loss of not just a boyfriend but also the loss of a plan I was so sure of after the loss of soccer. It felt like too much. I didn't want to feel any of it. Where would I run to now? Where would I hide now?

Lindenwood was my ticket to get everyone off my back about what I was doing with my life, and Chris was my ticket get society off my back about who I was going to marry and when, but Lindenwood was *his ticket* out of our relationship.

I was shocked and confused. I was angry at him, yes, but I was angrier at the fact that I lost a distraction and a huge part of my "rock solid" plan had just failed…not realizing that diamonds were forming and had been for years.

I thought it was some sort of cruel joke. I thought he'd call me the next day, saying he was joking, but he never did.

I had just lost soccer, and now this? Right before my birthday, too. That was one way to get out of buying me a present. Other than my plan falling apart in seconds, I was angry that he couldn't tell me in person the previous night. However, I'm grateful that he allowed me to weep in the comfort of my home and my mother's arms instead of potentially being seen by dozens of elderly people scooting around their living area.

We never spoke and I never saw him again. I never reached out to him to talk things over. There was no looking back. I was only interested in looking forward, and I started the second I realized he was never going to call.

Hot frustration and confusion mixed with some relief but mostly because I knew I'd rather be there, hurt and alone without him than ever to be seen in a relationship with him or any man ever again. That was the deep truth, and I knew it, but instead of feeling liberated, I was terrified. Not ready to accept. Not ready to admit. Not ready to be even an ounce aware.

Chris wasn't the last guy I dated, but it was the last formal relationship with a man that I ever had.

The next day, I found myself replaying the last several big moments of the last few months. That afternoon, I sat in the soccer house on the kitchen counter and recounted what happened in the last forty-two hours. My teammates listened, but no one really knew what to say. What could be said? I didn't need anything from anyone other than an ear to burn at that time. I just needed to talk and have someone listen, and they were there for me.

Over a pitcher of margaritas a few weeks later, though, I got some feedback from one of my male friends. He said to me, "We all need to get dumped sometime." Although I was annoyed at first, I wasn't mad at him for saying that. I needed to hear it. He was right.

In the first few weeks post-breakup, though, I felt even more lost than I had been. I wandered around St. Louis. Crying. Being. Frantically trying to find my next hiding spot.

One morning, I gathered things for a picnic by myself: a large beach towel, tea, water, a sandwich and some fruit. I drove to Forest Park and sat underneath a big oak tree on top of one of the park's many hills. I took out my sandwich, having been eager to eat it just an hour earlier, but suddenly I couldn't take one bite before I sobbed. By myself. In the middle of the day. In the middle of the country's largest and nicest park.

A woman and her two kids ran up and down the hill several yards away from me. I turned away so they did not see my face, hiding my pain in plain sight.

I was mourning. I thought Chris was going to be my ticket to a comfortable, heteronormative life. It was certainly not a life that I truly wanted to live, but one that would save me from facing myself. And I was pretty good about convincing myself that's what I wanted even though I was hurting myself in the process.

He was going to be my lifelong hiding place: the biggest Wall I could hide behind. He was the marathon of my running away from myself, but he stopped on mile two while I was the only one who badly wanted to make it to the finish line.

I wouldn't give myself permission to do what I really needed to do. I needed to stop on the path I was on and take another one, one without any detours, one with thorns. One without lights for miles in a vehicle that had numerous blind spots. A road without any U-turns. My own highway.

A long ass one-way road. The only way out was through.

I started counting each day without Chris. He didn't die, but I lost him. I lost someone I talked to every day for nearly a year. I'd never cried so hard after a breakup. I stopped counting after the ninth day. I told myself I did not need him, which I only believed to be partially true. This was yet another truth I didn't want to believe because I didn't want to address it. I didn't want to address the fact that I was capable of doing what I needed to do without him.

I was afraid of failing. I was afraid if I broke down the doors and tore down the walls that I'd fall out, and I wouldn't be able to catch myself. And since I wasn't inviting anyone behind those doors or walls, there would be no one there to catch me either.

I wanted to blame someone else. I was mostly mad at Chris—not so much for breaking up with me but for letting me be by myself, for pushing me back to asking these questions I didn't want to answer.

Back to these questions I only asked if I was alone or still.

Who would I end up with now?

Why didn't he want to be with me?

Didn't he say he loved me?

How could someone be so cruel?

What would this mean for my mind?

Could I outrun this pain?

Where will I distract myself?

I must find somewhere to go. Somewhere to be. Somewhere I cannot let heavier feelings make their way back up. I'm not ready to face the answers to those questions.

Anger grew even more when I started thinking about Lauren again. I pulled her profile up on Facebook. She looked as though she was doing just fine. I so badly wanted to reach out to her, but I didn't.

I was back to digging my way to the root of my big feelings. Well, actually no. Not *back to*. I never really went there. Not fully, so I couldn't go back to a place I had never been.

I was alone and still. The thoughts and feelings quickly became too much. Instead of getting to know the path to the root of my feelings, I started drinking even more. The breakup was the tipping point that sent me further into the unknown, a cold black hole of mystery that I procrastinated solving with each and every sip of liquor. I felt like I lived at the bottom of deep well with dampness enough to make me cold but not with enough water for me to drink.

I wondered if Lauren was fully out yet. I wondered if she was living her truth completely, unlike I was. I hoped she was. She deserved that. All queer people deserved to live fully without harm and fear. I wanted to live fully, but I wasn't ready yet. There was too much unknown even thought I wanted to be freer. The only thing that will set you free from the lie is the truth. Lies are lies, and they only die when the truth comes out.

CHAPTER XXX

I worked until 11 p.m. at the nursing home the night before my twenty-second birthday, just a couple weeks after Chris broke up with me. The last hour of my shift, I couldn't decide whether to meet my friends downtown at Ball Park Village aka BPV or not. I knew tomorrow would be a long, but fun day and I did not want to spoil it by staying out late that night. But I called a cab anyway to make last call.

When I arrived downtown, the bouncer checked my ID. It was just after midnight. Officially my birthday. I had no intentions of drinking for the majority of the next eighteen hours, but hey, what else was I going to do? I had triple the number of reasons to drink: 1. I just got dumped. 2. It was my birthday and 3. I was graduating in a few weeks and still hadn't found something to fill the gaping hole soccer left.

I found Timmy and Sammie immediately in the middle of the first floor. Before I could even go to the bar for a beer, an arm wrapped around my shoulders with a drink for me. I turned around and thanked Logan for the drink. He wished me a happy birthday and spun me around to dance. I downed that first beer quickly in order to catch up with everyone else. The only person who was making me drink, thinking I had to catch up with the others, was me and only me.

I ended up having six beers and at least one shot of whiskey in the ninety minutes or so I was there. Timmy, Sammie, Logan and I made it back to the soccer house around 1:30 in the morning. After chugging a few glasses of water and eating a half-baked pizza, we each found a spot to sleep. My spot being in an empty bedroom off the garage with Logan. When I first saw Logan that night, he showed up for me as a friend who had recently gotten dumped. He immediately took my hand and danced with me in the middle of BPV. The dancing led to flirting, which led to him hitching a ride back to the soccer house with Sammie, Timmy and me.

The next morning, I woke up half naked next to Logan on the floor of an empty bedroom at the women's soccer house. Laughter hid my utter disgust with myself. I realized that the condom got stuck in my vagina. After failing to fish it out with my fingers, I quietly went to the kitchen, just outside of the bedroom door, and I fetched a spoon. Scooped it right out. *Never again.*

I was still a bit drunk from the night. I looked like I was having fun. I wasn't. I was just hammered and happened to not ignite the runner part of my drunk self. I was glad for the distraction this drunk gave me. I was glad for the distraction my friends allowed, too.

One of my teammates took me and Logan to my car the next morning. After dropping off Logan, I arrived back home. I avoided a hangover by eating a breakfast sandwich as soon as I got there and by drinking as soon as I got in the car to go to the stadium.

To my disbelief, after binge drinking beer and bourbon all day and the previous night, I was a happy drunk on my actual birthday. I bought Tsuki, my brother and Jacq tickets to the ball game. Jacq is my younger cousin that I often refer to as my sister. We are four years apart, and she is as stunning as she is goofy, smart and caring. She and I have been close since she was born.

My brother reimbursed me for his ticket with bottomless bourbon that came in a plastic barrel cup. My mom and Aunt got their own tickets and sat close by to our section so they didn't hear me as I drunkenly rambled about how Chris never wanted me to suck his dick. I was totally okay with not sucking his dick, but I was curious as to why he didn't want me to. I've never met a straight or gay man (to my knowledge) that was not into receiving oral sex.

"Isn't that weird he didn't want a BJ?" I asked a little too loud that the fans in front of us turned and glanced my way.

My brother replied with a laugh, "Yeah, that's really weird."

As the drunken fact spewed from my mouth, I felt my shoulders loosen. I didn't realize I had been thirsting to tell someone about the sexual aspects of my relationship with Chris. I hadn't cared so much about everyone's reaction, but I remember it felt so good to let go of some thoughts I had been having.

My brother and my relationship at that time didn't make it weird for me to drunkenly chat about sex. We were close enough to laugh it off. It wasn't a deep or serious conversation and hadn't lasted that long. I didn't go into much detail with them other than the oral sex tidbit, but I wish I had. Maybe not more details with my brother, but I would have told Tsuki or Jacq that sex with Chris felt disconnected. That it felt boring and unadventurous. It felt like it was something we did just because we were in a romantic relationship.

It started raining during the game. Absolutely pouring. The rain came down as fast as the liquid left the bottles in my hand. I was hammered…again. Underneath a pavilion, Mom and I surprised Jacq with the news about New York. A trip to New York was my parents' graduation gift for both of us. Jacq was four years younger than me and had just graduated high school.

I don't feel that I deserved the gift of this trip. Plus, I was afraid that I would feel so many things in New York, good things that I'd have to leave there when it was time to go back home. I didn't want the good feelings. Instead of embracing and showing gratitude for the good feelings, the good feelings made me sad a lot of times because the good feelings don't last. They were just a reminder that bad feelings were just around the corner.

Part THREE

MAY 2014 – AUGUST 2015

CHAPTER XXXI

One of the big reasons I said yes to Lindenwood was because it would land me closer to Chris. And that became the exact reason that I no longer wanted to go. One of many. I also had big dreams. I still have big dreams. I envisioned myself going to grad school, but I didn't envision that I'd be hanging around St. Louis for three more years.

Call me bougie, call me a brat, call me entitled, privileged, or spoiled. I knew what I deserved; that was a shot at life in the big city. I'm not saying that my dreams wouldn't happen if I ended up at Lindenwood or stayed in St. Louis, but my heart wasn't in it. That was not a stop on my journey that felt right. I also couldn't help but think of the dream I had when I my grandpa came to me almost three years earlier. *He was singing, and he told me to leave.* I wanted to meet new people not follow in the comfort of connections I had already made despite good intentions. I wanted a bigger stage. I needed strangers to see my worth. I needed a glimpse of being good enough in a field unrelated to my athletic ability. And that started with turning down that scholarship to Lindenwood.

I was glad to near the end of this chapter in my life despite not knowing where I would end up next. I had said yes to Lindenwood because that's what I felt nonverbalized pressure to do. The pressure I mostly had put on myself. I did not know where to go from there, but for the first time in a long time, I trusted myself.

I had faith. I didn't know where I'd land, but I knew something better was waiting for me, even if I couldn't put it into words yet or see it physically in front of me.

Just a couple weeks before graduation, I broke the news to my mom on a Sunday before dinner. She was not happy, especially when I told her that not only did I not have a backup plan, but I didn't have any plan at all. I didn't know. Just like my mom, I wish I knew, too, but turning down that offer and trusting my gut instead felt great. I felt lighter. I felt freer. I hadn't realized it then, but I felt freer because I had faith in myself over the unknown. For the first time, I listened to my gut with every fiber of my being. I let go of the what-ifs. I let go of a plan that I could see clearly. I let go of knowing what was going to happen. I let go of all that, and I started holding on to where my gut was telling me to go.

I knew there was something that would get me to my higher self. Something for me out there even though I had no idea where exactly it was. All I knew for sure is that it wasn't St.

Louis. Not right then anyway.

Even with that, I knew I was opting for more distance between myself and where my problems began. A fresh start would keep me from drinking. A fresh start would cure my depression. A fresh start would make me happy. However, fresh starts, and I only work well together until my problems figure out where I am. The fresh starts were only another way for me to run. Those adjustments to new places and people gave my mind somewhere to focus and let me easily suppress the feelings that needed to be addressed: i.e., sadness, misery, self-doubt, insecurity, etc.

However, we all know you can't put miles between yourself and your problems. You carry them with you wherever you go until you finally pull into a rest stop and address them head-on before continuing on your way. One thing I was proud of myself for that I had worked toward was confronting people with my decisions when I had put my best interest in front of theirs.

The Professor and I met for coffee at St. Louis Bread Co., aka Panera Bread. It was a hot, sunny St. Louis afternoon. It was still May, but summer had already arrived. Springtime in St. Louis usually only lasts a few weeks if we're lucky. We sat at a four-top on the patio across from each other. I kept my sunglasses on, as did he.

His expression turned from hopeful to disappointed as I told him the news of not going to Lindenwood. I could see his eyes narrow and look down behind his lenses. I thanked him for the opportunity and told him this was best for me.

Sure, I may have been running away by not staying in St. Louis, but I also felt deep in my bones that I was running toward something. I started to realize something during this conversation. Something that would give me profound growth and breakthroughs. I didn't want that growth and those breakthroughs to come in the comfort and safety of my hometown. I wanted to explore a city that I had bonded with for years. I deserved to do that.

Shortly after I explained to him that I had no idea what I'd do in the long run, I got up and walked back to my car. My shoulders back further, and my head held high. I drove home with the windows down, radio blasting and felt a sense of relief. I didn't feel stuck in that moment. I felt hopeful and excited about the possibilities of leaving St. Louis.

CHAPTER XXXII

I could have worked a hell of a lot harder in college. My all-girls catholic high school education had a strict GPA policy for athletes; besides that, I always felt worthy and rewarded for getting good grades in exchange for hard work. It was not until I got to college that I realized that high school truly did prepare me for college. Academically, college was a snooze fest. I should've tried new things. I should've studied harder and taken more challenging classes. Maybe I should've played another sport or gotten more involved with other things on or off campus. Instead, I did the bare minimum in the classroom and overworked on the field. When I wasn't doing those things, I wasn't doing much else other than drinking and daydreaming.

I dreamt of packing my bags and moving to Chicago or magically being discovered by a television producer and being plopped right on the set of my own show. I'd spend hours watching old episodes of SNL instead of writing sketches and putting on shows of my own. I just assumed because I was funny and a good writer that things would fall into place for me. And maybe they would someday, but not without years and years of hard work. Unlike high school and college, adult success is a long game, especially for someone who wants a career in writing and the entertainment industry.

I considered dropping out of college dozens of times, but I was too depressed (and scared) to make any big decisions. I may have been running at times from myself, but I didn't have the energy yet to actually run away from St. Louis to the big city.

I tried to want the full college experience: a perfect balance between fun and academia. I am glad that I stayed in school and was able to play soccer, but college let me down in ways that I never could have predicted. I craved to be in thought provoking classes. What I learned as an undergrad should've been so much more. However, I was afraid. Afraid that if I did more challenging schoolwork that my depression would keep me from excelling—a constant pull between my poor mental health and longing for an educational challenge. I took college for granted at times and didn't realize how much of a privileged position I was in.

The morning of graduation, my mother was ecstatic. She was proud of me, but I was not proud of myself. I simply showed up and only did the work as a distraction from the emptiness that consumed most of my college days. She pulled out her camera, and after one attempt to protest a picture, I faked a smile for her collection of important moments in my life.

I looked beautiful. I was radiant that day. I wore a comfortable and fitted navy-blue sleeveless dress with a lace trim and my favorite nude heeled sandals that would later break on a New York City grate like I was in the cast of Sex and the City. My longish blonde hair sat in perfect golden waves. My nails were polished with a soft pink, and I put on a smile so fake that it looked real.

Saint Louis does not have a springtime. Well, maybe for a day or two, then it's straight into summer. On my graduation day, May 10, 2014, summer in Saint Louis had already arrived. I remember that day and night as clear as the water I drank after drinking for twelve hours straight. I was too hungover to not let myself go without water.

I left a little earlier than my family, mostly so I had time to stop to pick up a pint of whiskey. I wanted a pint, but a pint wouldn't fit in my wristlet wallet. I settled for a handful of airplane-sized bottles instead. I blasted my favorite Lady Gaga playlist and drove to Forest Park for commencement. I imagined I was on stage singing her song. I'd like to be there, but I wasn't.

I was here about to binge drink yet again.

By the time I got to the Muny, a local outdoor theatre in Forest Park where graduation was held, all the shaded parking spots were taken, so my car had no choice but to bake in the sun. As soon as I shut the car off, I opened one of the bottles of Jack and downed it in one long ass gulp. I placed two more in my wristlet and slid another in my Nike sliders underneath my dress, which I had spent the last three years with me on the field. I kept the last bottle in the car for later. No matter how warm it would be in a few hours, I knew I'd drink it anyway.

I was too depressed to speak up. I was too depressed to let anyone know. I did not want to disappoint them. I even said to my parents at brunch afterwards: "I didn't really learn much." Those were harsh words, but it was my fault. I didn't learn a lot academically, but I did learn a lot about how much life can kick you around. I learned a hell of a lot more about how your mind can kick you even harder.

I should've been graduating from Ole Miss with a theater degree and a plethora of memories and friendships from a stellar soccer career in the SEC. I didn't get any of those things. Instead, I got a communications degree, finished my soccer career at a division three school, a drinking problem and one dead grandparent. *Now what?*

But the thing is, among all that disappointment, I also walked away stronger. I walked away with a deeper understanding of how my mind works when I go through a depressive episode. I walked away from college with a few great friends and a lot of good memories. It's easy to focus on the bad when you're majorly depressed. Depression feeds into pessimism and eats it up like a pint of my favorite chocolate peanut butter ice cream from Oberweis.

As I entered The Muny, I struggled to find my righthand woman, Tsuki. I was lost in a sea of people, many of whom I didn't know at all—maybe myself included. Well, yes, I did know myself, but I didn't want to talk to the real her.

Before I found Tsuki, I saw a woman I went to high school with. Uncomfortable standing by myself, I approached her. We used to be friends and even went to a two-week-long theatre camp together at The Second City after we graduated high school. I didn't know she was graduating that spring, so I said just that and congratulated her. She replied with a rude remark that, apparently, I couldn't count how many years it took to finish an undergraduate degree. I smiled and walked away, grabbing one of Jack's bottles and immediately emptying it in my stomach.

Maybe she was hurting, too. Maybe I hurt her without realizing it. We didn't exactly have the best time together in Chicago that summer four years earlier. I eventually forgave her for being rude to me, but it's been hard to forget the sting of the tone in her words. I briefly wondered if I had hurt her or said something to her when I was drunk, but I couldn't remember any instance. Might have, or maybe she was just a bitch.

I wish I could give my twenty-two-year-old self a big ass hug and a gallon of water and tell her that she doesn't need to wash down the pain with booze. I want to tell her that she can get through the unknown. I want to tell her that she will be safe, and while it's still going to hurt at times and a lot, it's going to hurt a hell of a lot less without the alcohol. Let it go, I'd say. Let it all go.

Surrender. Fall down. Let others catch you. You've been catching yourself for way too long.

Aren't you tired? It's okay to feel what you're feeling. Let someone help you.

Let you help you.

I found Tsuki just in time to not be completely alone as I graduated college. When we sat down, I shared some of my second bottle with her. I finished the rest and tossed it on the ground for someone else to clean up.

I smiled for my mom as she took more pictures of her only daughter, marking what most call a major milestone. My closest neighbors surprised me at the ceremony. I was not expecting it, but I was glad to see them. *Maybe today won't be a total suck fest.* It was truly so nice of them to come.

They came to celebrate and cheer me on, and I wish I had been more present enough to celebrate maturely. At the very least, I wish I had been more reflective. I wish I had taken the time to see that after the rough mental and physical few years I had, I still graduated on time. I still had done the work I needed to get to the next chapters, and I was successful in a lot of ways. I managed good grades even though I should've done better in school, and I made an unbelievable impact in their soccer program. I am so much more grateful now for that graduation day than I was in 2014, and I am proud of myself for who I was then, even though she was hiding.

I wanted to leave immediately after the ceremony and start running to the next chapter, but I was stopped by friends and various faculty members afterward.

Two of them came up to me, and after congratulating me on my degree, one of them announced that I was named 'Senior Speaker' by the entire department, an honor I'd only just found out at that moment. Essentially, the award goes to a graduating senior who stood out during their time in Webster's Communications department. She apologized for not letting me know sooner. Time escaped her, like it does to all of us. I thanked them and thought, *that's definitely something I can at least put on my resume!*

Since I was already tipsy, my brother drove my car to brunch. During this post-grad brunch with my parents, brother, and grandma, I took a brief break from the whiskey only to consume bottomless mimosas. I had already ordered a cheeseburger and forced myself to eat every bite, fully aware that it would look bad to keep drinking on an empty stomach.

After a two-hour power nap, I freshened up and headed back out for an evening and night of more drinking. My parents and I parted ways after a few hours of drinks at a local pub with the rest of my graduating teammates. A baseball player was having a party that night, so my brother and I headed there with a group of now former classmates. On the way there, we picked up another handle of whiskey.

In hour eleven or twelve of my whiskey marathon, there I was, stumbling up a staircase to prove that I was straight, one last mark on my college experience to leave with people who probably didn't give a shit about my sexuality nor remember me even being at that party. That guy just wanted to get laid. I cared so much about appearing straight because I was afraid of what would happen if I pulled back the curtain. The kissing I didn't mind, but it quickly led to twenty-second sex with a guy I didn't even know. I don't remember saying yes. The only reason it lasted twenty seconds was because I was physically stronger than him and was able to push his scrawny ass off me, sending him flying into the dresser behind him. He immediately apologized and ran out of the room. *Time to go home.*

I should've gone with my brother when he tried to get me to leave with him. But he should've been a better brother and carried my ass out of there. I called an old friend to pick me up. He came immediately and got me home safely after I tried running from him, too. The next day, I texted and thanked him for the ride and the late-night breakfast and coffee to help sober me up before I got home. I then did something out of my typical hangover routine. I asked him to dump out the rest of my whiskey that I left in his car. I trust that he did just that.

I spent the next day avoiding my mother and punishing myself for the inability to blackout. I inflicted upon myself my usual hangover punishment: barely any food and water with a side of negative self-talk. When I think about the way I talked to myself during that time now, it makes me want to cry—I can't believe how cruel I was to myself, how little compassion I held for myself, how I talked to myself in ways I'd never dare speak to or about a friend or loved one.

CHAPTER XXXIII

By the time I flew to L.A. for a week, the sore throat had worsened, and I could feel myself getting worse after partying for the last month. The sore throat I had been ignoring couldn't be ignored for much longer. Yeah, I also ran from physical sickness instead of addressing it before things got worse. I didn't want to miss out or get left behind. I didn't want to be seen as weak.

I opened one of the many Emergen-C packets I brought and mixed it into my water on the plane, knowing full well that the only cure for my ache was rest with a significant dose of down time and self-love. I pulled my headband over my eyes and fell asleep until we landed in Colorado for our connecting flight.

I had been to Laguna Niguel, Laguna Beach, and Malibu, but this was my first official time in L.A. The first night there, Blair made us chicken enchiladas for dinner and then gave us a tour of her apartment building and neighborhood. I totally was into the L.A. vibe. I wanted to stay there. I caught a feel of Hollywood, and I didn't want to leave. Everything looked like it was kissed by the sun. I was enamored by the blue, sunny skies woven in between mounds of hills and palm trees. I loved being so close to where my favorite films and TV shows were made. I loved that the ocean was drastically closer than it was from landlocked Missouri. Also, being that far away from home felt like freedom; I couldn't touch my problems, and they couldn't touch me. I wanted my energy to match that L.A. vibe that L.A. gave. Southern California made me want to feel warm nearly every day, and being there convinced me problems could disappear, even if it was just for a little while.

Once the sun went down that first night, we took an Uber to a bar downtown. The crowd was thin for downtown L.A. at 9:00 p.m. on a Tuesday. We were over dressed for a weekday, but can one be over dressed in L.A.? I don't think so.

The band played cover after cover, and we danced just the three of us. We joked around, claiming that it was *our* bar, *our* territory, because there were so few people there. So, when another group of club-esque dressed young women walked in, we scoffed at them…jokingly, of course. Ten minutes later, we were all doing a round of shots on the house. The band let us sing a few lines, allowing me to briefly live out my dream of being a pop star just blocks away from Capitol Records. We were turning up on a Tuesday when all I'd ever truly wanted was to turn down the bed and crawl in it with popcorn and a movie.

A few hours later, we floundered out the door together to squeeze into the back of another Uber. We were comfortable enough to sit in the backseat of a stranger's car but not comfortable enough to sit shotgun.

Heels were kicked off as soon as we got back in Blair's apartment. I took mine off in the car and carried them inside, walking barefoot through the lobby and garden area to get to Blair's unit. Famished, we immediately polished off the rest of the enchiladas. I couldn't get to bed fast enough. I even contemplated not changing the clothes I was wearing. I needed sleep. I half-washed my face, grabbed some water, brushed my teeth, and prayed that my body wouldn't spin once I got into bed. *Please let me sleep well. Please let me sleep a little. Please, dear god, let my mind be okay in the morning. Please let my throat not feel worse than it did today.*

I shed a few tears quietly that one of prayers was answered once I laid down. I was spared the spins during this drunken slumber. I fell asleep easily and woke up with only a slight headache, which was soon taken care of with an egg sandwich, Tylenol, and thirty-two ounces of ice cold water. Oh, and coffee, of course.

I remember having a good time that night, but I also knew there'd be hell to pay the next morning. I also knew that I spent every second inside that bar running from my feelings. Wishing I was someone else. Wishing I could stay there in California and not go back home, thinking *if I run away from St. Louis, then I run away from my problems, too.* And I thought back then that if I were to run away from my problems, then that equated to resolving them—not having to deal with them at all.

I powered through the next full day at Universal Studios. We also took a tour of the studio lots, and that's when I fell in love. It was love at first sight when I laid eyes on the TV and film sets: *Desperate Housewives'* Wisteria Lane, a crash scene from *War of the Worlds* and from *Pyscho:* the Bates Motel, and *Jaws*.

It was absolute magic. Finally, a tangible representation that maybe I could someday become a professional screenwriter.

I dreamt of being on set, of my words being spoken on screen, maybe even by me! Oh, the possibilities. I felt so much hope and fire after seeing those sets. I also felt lost and afraid and so far away from it all. I was so impatient. I still am with a lot of things.

I didn't understand or know that while I could get there someday, I had a lot more to learn before I got there…before I got even close to being there.

By the time we got back to Blair's, I was exhausted. I took a shower first, and when they were getting ready to go out, I pretended to be asleep. What I was really doing was racking up all my courage to speak my truth at that moment: *I'm not going to go out tonight. I'm exhausted and not feeling well.* Gosh, I probably said those lines a hundred times in my head, followed by words of encouragement: *It's not that hard. Just say it. You can do this. They'll get over it.*

Blair asked what I was going to wear. "Nothing," I replied. "I'm not going. I'm exhausted and not feeling well." *See, Al! You can do this. Easy, peasy.*

They both looked at me, disappointed, but my body could not hang. I wasn't afraid of being by myself because I knew I'd fall asleep immediately. If I had gone out that night, I probably would've passed out somewhere in public. I didn't want that to happen. I knew what my body needed, and I knew what would happen if I didn't give that to her. At least this was something; a few years prior, I likely wouldn't have been able to say those words. They went out, and I took a shot of vodka and fell asleep within ten minutes of them leaving, again not remembering the feeling of speaking the truth. Not being aware of its power. Still so eager to move on to the next thing. Still running as fast as I mentally could.

About four hours later, my phone started to ring. I ignored the first few calls because I could not tell if I was dreaming or if they were real. I finally answered. It was Blair. She lost her wallet and needed me to come down to let her and Sammi inside. I threw on some shoes, rubbed my eyes, and went to get them.

They were sloshed.

"You have to come help me!" she cried.

Blair grabbed my arm and pulled me down the front stairs of her building. We don't get far before I suggest looking for her wallet in the morning when we have more light.

"How was your night other than that?"

"Sooooo GOOD! So. Fun. You should have come!"

"I'm glad I didn't. I would be dead tomorrow even more."

Not going out that night didn't keep me from getting sick, but it did allow me to enjoy the rest of my time there with my friends.

We spent the last two days in L.A. at the beach and pool, and I had nothing but the future on my mind. Somewhere after graduation, while I was still running from my emotions, I felt like I also started running toward my life purpose, too. My biggest flaw in that plan was not realizing that I needed to run through and work through my emotions while on the path to fulfilling my life's purpose. I didn't realize that running from my truth and emotions could possibly be keeping me from that purpose…and maybe something even bigger. I also didn't realize how huge mind body connection is and that ignoring emotions could cause chronic, physical pain.

I wish I could've let my friends in more, too. I was afraid. That fear could also be one of the reasons I'm no longer in touch with Sammi or Blair and most of the people I went to college with. It makes me sad sometimes thinking about it, but we laughed just as much as we partied. We spent quality time together just as much as we worked out together. Life was easier, and a lot of light during those times came from laughing and bonding over a sport that we all loved.

I wish I was brave enough back then to speak up. I like to think that my teammates would've been supportive if I opened up a bit more, but I wasn't ready. Not fully. So, Blair, Sammi, Timmy, Alyssa and Faith, if you were ever wondering why we grew apart, it's because I'm gay and drink water.

If growing apart is one of the many sacrifices I had to make to get where I get to, I'd do it again, but we're older now and all in different areas of our lives. I'm happy for all of you.

CHAPTER XXXIV

Coffee. Coffee. And more coffee. The one essential to get me through working thirty hours that weekend before jetting off to New York City. Because sleep was not on the table. I had been back from L.A. for less than two weeks. To make up for lost wages, I overworked myself when I got back and because I was leaving for New York, which meant more wages would be lost soon enough.

Friday, I closed the gym. Saturday morning, I taught a spin class and worked a few hours at the gym again. I ran home to shower and eat and pack more food for later. I returned to my car and drove to the assisted living facility by 3 p.m. I was there until 11 p.m. I got home as soon as possible to sleep less than eight hours before returning to the assisted living facility by 7 a.m. where I'd stay again until 11, working a double.

I threw myself into work. I threw myself into distractions to not face the detrimental pain of the change from not playing soccer and going to school full time. I was avoiding facing the change.

The assisted living facility was top of the line in housing for old people. A grand staircase hugged the right side of the foyer, and a large living room sat to the left, just behind the concierge desk, my desk. Past the foyer was the dining room. Near the kitchen entrance a table stood with three large thermoses of coffee on top. I loved that coffee.

I drank it black back then and sometimes still do. The after taste reminds me of cigarettes, ever so slightly. Cigarettes remind me of Maren and the better times I had in Mississippi. Pink Camels. We only smoked when we drank. We thought we were cool. We were cool, but smoking is very unhealthy, as you know...I hope. I was glad I did not get addicted to cigarettes. One unhealthy habit is more than I think I could handle. Plus, alcohol was so easy to use as camouflage.

I made sure to always use one of their small white cups as opposed to the thermos I brought with me. It forced me to get up and walk around more, leaving the chances of me falling asleep at the desk minimal. I filled up my third cup and walked back to the desk. I pulled up my laptop and turned on *Orange is the New Black*.

Before the theme song ended, I jumped as someone said, "Hello." I turned to my left and saw Nita had shuffled ever so quietly from her room. Nita was all of four-foot-eight. Her pink night gown just might have come from the Big Girl section of an American Girl magazine.

"Oh! Hi, there, Nita."

"I'm sorry, sweetie. I didn't mean to scare you," she said with a chuckle.

"That's okay! I need to stay awake, so thank you."

I paused, noticing she didn't have her walker. "Where's your walker, Nita?"

She turned around and then back at me.

"I…I don't know." Her hand covered her mouth in disbelief.

"Well, I'll help you find it."

"Will you, dear? That is so kind of you."

"No problem!"

I closed my laptop, got up, and walked over to her. I was Gru and she a minion when we stood together. I extended my arm, and she looped hers in mine without hesitation. I sighed with relief that she walked all the way from her room without falling.

She continued to shuffle her feet, and I took the babiest of baby steps in rhythm with her.

Nita stopped at a bench just two doors down from her room.

"Are you okay, Nita?"

"Oh yes." She paused and grabbed my hand, then looked up at me, her green eyes meeting my blue ones.

"It's time. I can see the light dear. I am ready," she said.

I smiled and gave her a hug with my free arm.

"Thank you, dear."

We shuffled the rest of the way to her room. I opened the door. The walker was left right next to her bed.

Nita died two days later. She was 102 years old. I am so grateful for my many interactions with her. I didn't know much about her life other than where she was living when she died.

But Nita was happy to be wherever she was. She was kind and didn't take life too seriously. Maybe she told me about her past without even saying a word about it. This last interaction with her gave me a little faith. That maybe I could find peace, too...somewhere, someway, somehow. I only hoped it wouldn't take until I was 102.

By the time I got back to my desk, the coffee had become cold. This time, I grabbed my thermos and filled it to the brim. For the next twenty minutes, the lobby was silent, at least. I watched my show with one earphone in and the other hanging, gently swinging and resting, resting and swinging on and beside my shoulder.

Someone rang the front door. I looked up and noticed another resident's daughter and her husband. I buzzed them in, and they signed the visitor log on their own, familiar with the process. They had food with them and let me know they were just dropping it off. I barely heard what they said next because the phone rang at the same time as someone else ringing the front door. My anxiety went from zero to fifty as I reached for the phone and door button at the same time. BUT not without knocking my thermos of hot coffee all over my laptop.

Ah, shit. Well, at least I just graduated successfully. I don't NEED this laptop.

I played it cool as I spoke with the person on the phone and silently greeted the new visitors with a wave and motion for them to sign the visitor log. I answered the person's question and was once again by myself after a whirlwind. I looked at the pool of caffeine swaying in and on my laptop. I fetched a handful of napkins off a table in the dining room. I dabbed, wiped, blew, shook, prayed, and chanted that my Mac would be saved, knowing that it was a lost cause. It was soaked. R.I.P. We had a good run. Thank you for your service.

After most of the liquid dried, I closed my laptop and slowly put it in its case. Defeated. I sighed and made a mandatory rule to never keep liquids on the same table as my computer ever again, a rule that

I break nearly every day. Such an adrenaline junkie…or am I just continuing to not listen to the rational part of myself?

The next morning, after my laptop was laid to rest by the caffeine gods, I left for New York City with my mom and Jacq. Until then, I had only visited New York City in movies, books, and my dreams. It was just like how I'd seen it and dreamt about it, except it is way better in person. I can still hear the cab drivers; I can feel my heart beating as they swerve in and out of traffic; I smell the street food and taste it on my tongue, but not without the stench of urine and trash.

I loved how I felt in that city. I felt that I could do anything there if I worked hard enough. I wanted to be there, to stay there, but I knew I couldn't stay that time. I asked myself, *How do I get here?* And I meant it literally, as in, how do I move to New York, but I also meant something more ambiguous here, as in, how do I get my mind to where I went? How do I feel good and free all the time, as I did when visiting New York?

I cried on the plane ride back to St. Louis, hiding my face so no one would see. My heart broke a little more because I had no idea how to get to where I wanted to be. I longed to live in the city. I longed to write words with other writers. I longed for the grind it takes to get there. I longed for the city to harden me, make me tougher, prepare me for what's next. I longed to fulfill my purpose and find peace. It never dawned on me that finding peace was not a destination.

As I dried my cheeks, I made a promise to myself: *a year from now, I will be living in L.A., New York, or Chicago. No matter what.*

By the time we landed back in St. Louis, I had a plan again. The day after I returned to St. Louis, I pulled together my finances. I had about $1200 to my name. But my responsibilities were far from troublesome. I did not have to pay rent, nor did I have a car payment. I was financially well off in those terms, but I resisted earning more money because I was so paranoid that I'd get stuck somewhere I didn't want to be, so I avoided a corporate full time office job at all costs. I thought through and through about what could get me to the city without a job lined up. The answer? The hiding spot?

School.

CHAPTER XXXV

As the days got longer during the summer of 2015, so did my sleeping increments. Just a couple of weeks after our New York trip, my energy depleted after just a few hours of being awake. Hungry for answers, I tried nearly every kind of cleanse you can think of: candida diet, lemon juice cleanse, gluten-free, dairy-free. I was tired, and I was hungry.

I spent all my time between work and naps researching different grad programs, and my worry growing as my energy stunted. *How can I move to a new city and start grad school when I spend most of my time sleeping?*

I originally thought that this extended slumber party was left over from depression, but this tired felt different. It was thicker. While I can sleep a lot during a depressive episode, I never went back to bed after a few hours only to sleep another six. I could be awake longer when I was depressed. Perhaps, depression was a part of this tired, though.

This tired felt heavy in the head and the fatigue caked on to every single inch of my body. It felt like a full days' work was executed by hour three of my day.

Despite that, I kept going. I kept looking for answers while figuring out where I was going to go to grad school. I'd love to go for theatre, but most, if not all programs require a Bachelors in Theatre upon application. I looked at various mass communication degrees and considered getting a PhD.

One afternoon, in a moment of clarity, I remembered my visit to L.A. just a month before. I had been writing stories, songs, poetry, and jokes ever since I could write. Writing brings me great joy and satisfaction, and I knew I'd be published in some way, but it never fully dawned on me that I could get paid to do the thing that I loved most until visiting those TV sets in LA. I love performing, I love singing, but all my work comes back to writing. That has been the only constant in my life outside of soccer. Writing is my escape. Writing is my love. Writing is my purpose.

Curious, I searched screenwriting programs, and to my delight, there were many. I immediately made a list: USC, UCLA, DePaul University, Northwestern, and NYU. I crossed off Northwestern first. I didn't think my undergrad transcripts would do well there. I guess I'll never know for sure since I didn't apply.

Not as much now, but in the past especially, I tended to make plans for myself and big decisions without always fully thinking about how it'd impact me financially, mentally, and emotionally. When it comes down to decision-making time, if I don't have all the answers, I rely on faith. I rely on my feelings. My faith lets me face the unknown and know that it'll all work out. Maybe not in the way I envisioned, but it still works out. My faith keeps me going. My faith in my gut, in my future, in myself. My faith in the universe, faith in God, and faith in my spirit guides.

California, Chicago, and New York, of course, have the most options and best programs, but all three of those cities are crazy expensive, and I had no clue how I'd afford not only to live there but also to move there. Even though I was saving as much as possible, I was also still having fun when I felt up for it. I also spent copious amounts on the cleanest of clean foods my budget could buy.

I didn't know anyone in California at the time. Some people I knew from high school lived in New York, but we hadn't talked in a while. My brother had moved to Chicago the year before. Chicago is closest to home. I love Chicago. I also knew on a deeper level that I did not want to be rejected from schools. Getting in was not a sure thing for me, but I had the utmost faith in DePaul and knew it would be a good fit for me.

I tried writing on the computers at the local library, but I felt like I was on display. I was used to writing in the comfort of my own four walls. I could use one of mom or dad's computers, but they're both for work, and again, I would probably feel as though I was on display. I needed my own device. From my iPad, I ordered a $300 HP touch screen laptop. I kept that sucker for eight weeks and then resold it for a lesser price.

I put everything I had into applying to one school and one school only: DePaul University. The application process strengthened my sense of purpose, gave me hope, and gave me something to look forward to.

I recently looked at those pieces I used for submission…oh…my… stars were they atrocious! Total shit.

Prior to the December deadline, I submitted my online application. The notification of acceptance or rejection would be coming March 2015. And thus, began the longest waiting period of my life.

I spent the first week of December in Laguna Niguel, visiting Maren. I was drawn to the holiday decorations when the weather was still quite warm compared to St. Louis. I will always adore a Christmas tree on a beach. The second guessing settled in when I saw the west coast palm trees.

I immediately questioned why I didn't apply to more schools. I should have applied to one in California, one in Chicago, and one in New York. And then a backup school in Florida or somewhere. *Crap. It's so warm here; why didn't I apply to a program anywhere in this state? After all, Los Angeles is home to entertainment.* I was incredibly more anxious in the months between hitting submit and the phone call that changed my life.

From mid-February to the date of admission or rejection, I checked the mail every single day that I was home. At first, my mom thought I was being helpful, knocking one thing off her to do list, but she quickly caught on.

When I was not at home, the first thing I asked my mom when I got there was: "did anything come in the mail for me?" Some days she'd say yes and laugh when she handed me a postcard from my dentist for an appointment reminder or a letter from my youngest cousin, Sophia.

My letter did not arrive early, nor did it arrive on time. On the day we were to find out, the mail contained nothing but bills and junk. Grandma was visiting that week, and she and I fed off each other's nervous energy about my application status and whatever health concern she had at that time.

I entered the house, tossed the mail on the kitchen counter, and huffed into the other room. As Mom cooked Grandpa's famous firehouse spaghetti, she asked: "I'm guessing it wasn't in there?"

"Nope! I'm calling now."

My heart pounded as I dialed DePaul admissions. A woman answered. I was caught off guard by her politeness due to the stark contrast of my angst. My leg shook as I sat on the couch. I asked her about my application status and said I was under the impression I would be finding out today. She put me on hold for what seems like ten minutes, but in reality, it was probably one or two. The woman returned to the phone and cleared her throat.

I didn't get in.

KIDDING. I did! I thanked her. She told me the letter should be arriving within the next day or two.

Great! Now, I can move forward. Finally, I am going to leave here. I am finally going to be in Chicago, where I belong. My plan was working, and once again, I thought this news would solve my problems.

CHAPTER XXXVI

A perfect summer night was before me. I made a decision I had no right to make, and I closed the gym early so I could go eat a sandwich with a coworker. In my juvenile defense, I only closed ten minutes early, but that coworker was trouble.

Crickets chirped throughout the gym starting at 9 p.m. Literal crickets. The gym had a bug and rat problem. No, not gym rats. Actual rats. At the beginning of our relationship, I ignored that coworker because I knew he was trouble. I could smell his arrest warrant from a mile away. You haven't seen crazy eyes until you've looked into his. Most nights, he and I were the only two workers left after the manager went home around 8 or 9, depending on the flow of foot traffic.

Just like my feelings and my sexuality, I ignored the red flags that came along with this one guy. I ignored them because he had weed. It wasn't hard to get him to invite me to smoke with him.

I had two rules about smoking weed in my late teens and early twenties, nearly a decade before it was legal in most states: *never seek it out unless it is presented to you, and never pay for it.* I honestly did not see anything in Nathan until he offered me weed.

Weed was a safer option than alcohol—always has been—but still much of society sees it as a bad thing. Tell me what's worse for the mind and body: .25mg of an edible or a six pack of beer over the course of a night out?

Although weed was probably a more reliable, safer option of the two, smoking weed with this one guy definitely came with danger.

Danger's name was Nathan.

At that time, there was no medical reason for me to use marijuana, and I certainly did not get high a lot because alcohol was my go-to drug of choice.

I should have known better about him. A few weeks prior, we'd ended up in a bar while on a coffee run for our coworkers. I offered to drive, mostly because his car looked just as unsafe as he was. We drove to the Starbucks up the street and ordered all the coffee for ourselves and the trainers back at the gym.

We headed back toward the gym, but he told me to pull into the next parking lot. I did. He looked at me and asked: "Wanna take a shot?"

"Fuck yeah I wanna take a shot!" I replied, nodding enthusiastically as we ran into a Mexican restaurant. The bartender greeted him by name, and he ordered us two tequila shots. One each. We threw them back and rushed back to work.

At the time, I felt invincible. I felt fun. I felt daring. I felt like I was doing something right. Looking back, though? It was pretty fucking dumb. I was not cool taking shots during working hours. Although some may argue that they drink alcohol at work weekly, that's not an image I was wanting to paint. I kept it my secret. No one knew about those shots.

Just me and Nathan.

So that night, closing with Nathan, right before I locked up for the night, I grabbed a peanut butter and chocolate Muscle Sandwich for my breakfast the next day and lied to myself, saying that I would pay for it then. I stole so many protein bars from that place.

Nathan tossed out the last of the trash, and we hopped in my car. Nathan may have had crazy eyes, but he was a pretty boy. He had a face made up of sharp cheekbones and a rigid jawline. Unless you count his floppy balls, there wasn't a physical flaw on his body except for a few scars from his time in the Marines. I could have done without knowing about his floppy balls, but get a few drinks in me, and you know I ended up sleeping with him eventually.

Nathan and I got sandwiches from Snarf's Sandwich shop on St. Louis University's campus. I finished my sandwich, and Nathan wrapped the second half of his to save for later. We walked to my car, and before starting it, Nathan and I made out a little bit. We were excited to get high when we got back to his place. It was a hot summer night, so I rolled the windows down to soak up the summer heat as I exited the parking lot.

Lights from the small city glistened and soon most of the lights were behind us. A normal scene quickly turned out to not be normal at all. A bus in the distance continued on its route.

A distraught woman on the side of the road screamed for help. A case of beer and a bag of groceries sat next to the bus stop. Just ahead of the woman, a man twitched on the ground. Now, just a hundred yards away, I could see that this man's leg twisted unnaturally at his knee. As we drove closer, we saw blood surrounding the man. The leg was worse than what I saw several yards back. It was twisted behind him in a way no man or animal should ever experience. I drove past the man and put the car in park. I put my flashers on and called 911. Of course, no one else seemed to be driving at this hour. It was just me, Nathan, a distraught woman, and a dying man—all together on a dark city street at 11 at night. Nathan raced out of the car and gave the man CPR. I hung up with the dispatcher, looked up in the distance, and saw the bus lights get dimmer and smaller. It must have been a mile up the road by now.

I turned and looked behind me down Grand Ave, the sign to Cardinal Glennon Children's Hospital illuminating brightly. I thought about running in there for help. The woman on the sidewalk was still in full on hysterics. I decided to stay with the woman. I kept a couple yards distance from her but approached to console her with my words instead of a hand on ger shoulder. I asked her what happened.

Through her blubbering voice, she told me she exited the front of the bus while the man exited the back of the bus. He set his beer and groceries down before evacuating, but he tripped as he stepped out of the bus. The bus dragged him thirty yards beyond the bus stop before it spits him back out on the street. She assumed the driver hadn't noticed, thinking he'd hit a pothole or ran over some sort of debris. I suppose it would be hard to make out what you'd run over while driving a bus. It could be anything, but if it were me, I'd convince myself it was just trash or something.

But I also would have stopped to check out what was behind me.

Just a few feet away from us, I watched Nathan vigorously continue to press on the man's chest, glad that it was him and not me performing CPR on this stranger. I had been CPR certified since

I was fifteen, but this was way above anything they taught in those classes. You can't really prepare for real-life, real-time scenarios at your neighborhood CPR training.

Blood covered the ground. Blood covered the man. Within minutes, paramedics and police arrived. Nathan, now covered in blood, talked to the cops, and rambled on about his service in the Marines.

No one was a hero that night. The police escorted the woman into the back of the cop car and got her statement as she tried to calm down. They offered her a ride home, and only once she was out of sight did the paramedics cover the man and zip up the body bag.

The officers, paramedics, and firemen thanked us. We thanked them, and I think I even said: "Oh, it's no problem. Have a good night." Nathan told the officers he knew how to properly clean blood off his person. So, still covered in blood, Nathan got back into the passenger side of my car, and I, in the driver side.

He did not say a word the rest of the six-minute drive back to his apartment. I had no idea what to say, so I was also silent. I wanted to go home to my own bed, to my dog, to my safe place, to the dinner plate I knew my dad left for me in the refrigerator. I considered it some sort of BBQ or only famous to our family: my dad's wing-it pasta dishes. How was I thinking about food even though I had just eaten?

But I knew not to leave Nathan alone right then. Honestly, we had just planned to grab a bite to eat after work. We didn't plan on smoking. I didn't bring a change of clothes, and usually, I had no problem crashing in my work uniform, which is basically pajamas anyway: yoga pants and a tank top. But I'd like to change my clothes. I'd like to take a shower and have some ice cream for dessert. But I stayed with Nathan instead.

I turned on Nathan's street and parked in front of his building. It was far too quiet for my liking, and it didn't get much louder once we get into his apartment. His place was dusty and would have appeared unkempt if he had owned many possessions. He had the essentials and the essentials only…plus a cat.

What am I to do? I poured us both a glass of water. I sipped on mine while I watched Nathan chug his in two big gulps, toss his cup in the sink and lean over it. He grunted and exhaled, and I was careful not to look him in the eye. I did not want to touch him, just like I did not want to touch the woman on the side of the road just fifty minutes earlier.

I realized in that moment that I hardly knew this person, and I honestly did not think I ever had the intention of getting to know him. I just wanted to smoke a little weed a night or two a week to pass the time before I moved to Chicago. How stupid of me to let my focus and purpose veer elsewhere, especially in a negative light.

Nathan gripped the edge of the sink so hard I thought he would crush it like The Hulk. He pushed himself off it and grabbed a pipe on the table that I had just noticed for the first time when he picked it up. He then grabbed a bag of weed on top of his fridge and hastily shoved it into the pipe. He then looked for the lighter. I'd help, but I was scared. I didn't want to open a drawer to find a gun.

He told me he had a gun but didn't say where he kept it. *Why the fuck am I here? How…why did I let myself get here?* I had only been in his apartment one time before that, and I had no intention of returning because I did not feel safe there. I did not want to be there. More than that: I did not want to say anything else that would push him over whatever edge he was inching toward.

Nathan opened all the cabinets and drawers in this tiny kitchen. He ended up ripping a drawer out completely, and that only made him more upset as forks and utensils sprayed across the kitchen floor, covering the small space entirely. In one of the opened drawers, I saw a lime green lighter, and I carefully picked it up and handed it to him. He walked out the far end of the kitchen onto the tiny deck. The only light out there came from another apartment until he flicked the lighter on and lit the pipe.

I looked at the clock. It was almost midnight now.

After swallowing another glass of water, I joined him on the deck. It was so tiny that the two of us barely fit. I took the pipe and light it for myself. I could tell Nathan wanted to say something, and he reassured this observation by beginning sentences and never finishing them several times.

"He - he," he started and stopped several times and then said, "He was dead before I even started…"

I didn't say anything because I still didn't know what to say, afraid of saying the wrong thing, so it was better to just not say anything at all. Neither one of us spoke again before we fell asleep in his bed.

If I did sleep that night, it wasn't much. I woke up early the next morning and laid in bed, saying nothing until he woke up.

I didn't have any clients that next day, but I was working the second shift of membership from 3 till close. Nathan had to be at work at noon. We decided to get breakfast up the street around 10 a.m. and head to the gym right after. Once our food arrived, I was careful not to eat too slow or too fast. He vented a little bit but stopped himself from talking too much about what happened and how he was feeling. Not once did he ask how I was doing. I wouldn't know how to answer anyway. I was already working overtime to shove last night into the depths of my memory, hoping that I'd forget it. After we ate, I dropped Nathan off at the gym. I ran home, thankful no one was there when I got there. I quickly showered and changed. I opened the fridge to see my dinner plate from last night. I tossed its contents in a Tupperware container and headed back out the door.

Nathan worked for fifteen minutes before he told our boss what happened and said that he needed to take the rest of the day off. He left my name out of the conversation, which I am grateful for because I didn't want to be sent home. I didn't want anyone to know I was there. I had already tried to refocus my priorities, and I did not want to bail on my shift. I needed the money. Even more, I needed the structure. Even though I'd just showered, I planned on working out before my shift started. I had about three hours to kill in addition to my workout. I needed to buy myself a few hours of distraction, and I got just that when I pulled into the parking lot just as Nathan was running out of the building.

And like some schoolgirl idiot, I followed him. He asked if I wanted a drink. Hell. Of course, I wanted a drink. I skipped my workout and drove us up the street to Hot Shots, a local sports bar. I ordered a Budweiser. He ordered the same. We sat in silence for a bit at the bar before I suggested a game of pool. After a few shots into our first round, I finally saw him calm down for the first time since the previous night. We played three rounds. I let him win two out of three.

I only had one beer even though I wanted a whole bucket. Other than the occasional mid-shift tequila shot, I had rules about drinking before work, but I somehow never managed to implement a rule fully enough to not drink the night before work. Maybe I'd learn someday, but then I'd tell myself: *Fuck it. I'm twenty-three. I am sup-*

posed to be drinking and partying. That's normal. Before long, I needed to leave to go back to work. I offered him a ride back, but he said he was going to stay for another round and would walk back.

My shift was slow as hell. I kept finding things to do. I did them. And then I did them again. There was not enough work for me to do to occupy my mind. I watched the clock tick by the second. That man hadn't been dead for twenty-four hours yet. His almost lifeless body flashed in my head. An hour into my shift, the events of the previous night started to really sink in. I walked outside and called my mom. She answered, and I told her that something had happened the previous night.

I recounted the previous evening's horrific hour as I sat on the curb in front of the gym entrance and lost control of my tear ducts.

"That's awful, Al. I wish I could give you a hug. I was wondering why you didn't come home," she said.

A middle-aged woman who was a member saw me as she walked toward the entrance. She turned around and slid open the door to her van. Within seconds, I was handed a few tissues. Despite being on a call, she whispered something kind to me—something like, "We've all been there. Hang in there!" Then she patted me on the back and went inside.

That simple gesture left an imprint of kindness on my heart. For some reason, I found it especially touching that she gave me her supply of name-brand tissues! She could have gone inside and grabbed some of the off-brand tissues the gym provides, which always make my nose so dry, but she used her own.

Heat rose from the blacktop in front of me, the curb almost too warm for me to sit. I didn't want to go back inside. I wanted to stay out there where it was warm, quieter, and without fluorescent lights. I took one loop around the building to catch my breath and dried my eyes even though most of my coworkers and gym goers already saw me crying on the curb.

Within the next hour, my mom showed up at the gym. She gave me a hug, and we chatted a little bit more. Her hug was warm, just like outside; it truly made me feel like everything would be okay. She told me to come straight home after work, and I did just that. When I arrived home at night, I opened the fridge, and there was another plate from my dad waiting for me to enjoy.

In the several weeks leading up to that stranger's death, Nathan and I had sex several times. I felt as though I owed him something for the weed. I should've known I didn't owe him anything, and he ended up just being one of two coworkers I slept with while working at that gym.

If I didn't have weed in my system, I had at least a beer or two, but it was never enough to escape from him escaping in me. Something new came up when we had sex, too. Something I noticed but didn't pay much mind to and something I would add to my *things to ignore and run from* list.

The penetration hurt. In the coming days and weeks, I noticed Nathan's behavior becoming more sporadic. Some days, he greeted me at work with a smile. I was cordial but didn't start any conversations. I only spoke if spoken to. I was careful not to hang out with him outside of work anymore.

I reminded him again that I was moving to Chicago in August. I told him I needed to focus on my move and going back to school, and I couldn't hang out anymore. He would not take no for an answer. After a few days and nights of avoiding him, he came up to me at the desk. The front desk was a triangle, and the tip of the triangle was where I would normally stand during work in front of the computer. One way in. One way out. That is exactly where I was when I heard him say my name.

"Ally," Nathan said from behind me.

I turned around to see him just a few feet away from me and blocking my only exit. Technically, I could have jumped over the counter, but I was not going to do that during work and at our busiest time of day.

"What?" I asked.

"Can we talk?"

"No. I'm done talking to you."

"Please."

"No. I am working."

"You can't just ignore this," he sighed heavily. "We've been through so much together."

He cannot seriously be trying to trauma bond with me now.

It was 6 p.m. on a Tuesday—peak gym time. This was not the time nor place to be sewing friendship bracelets with the blood of a man we saw die.

I tried to move past him, but his hand touched my hip, and I froze.

"Don't touch me. I don't want to be with you. I don't want to be your friend. Leave me alone."

I grabbed a binder from the ledge behind him, and he walked away. Twenty seconds later, a loud sound stemmed through the space. I looked at my boss, who had just come out of his office. "What was that?" he asked.

I leaned over the ledge and looked down the stairway.

"That," I said as I pointed to the wall of trainer pictures, and below the last row of framed photos was now a new hole made from Nathan's fist.

By the time I left for Chicago, that hole had still not been repaired. An expired flyer for kickboxing lessons covered it up.

A few days later, I met with my boss in his office during a shift that Nathan was not on. I told him that I was with Nathan the night that man died, and that Nathan was now using that as leverage over me to get closer to me even though I refused.

"I can no longer work with him. He punched a hole in the wall after I told him I didn't want to be with him. As friends or anything else."

"Well, I'm not going to fire him, but I can change your shifts around."

"That's not good enough. He's here all the time. If he's not working out, then he's working.

If he's not working, he's working out. That's all he does."

"I'm not going to fire him."

"He punched a hole in the wall during the busiest time of day. The kids' classes were going on!"

Silence.

"Well, since that's the case, I should let you know that I am moving to Chicago for grad school. I quit. I'm not giving you two weeks notice. Please mail me my last paycheck and give someone else my last few client sessions."

I walked right out of there after that, with all my things, three hours before my shift was supposed to start.

My craving to live in Chicago was much stronger than my desire or need to work at that gym. The few hundred dollars or so I'd collect between then and moving wasn't enough to continue to put up with Nathan. I deserved better than that place. I definitely deserved better than him. Walking out of that gym and away from Nathan, I felt I was returning to my 14-year-old self, who promised never to let a man get in the way of what she wants. I felt empowered, strong, and freer because I walked away while also standing up for myself. And I did so without a soccer field in sight and without an ounce of alcohol in me.

CHAPTER XXXVII

Karen was the next therapist that I saw three and a half years after Melissa. Enough time had passed, and I was more open to trying therapy again with someone new. Karen came recommended by my new doctor. I trusted my new doctor, so I decided to give Karen a chance, hoping we would connect. I was anxious for that first session, and the lobby of her office only added to my anxiety.

The plethora of relaxing things overwhelmed me. Had this woman ever heard of *less is more?*

A doorbell hung on the wall next to the door that serves as an entrance to three or four different offices. I rang Karen's office and took a seat. I picked up a mental health pamphlet and skimmed through the pages of things I already knew as water fell onto rocks from a vertical fountain a few feet in front of me. I read on the pamphlet: *10 ways to feel less anxious* Right Now! Another said, *Feeling Depressed? Here's why you should tell someone.*

The dim lights made me sleepy. *Why are the lights dim? It's bright, hot and sunny outside. God, I am so tired. I am tired nearly all the time now. Her office better not be dim like this waiting area. There isn't even a window in here.* I waited almost twelve minutes before I rang the bell again. I should not have shown up early. Being too early meant waiting longer. Waiting longer meant ample time to overthink. *Did she hear my ring? Is she even here? Did I follow-up with her to confirm our appointment?* I scrolled through my e-mail to confirm my confirmation. A man exited the door to the offices. Two minutes later, Karen opened the door and summoned me back.

Karen's office was huge, like the size of a living room in an upper-middle-class home. A long couch centered the room, and to the left of it was an oversized chair. In between her chair and her patients' seating options, was an oversized wooden coffee table. Almost everything was OVERSIZED.

A dish of sand with a rake (too big for that table), a normal sized Rubix cube, and a huge ass glass paper weight weighing down nothing sat on the table between us. Oh, and her chair was also her desk chair. Every time we began our sessions, she wheeled it over from her desk all the way across the room.

I gave Karen the 411 on everything that happened with Chris through the latest with Nathan over the course of our half dozen or so sessions. She sat the same way every time we met: knees together with her hand folded or placed neatly on her lap. Karen usually wore a skirt with a sleeveless top and cardigan. Glasses balanced on her button nose. Her lips were thin and rarely with color.

Every session, I sank into the couch and stared at the dish of sand. My fingers laced each other neatly on my lap, and I played with my thumbs, still eyeing the sand wanting to play with that instead. My only goal with this therapist was to work through the last year and a half before I moved to Chicago, ignoring the fact that therapy and healing cannot be rushed and are not linear.

I never told Karen that I thought I had a drinking problem. I never told her that I thought I used alcohol to mask a deeper truth. I never told her that I could only tolerate sex with men when I was under the influence.

I never told her any of this because, for one, I did not completely trust her, and two, I also knew that if I said it out loud, then it would be more real. I still wasn't ready to admit any of it, but I was all for wanting to see a reaction from her.

To fill an awkward silence, I said this instead:

"I dated a girl once. I was in love with her."

Her thin lips disappeared into her face, and she began to fidget in her desk chair.

"Oh…really?" she asked, clearing her throat in the process.

"Yes."

She was all ears with willing insight on standby after I told her about Chris and Nathan, but when I proudly told her that I dated a woman a few years ago and think about that relationship a lot, she was speechless. Shocked. Wounded like I replaced her huge sand box and paper weight with their regular sized counterparts without consent.

Seeing her reaction, I thought to myself, *Oh, this should be interesting.* I went on to tell her most details about Lauren and our relationship. It felt just as good telling the story of us as it did to watch Karen struggle to hide her discomfort from my truth.

This is what she said when she finally did speak: "my daughter sees a therapist."

She then focused the conversation back to Nathan even though she successfully distracted me by that comment. Was she trying to make me feel more comfortable? Was she trying to become a mother figure? I hadn't mentioned my own mother other than that she was encouraging me to go to therapy.

I had started seeing Karen a month after I started hanging out with Nathan.

I didn't mind Karen's discomfort from my truth, but I did mind when I told her how unsafe I felt with Nathan, and she told me:

"It sounds like Nathan just needed a friend."

"Um. I wasn't safe. He punched a hole in the wall at work after cornering me at the desk." "He was just lost."

"Him being lost or whatever the fuck he is doesn't mean that it's okay."

To make her believe me, I finally said, "he has a gun." I immediately regretted telling her, though, because now she was really listening.

She quickly leaned forward and lightly pointed a finger. She meant well, but I was hung up on the fact that when I told her about dating a woman a few years ago, she tensed up! But bring a Glock into the conversation, then she's triggered in a totally different way.

I jokingly replied, "I can outrun him."

"You can't outrun a bullet, Ally."

Touché, Karen. Touché.

She failed to convince me to get a restraining order on him; it was probably a good idea, but I didn't want to go down that road. I was a month away from moving to a different state. I wanted to move on. I didn't want to deal with what I was leaving behind. I just wanted to leave it there and be done with it.

What I was really doing, though, was continuing to run from all my problems and avoiding processing any and all emotions about what happened. This time, however, I started getting tired of running. I started getting off carrying the weight of worn-out legs. Continuously not speaking up, I began to feel like a wet blanket was draped around my shoulders. That physical toll was exhausting me.

I hadn't brought up this fatigue in therapy, but I did start noticing the toll it took. I was getting tired of seeing myself repeat the same patterns. I was getting tired of the growing space between where I was then and where I was almost five years earlier with Lauren. I started worrying that Lauren would be my, for lack of a better term, one-hit wonder. I wanted to not have just one ex-girlfriend. I wanted new memories with a new queer person. I wanted more for myself. I wanted better. I felt so far away from that, though. I also wanted to go to Chicago without any distractions dating-wise.

In one last attempt to get me to talk to him, Nathan dopped off a book for me at the gym as a going away gift. I never went to pick it up. I had already quit and didn't plan on ever going back there.

My sessions with Karen ended just under three weeks before my big move. I lied and told her I was too busy to come back before I left. Even though I didn't talk much about my feelings, I still felt better talking out most of my shit, and I felt freer from Nathan and with the poor judgement and choices I made with him. Unfortunately, I bumped into him one more time before I left town.

Dozens of barely of age and underage co-eds were at Laclede's that night for penny pitchers. Laclede's was notorious for accepting even local library cards as a form of accepted ID. Well, that's what the rumors were anyway. He was at that bar with a buddy to celebrate Nathan's release from jail.

Tsuki and I decided to hangout for a bit before going to the gym and meeting up with some of our former teammates. Since we had plans to work out, I didn't plan on drinking, but that changed the second I caught a glimpse of Nathan across the room.

Okay. Where's the beer. I froze.

I did not know how to walk away from him nor this bar that I did not drive to. *All I know is that alcohol is aplenty, and I am one penny away from calming down.* Even if the calm lasted a few minutes, I desperately wanted it. I wanted the mask back. I wanted the mask that would help me get through whatever the rest of this night had in store.

Tsuki had a drink, too, and we ended up forgoing our workout. Who the heck thought going to a bar before the gym would lead us to actually going to the gym? So silly.

Not even an hour later, I was noticeably drunk. I justified this by reminding myself I hadn't driven there that night. I didn't want to be forced to leave a bar because he was there. I didn't want to physically run, but my mind was racing so fast, and I needed to slow down for once. But slowing down my racing thoughts came at a price.

Not so oddly enough, Chris' sisters were at the bar that night, too. I saw them long before I saw Nathan. They weren't the reason I drank, though; I'd finally healed from the broken heart their brother gave me. In a way, he set me free, and I was grateful. I'd take an awkward run in with them over seeing Nathan ever again.

I tried to hide, but since I couldn't, I drank. The bar wasn't that big. Most of my friends were shorter than me, and I stood out in a crowd with or without heels. I pretended to be overly engaged with my friends' stories and party antics while keeping tabs on Nathan out of the corner of my eye. In a moment of distraction from a friend's joke, I lost him, but he was closer than I thought.

I turned around just as he walked behind me. I held my breath until I felt him pass. I told myself that he'd left for the night. An hour or so later, I was hammered, and as the crowd started to disperse, I looked over and saw him staring at me, sitting at a table by himself.

He smiled at me. I didn't return the smile, but something possessed me to make a beeline straight for his table.

After I drunkenly told him that he needed to get his life together, he told me how much he'd miss me, and a wasted thought entered my head: *it would look good to leave this bar with a guy.* So, I did.

Well, I tried to. All the other males in the bar had left except for a few that were too young or some that I already knew, and so I decided to use the trouble I already had in front of me.

Just as I was about to get in Nathan's car, my boss ass friend, Tsuki said: "Ally, get the fuck in my car or I'm never speaking to you again." She didn't have to tell me twice. I got in her damn car.

The scrappy little woman Tsuki has always had my back, no matter what. She still does. Thank you, Tsuki. I didn't completely hit the Wall, but I was actively running toward it.

Tsuki was there to stop me, unlike many times previously when no one was there to stop me. This was new for me. I did not run from her even though I tried to. I listened, got in her car, and apologized. I puked as soon as I opened the door to get out. Tsuki tossed me a T-shirt and got me some water. I put the shirt on. I chugged the water in two gulps, and I passed out on her couch.

I never saw Nathan again after that night, other than a few frantic late-night Google searches several months later. The last I heard was that he had another warrant out for his arrest for possession of drugs and was prohibited from leaving the state of Missouri. So, I felt somewhat safer another state over and with hundreds of miles between us.

Even with the geographical space, though, I still found myself many nights walking home from class checking my shoulder as if I was back on the soccer field looking for a defender behind me.

CHAPTER XXXVIII

Another reason to celebrate with alcohol: weddings. It was a beautiful October day in 2014, warm enough not to need a jacket and cool enough not to sweat my makeup off. The day was perfect, and it was the first wedding I had been to in over a decade. I met with my co-captains, Timmy and Sammi, and we drove downtown to the hotel. A teammate that was a senior during my sophomore year was marrying her high school sweetheart. I cried during the ceremony. She looked beautiful. The whole day was beautiful. It was all beautiful, but I was jealous of how easy it all looked.

How did she get here? What a beautiful life she has. I wanted to enjoy that day, but I did not know how to without alcohol in my system. College had passed me by, and so had my excuse that the lifestyle I led was the college experience. *Why am I still doing this? My age? Wanting to fit in? Society? Why?* I was twenty-two. *Supposedly* an adult. If I'm still doing this shit now, would I keep doing this throughout the rest of my 20s, my 30s, God forbid if I make it to 40?!

I felt like a bum at that wedding. Not physically. I looked beautiful. I wore a black mid-thigh length lace dress with long sleeves and an open back that I would end up losing by the end of the night. Never to be seen again. My shoes were somewhat comfortable black velvet heels with plastic gems sprinkled about. My hair was twisted into a perfect and tight low bun. I always looked beautiful even when I felt messy, but the messiness of my insides rarely matched the outside, mainly because I had been sure to keep it that way for so long. I was an expert at playing the game of looking fine and feeling just fine, so I wouldn't disrupt anyone else's life.

I hadn't done much with my life yet. Still, I hadn't learned how to not drink when I didn't want to. I hadn't written anything close to being published or sold. I hadn't done anything except run and kick a ball on a field. Damn, I was so hard on myself. I'm far less harsh on myself today. I had just graduated college, where I played soccer for another four years, which was my goal and dream all along. There was so much time left, and there was still so much to learn. I was just getting stared in adulthood. I was in its infancy.

My college coaches were at this wedding, along with several women I played with. *I must show them that I'm okay, that I'm thriving in this life.*

So, I drank. I danced. I drank some more and some more and some more.

My downfall this day was going hard between the ceremony and reception.

What were we to do before the reception? What else was there to do besides day drink? After we settled into the hotel, we headed to Washington Ave in downtown St. Louis. I decided to start with whiskey and drink beer at the reception. *Hard stuff now. Lighter stuff later.* Although the Wall and I had gotten to know each other quite well those days, hitting it did not cross my mind. That's the thing about the Wall; I never really remembered it was there until I hit it. By the time we got to the reception, I was a happy drunk, still in control, until the open bar freely poured me more whiskey, drinking me closer to the Wall. Yeah, I didn't really switch to beer, and I certainly did not have any water like I initially intended. I kept binge drinking whiskey for hours and hours.

Some of my coworkers were a few miles away at an event that I was trying to go to. I had no reason to leave the wedding other than the habit within my habit: drinking and then running. By 9 p.m., I had reached the running part of my evening.

I attempted to get strangers to take me by opening their car doors at a stoplight outside the reception hall; I had no clue how much danger that put me or others in. Finally, my college trainer pulled up with her husband and my two co-captains. I did not realize it was them at first. And even when I did, I thought *they're tricking me. This is a trap.* So, I ran.

She ran after me. She can outrun anyone on or off a soccer field. She may argue that isn't true, but I believe she will kick ass until the day she dies.

Silly drunk me thought I could outrun her that night, but shortly after she chased after me, I didn't want to run anymore. Not from her. Not from my friends. So, I stopped and let her guide me back to her family's minivan, which her husband was driving while my two co-captains sat in the back seat.

Even years later, after having twins and bringing her child count to five, she's one of the strongest women and humans with whom I have been blessed enough to cross paths in this life. She cares for all children and players: her own, her friends, and her players.' She's incredible.

She was genuinely concerned about me that night, and I trusted her. I still do. She was the last person I wanted to disappoint, and the following days, I was nothing short of devastated by my behavior that night.

I had no reason to run away from my company that day. Someone at some point had called my dad. I don't recall much of the car ride home, but I remember sitting in the hotel hallway in my pajamas and seeing my dad walk down the hall. I was shocked that he came to fetch me. I felt loved. No more running—at least for that night.

I was running because I was drunk and did not want anyone to see me like that. I was running because of what drunk me runs from: my fear that someone would figure me out. Afraid that drunk me would tell my truth. A constant cycle of feeling, then not feeling, then drinking, then drunk feeling, then running to not feel. There are only two ways to avoid that coming out: 1. being sober or 2. running and running and running.

It was such a catch-22 though, because if I were to choose option one, I was also avoiding my feelings. It was like a ticking clock. The more I felt, the less alcohol-free I wanted to be.

With each sober hour that came next, each drunken memory came back. Not once ever during my alcohol consumption did I think: *You will remember almost everything you say and do, Al.*

While drunk feelings were embarrassing and ugly and gross, they weren't nearly as hard as the much realer sober ones.

I ran away from my decisions. I ran away from my feelings. But I was DRUNK, so that feeling of not wanting to be drunk would only happen if I was sober. When my dad and I got home, he graciously made me a breakfast sandwich. A co-worker, who I had been calling several times throughout the night, called me. I answered and walked out to the back patio with my sandwich and a glass of water.

Something was different this time, though. I felt like a little kid, and I wasn't too fond of that feeling. I was embarrassed for how I behaved at the wedding and after, and I was embarrassed as my parents looked at me at 2:00 in the morning as I sat on the steps of the back patio. Their faces looked tired, and I felt horrible for ruining their evening and disrupting their sleep.

I don't want to do this anymore. Why can't I drink safely? What must I do to not be in this position ever again?

After several years of binge drinking on and off, I was finally coming to a point where the booze was no longer working to suppress my emotions. The tiredness of running away was started to get stronger than my willingness to run.

I did not love my sober mind because it was filled with so many emotions I did not know how to navigate. Being sober was uncomfortable because being sober meant feeling. I didn't want to feel those feelings because they were all so painful, scary, and unknown. I was afraid of being sober because I thought I would grow further away from people. I felt that my connections would fade, which turned out to be true, but also not bad either because it left room for new connections to be made.

Twenty-two-year-old Ally did not necessarily think it was a bad thing to grow apart from people. Even with a new sense of not wanting to drink so heavily, the unknown was something she really did not like.

Sometimes, growing away from people means we are growing into ourselves. Sometimes in order to grow up, to grow true means letting yourself go in a better-for-you direction.

CHAPTER XXXIX

The rest of the winter was spent on the go. I went out a lot. I drank a lot but not too much after that wedding. I threw myself into work, picking up more hours and keeping myself busy by working out. I distracted myself as much as possible and ignored the fatigue that grew harder as the days grew shorter.

Spring had arrived, but it was still cold during the Easter of 2015 when my parents and I traveled to Chicago to visit my brother. On that Saturday, Mom, Eric, and I looked at one apartment building that I could potentially move into later that year. I slept in that morning, and we left the hotel around 10 a.m. By 12:30 p.m., I was back at the hotel and back in bed sleeping. My mom woke me up for dinner just before 6 p.m. I cried in confusion and fear. I had no idea what was tanking all of my energy. I had cut back on drinking. I tried to work out, even if it was only for twenty minutes at a time. I tried different diets, eliminating *bad* things. That was all I could do, anyway. I was eating cleaner than ever. Everything seemed so far away, even though I was closer than I ever had been to Chicago.

In fear of a shower rinsing off what little energy I had left, I skipped it but changed into fresh clothes. As I pulled on a clean sweater, questions ran through my mind: *How am I supposed to move to a new city, go to school full time, and do all the other things I want to do when I am just up for less than four hours and already need a bed?* I convinced myself that depression delivered this extreme fatigue. It felt like I had mono again like I did my freshman year at Ole Miss, or maybe it never even left. Brain fog set in, and it was so stubborn I let it win. I did not know how to fight this fog yet. I started seeing a new doctor.

In the three months I was her patient, close to 200 vials of blood were taken from my arm. The largest quantity taken at once was 120 vials. Thirteen, fourteen, fifteen vials of blood later, and I could no longer look at the blood escaping my body. My eyes floated to the ceiling, and I dreamt of French bulldogs and Alyssa spaniel puppies—in a field running toward me with open paws and kisses.

I took pride years earlier when doctors' visits were far and few in between. I loved how I could eat almost anything I wanted and still run miles and miles. I loved how my athletic body could combat any opponent on the field…and off the field if it came down to it. But I left everything I had on each field I played on. I was a fighter on the field and a lover off of it, but I could still be a fighter off the field when I needed to be, which frankly occurred nearly every day.

I threw slaps and punches at opponents when refs weren't looking. This was only if they were giving me or a teammate too much trouble. You're pulling on my jersey for the entirety of the first half? That's just asking for a slap in the back. I'd run across the field to tackle another when they did my teammate wrong by cleating her or pushing her down for no other reason other than to be petty. But now, my immune system had other plans. I was the one being attacked…by my own body.

I drank copious amounts of caffeine each morning. Day. Sometimes night. Zero effect. On a typical weekday, I woke up, trained my whopping two clients, attempted to exercise, then went home and slept six hours before teaching spin class. I loved teaching spin because I could act my way through a class, looking like I was working harder than I was. One of the trainers at the gym where I worked was a sponsor for Monster Energy drinks. A few times a month, he'd pop in the gym to drop of samples. This guy was ALWAYS amped. I couldn't believe I was jealous of an MMA fighter's energy. That had been me just a year prior. I trained twice a day, sometimes three, to prepare for season. Had soccer ending been the start of health issues laid dormant because I was in such great shape for so long?

I went back to the doctor for the blood work results. She said six little words that gave me *one* answer to my long list of health issues that were just beginning. She said, "Your thyroid is in the toilet." My doctor then prescribed me a medication to regulate my thyroid. However, it would take months before the right dosage was found.

Knowing that these medications take time to work and to narrow down the correct dosage, I forced myself to be patient with this medicine. It took over a year to find the right medicine and for it to start making a difference. Every three months, if I didn't see a significant change in energy, the dosage was switched.

The brain fog would subside eventually, but naively, I thought it would be gone for good once it was gone. Brain fog, as it turned out, was a symptom of literally every illness that lives in me. I was twenty-three at the time of this diagnosis, and at the time, other than depression, Raynauds, and hypothyroidism were all I for sure knew I had.

On a cloudy, cool mid-June weekday, Mom and I drove back to Chicago for one reason and one reason only: to find an apartment. The next morning, as we finished breakfast, I pulled up the address of apartment building number one on my phone. I struggled to locate the exact spot of the building. We decided to walk a few blocks, but then it started pouring. We hopped in a cab and learned that our destination was less than .2 miles away. We shared a laugh and paid $5 for the ninety-second car ride around the block.

I remembered it being loud right outside the building—I suppose this was typical for downtown living. Ten minutes into the first tour, the guide took us to the laundry room. To get there, you had to walk down a narrow hallway in the basement, making it awkward for laundry goers to pass by with their bins full of dirty clothes, passing others with their clean clothes. I suppose this was the case in any laundry facility, but the narrow hallway heightened the awkwardness. Across from the laundry room were a handful of offices, one of which was the maintenance office, and around one corner at the end of the hall was a loading dock. I was not into it. I realized in that moment I needed a laundry room that was above ground and with windows. I had seen too many murder mysteries to know better.

We toured the second building, and my mom picked up on my shortness of breath and lack of responsiveness to the leasing agent as she asked me questions. We finished the tour and canceled the rest of the apartments we planned on looking at. *I guess I'll live here because I am too tired to make another decision. I am too exhausted to go any further.*

As we got ready to head back to St. Louis, I said, "I can drive, Mom."

"You sure?"

"Yeah. I'm fine." I wasn't.

I felt bad that my mom drove 90% of the trip, so I offered to drive. It was the least I could do after she's helped me so much. I drove exactly one mile down Lake Shore Drive. Mom knew I could not go any further. I knew it, too. But there I was again, saying things out loud, hoping they'd come true. I pulled over, and we switched seats. She drove the rest of the five-hour trip home. I slept the entire time.

The lease was signed for a mid-August move in date. I could not wait, but I was worried. *My body should not be responding this way. I am twenty-three years old. I should be thriving, right?*

There was only one thing during this time that made my fatigue drastically worse: alcohol. On a Friday night in July, I found myself at another Cardinals game. My parents drove my brother and I downtown. They had tickets to the game, too, but my brother and I were sitting with a group of his friends. I made it until the last call without a drink. One of my brother's friends placed a beer in my hand. Even knowing the impact it would have on my mind and body, I didn't want to be rude. Plus, it was hot, and a cold drink sounded nice. I also wanted a beer.

The whole time I was at the game I thought, *I'm depressed, and alcohol is a depressant. Oh, and my thyroid is fucked.* Still, I did not know how to communicate my depression. It took over me like a thief in the night: *I feel it, I don't see it, and then suddenly it's there stealing my energy, my hobbies, my emotions. My own body and mind robbing me of my own life. At least the life I want for myself. Maybe I can still get there? But how? I dunno. I'll drink this beer in the meantime, though.*

It was after that night that I felt threatened for the first time. I felt threatened by my alcohol consumption. I felt my future was on the line. A career in entertainment? Gone. Finances?

Disappeared. School? Forget about it!

My last fourth of July living in St. Louis and I still had not learned my lesson, but it was one of the last times I hit the Wall.

The guys made plans to hit up some bars in Soulard after the game. My parents came over to our seats during the ninth inning to fetch me to take home. I wanted to go home. My parents wanted me to go home, but something rare happened: I was experiencing FOMO. I was moving soon, and I knew the nights out with the guys were numbered. Despite going against what my gut told me, I went out when I should've been at home, in bed at a decent hour, taking care of my mind, body, and spirit with a cup full of water on my nightstand. I was always safe when I went out or drank with my brother and his friends, even if I did not feel safe within myself when alcohol ran through my blood.

First stop: Molly's, a popular bar in the Irish Soulard neighborhood of St. Louis. Fearing my card getting declined, I quickly transferred money from my savings account to my checking while I stood at the bar. There's that finances disappearing thing I just mentioned. I bought a drink for my brother's friend as a thank you for buying me one earlier. I mentally told myself not to drink anything stronger than beer. This body could barely handle a bud light, let alone the whiskey that I really craved. For a mid-summer night in St. Louis, it was not as humid or hot. It was a perfect night to be outside. For that reason, I was glad I tagged along. *I deserve to be here. I'm young. It's summer. I deserve to be out and not cooped up at home.*

A handful of girls I went to high school with entered the patio area. I said hi to them, hoping we'd take a shot together as a toast to our days at the academy. But they barely acknowledged me, leaving me feeling invisible. That day at Ole Miss, picking up my books after I quit the team flashed in my mind. I could've just been reading too much into it, but that brief interaction made me feel like dirt stuck in the groove on the bottom of my favorite pair of running shoes.

Instead of chasing them or giving them any more of my mental energy, I ordered two shots. One for me and one for my brother. We tossed them back. He ordered us two beers, and we rejoined his friends at a table across the bar.

One, two, three hours later, I really didn't know for sure the exact moment this time, I hit the Wall. Even with my energy depleted, I could still outrun most of my brother's friends, including the one that was chasing after me in the streets of downtown St. Louis that night. I eventually found myself in the back of a cab and texted my brother's friend to let him know. It should be noted that my brother would've ran after me, but he was still at the bar, and I had gone back to the hotel room with the others with intentions of crashing for the night.

The cab driver pulled over on the side of interstate 270 so I could slide open the van door to throw up. I felt myself piss my pants as I hurled, too. *I am disgusting*. I dialed my dad's office phone. There's one located right outside my parents' bedroom. They typically left their cell phones downstairs at night. The Wall needed to let them know that I was on my way home.

I told the cab driver my neighbor's address. I did this a lot. I did not want this stranger dropping me off at my actual address in the chance of him coming after me later on.

I could get quite feisty when I was drunk, especially when someone tried to touch me when I was climbing, and then clinging to the Wall. So, even if this cab driver, who was actually probably a decent human, tried to take advantage of me, I was ready, even though I had throw-up dribble on my face and now wet shorts. I crawled out of the van and realized that I was just one house away from my own. I saw my dad walking towards me. He asked if I paid the cab, and I told him I did.

If my dad was worried about me, he didn't show it, nor do I remember him mentioning it. Of course, my parents didn't like how I acted when I got that drunk. However, I believe they knew I'd always bounce back and eventually grow out of it, and they weren't too far off from that.

The next morning, when I woke up, I immediately rinsed off my body at lightning speed, filled up a Gatorade water bottle with ice water, and left the house. I drove straight to the gym, where I worked, and sat in the sauna for an hour. Whoa, an hour?! The sauna was partially broken, and it took several minutes for anyone to break even the slightest sweat. After that, I went for a run and then grabbed an iced coffee from Starbucks. I called and texted some friends to hang out, but either they didn't reply or were busy. Without anywhere else to go really, I headed back home a few hours after I had left and quietly entered the house. With Fourth of July plays already curated, my options were limited for impromptu socializing.

Mom was getting ready for a party later that afternoon and dad was watching TV. I stopped at the fridge and opened it. I considered eating something as I hadn't eaten anything since the game the previous night and that food ended up on the side of the highway. I would have loved to chow down on a bowl of pasta salad I saw, but I told myself I didn't deserve it. *I don't deserve to eat.* I had not eaten anything all day, partially due to a queasy hungover stomach and partially due to punishing myself for my behavior. I would disguise this self-punishment as a detox. On the outside, I'd say: *oh no, I'm not eating to flush out toxins and make up for negative calories taken in last night.* On the inside, I really thought: *I deserve the pain the hunger causes because I cannot control my alcohol, therefore, if I don't eat then I'll learn my lesson.*

Our neighbors growing up were known for some of their huge holiday parties, and most years, they hosted a Fourth of July party. Toni, my neighbor texted me, asking me where I was. I would've loved to go over there, but I pretended my hangover was worse than it actually was. I didn't deserve to go over there and enjoy myself after how I behaved the previous night. Also, my mom was over there, and after waking her up last night, I thought it was best to avoid her. Seeing as she wasn't my #1 fan at the moment, I stayed home. She was upset with me for how I acted when I was drunk the night before, and I didn't want to be around her knowing she was upset because of me. So, I avoided her.

I joined my dad downstairs to watch a golf tournament on TV in the early evening. Golf was relaxing for me watch. All you have to do is watch the ball. You don't have to follow a story line, unless you care about the score and what the announcers have to say, like my dad does.

Without warning, the front door opened, followed by footsteps. My mom's footsteps. I could always distinguish who entered the house or who was walking up or down stairs based on what footsteps I heard. My mom's are heavy. My brother's even heavier. He walks with urgency, always on a mission. He also skips steps going up the stairs. Again, for urgency. His ankles and/or knees pop, too. I laugh thinking of the dozens of times each of us fell up the stairs during our time living under the same roof. Then, there's my dad's footsteps; they are much, much lighter and sometimes with a quiet shuffle.

I was still on the couch when Mom walked over. She stood over me with her arms crossed, looking down at me.

My parents had seen and/or heard of the Wall a handful of times: the wedding last fall, last night, Valentine's Day last year, and surely a few more that I couldn't remember. I really did not need a lecture from anyone. I knew what I did was out of hand and stupid and gross and unsafe and made me a fucking loser. I did not need nor want a goddam lecture from anyone. But that's exactly what I got.

"You can't be doing this kinda stuff in Chicago, Al," Dad said.

"I know."

"You don't know anyone well enough to take care of you when you do this."

"Yeah, I know."

"Someone is going to take advantage of you," Mom said.

"I said I. Fucking. Know."

What happened to me? In high school, I felt so proud saying no to alcohol, and when I did drink, I was careful enough not to feel more than a light buzz. The first time I got completely hammered was during my senior year off of Blue Moon and Captain Nora. I got so sick that I never drank either again. I think by that point, I knew how I'd gotten there, but WHY did I let myself get there…again? Why did I keep staying there?

After that day, I didn't drink for a while and refocused on my physical health. I researched different foods that caused fatigue and how to undo it. The first elimination diet I tried was the Candida Diet, "a low-sugar, anti-inflammatory diet that promotes good gut health and eliminates the sugars that feed a Candida overgrowth." This helped me tremendously. My bowel movements came with ease and regularity. Most weeks prior, I wouldn't poop at all, and when I did, my stool was hard as a rock. Something natural finally made me feel better, but I ignored it. I followed the cleanse and diet for a couple of weeks before I was back to eating whatever I wanted. When I started feeling better, I thought I was healed. I didn't realize that eating right for my body meant adopting a lifestyle completely, not a two-week semi-cleanse here and there.

Like most of my health issues, this one wasn't a quick fix either.

Again, I looked healthy. I still look healthy today. I have damn great hair and have still managed to maintain toned abs years after soccer ended. I guess I still did not know how to feel good for long periods of time. I didn't know what good even felt like because, for so long, I had felt a disconnect from my peers, from society, from my family. The disconnection of looking one way but feeling another. i.e., looking straight but feeling gay; i.e., looking healthy but being in chronic physical pain.

Sometimes, I thrived because of this disconnection, and I embraced it a lot of the time. But when I didn't embrace it, I sabotaged my capabilities, talents, hopes, and dreams. Because the surface is easier to face and think about, just like staying in the shallow end of the pool is easier.

I think I didn't deserve it. Which is bullshit because deep down, I know I fucking deserve all the love and happiness.

I was hungover for three days after hitting the fourth of July Wall—my longest hangover yet.

I guess you get what you deserve. Actions have consequences. With my health issues and my depression, my hangovers only got worse. In the few weeks leading up to the move, I tried my best to have just a drink or two, here or there, always with food, always with other people. And things were…okay.

I wrote quite a few journal entries around this time. Here are a few of them:

July 20, 2015: "The next time I'm in Chicago, I get to stay and live my life there…I am finally so close. 25 days."

July 24, 2015: "My energy has been up and down, but today was up! I hope it continues through the rest of the weekend 'cause I got lots of fun stuff planned! Tonight, I went to sushi and the Cards game with Tsuki. Tomorrow, I'm spending the day with Jacq…I am going to ease my mind to sleep now. Last night, I didn't wake up once in the middle of my slumber. I can't remember the last time that happened! Where there's a will, there's a way. God bless."

July 28th, 2015: "I am so tired, and I didn't do much today other than nap and watch TV. My head started to ache this evening, so I couldn't even read. How am I supposed to start grad school with no energy?"

CHAPTER XL

I cooled it on the drinking for the first couple of months I lived in Chicago. I made it a point that none of my classmates or coworkers would ever see me drunk, and very few did.

I did not want to burn any bridges caused by Wall Drunk Ally. Plus, getting drunk would not get me to where I want to be: a writer-actor and perhaps a published author someday.

One of the other reasons I chose Chicago over L.A. and New York was because that's where some of my favorite actors and writers got their start. So, prior to my big move, I signed up for an improv class with The Second City theatre.

The class started in August, just a couple of weeks before school did. Mine met Sunday afternoons from 3 to 6 p.m. Just before the term started, though, a fire broke out in Piper's Alley, the Old Town building in which The Second City lives. Conveniently for me, the class relocated to Tribeca Film School less than a mile up the street from my apartment, saving me time and more importantly, saving me energy by cutting my commute in half.

On the first day of class, I left early to treat myself to an iced coffee from Starbucks. Little did I know at the time, a lot of restaurants and shops in the Loop close after the workweek. I found this bizarre. Despite not getting my coffee, I tried my best to show myself some grace by not being annoyed that I could've rested another twenty minutes. Instead, I was looking at a positive note—arriving to class fifteen minutes early. The coffee wouldn't have done that much for my energy anyway.

I found my classroom, and I introduced myself to the few people who arrived before me. We chatted about where we were from and why we were there; you know, it was basic small talk. I was in the middle of a sentence when the instructor arrived, bursting and then skipping through the door with the most energy I had ever seen in a person over twenty-five. He had so much energy that I started to believe he was part Martian, part human, and part puppy. After his lengthy introduction, he announced one rule and one rule only: "Bring all of your energy to this class, my friends!"

All I can think was *how the hell am I going to do this? I'm finally here, where I want to be, and I can't enjoy it because my thyroid decided to give itself a swirly?* Not only was I trying to figure this out in this three hour, once a week improv class, but my schedule would become busier once I started school and working more at the gym.

I rested as much as possible on the weekends to accommodate my instructor's request and also to not look like I didn't want to be there; I really wanted to be there, in fact. I did. Fighting back tears, I walked back home after the first class. Improvising was essentially making things up in real time, so I guess I just needed to just make up fake energy and fake happiness a little more than everyone else—or I could just play a tired bitch in each scene.

Second City's prerequisite for their Conservatory program is the completion of a full year of their improv program. That was my goal eventually, to complete their Conservatory and their Musical Improv programs. So, I started at the beginning: improv level one. Improv was fun and light and offered a welcomed escape from long weeks of work and school. Even though I was dog-tired most of the classes. Improv helped me navigate certain made-up situations, but those situations were also inspired by real life events and experiences. Improv allowed me to test the waters in telling the truth, even if I was playing a character on stage.

I made it through the term and eventually found balance with my busy schedule. By the last class, I felt more energy make its way back to me. I tried not to get too excited, though. I didn't want to get my hopes up.

My cooling off period ended two weeks into September when my brother bought me a beer at my very first game at Wrigley field. I felt like I stepped back in time. I didn't want to turn down the beverage because 1. I wanted it 2. I was on a tight budget and gladly accepted a free drink even though it would hurt me and 3. Baseball = beer.

I didn't get trashed that day, but I did get drunk. And with the brain fog from my stupid thyroid, I was quickly reminded that alcohol does not help…really doesn't help in any situation, any circumstance I've ever been in. The warning signs were always there that alcohol isn't for me. My intentions to drink were rarely ever healthy or the right intentions, and the few times they were, I still binged only to repeat my behavior whenever I stopped wanting to say no. I knew the lesson, but I wasn't really learning it. I was ignoring it time and time again, repeating my mistakes instead of changing for the better.

After our last improv class of the term, everyone went out for drinks and appetizers. Going to this was extremely hard for me. After each class except for this last one, I went immediately home to crash. I didn't want to be around alcohol with these people. In my class, I was in control. At the bar, I was still in control somewhat, just not as much as I felt I could be. I also did not want to explain myself for not ordering a drink like everyone else. It was expected of me to drink with these people. This was my official first social outing with them and the comedy scene in Chicago. Like in many industries, it's an unofficial rule that participants must drink and/or smoke something.

I stood my ground and ended up not drinking that night because I did not want to. It felt good standing my ground and sticking to it, but I did not make a big deal out of it. I didn't want to dwell on it and have that attention on me. I wasn't comfortable answering questions, and there were almost always questions as to why I wasn't drinking.

Most people in the group, especially the men, thought this was odd. Two guys specifically started grilling me about not drinking like I was an alien that had just landed from planet prohibition. They made plans for me to come out the following weekend to go drinking and bar hopping, clearly wanting to christen my official move to Chicago. I complied, excited for potential new friends.

The outing felt like another test: me vs. alcohol. I wanted to pass so badly to prove to myself that I could handle a night out without escaping reality completely, and I succeeded. I ended up not drinking that much. I had maybe one shot at the bar and a couple of beers over the four hours or so I'd been out with them. In between drinks, I was flirted with by one of my classmates. He claimed he didn't want to pursue anything during class, so he waited until it was over. I perked up. I was drinking *responsibly*, AND I had a potential suitor that I could use as a shield, to thicken the mask.

I turned him down at first, making him chase, but we ended up dating for a few weeks after I caved to his persistence and my want to prove that I could hold a job, be a full-time student and date someone. He was nice and cute but that's about all he had going for him.

His persistence to date me quickly turned into persistence to fuck me, which is what he was probably after all along. I wanted to wait to have sex because 1. I didn't want to have sex with him ever, and 2. I rarely get naked with someone I am just getting to know personally.

One chilly fall afternoon, he did not want to leave me alone. I offered him my time in the morning for breakfast, and then I told him I needed to go to the store and then get some work done before class. He followed me to the store, and then *helped* me carry my groceries back to my apartment! I repeated that I needed to get some stuff done before class and that he should probably get going. I could not have been any clearer about him needing to GTFO. He lingered briefly and then started making out with me, eventually guiding me to my bed.

We had consensual, crappy sex. Consensual because I said yes when he asked me, when I really was just doing one of the things I do best: lie to myself to accommodate others. *If I say yes, then he'll leave.* Just because it's technically consensual does not mean that I wanted it. I could've spoken up about not wanting sex. I could've said no. But again, this is what I was supposed to do, right? Have sex with the men I date? *At least I'll have something to share next time my straight friends and I talk about sex.*

I hated every second of the ninety before he ejaculated and the ten seconds after of his post-sex sticky breathing. My mind was elsewhere. My body wasn't mine in those seconds. I thought about my schoolwork and schedule, and did a mental run-through of what I needed to get done that afternoon for class.

I was sober for all this, never having wished for a drink more in my life. *Next time, I'll be sure to have a few drinks beforehand.*

I felt like a fraud. My mind also took me somewhere I hadn't been in years, Disney World. My mind entered a dream-like state after I finished the run thru of my to-do lists. My gut twisted as if I were getting ready to drop on Blizzard Beach's Summit Plummet water slide. On my way up the staircase to the top of the slide, I wasn't met with strangers standing in line. I was met with future versions of myself, cheering for me.

"You can do this, Ally!"

"We can do this together!"

I was so disappointed in myself for wasting that opportunity to fall towards my truth and my desire in the pre-sex moments with Afternoon Delight Guy. Once the intercourse began, I froze and didn't feel like I could stop until he did.

Instead of plummeting down the summit, I turned around and walked back down the staircase, having to face a long line of now past versions of myself. All of whom wore disappointed expressions on their faces, but some met me with empathy more than regret. Their mouths opened to say something to me, but no words came out no matter how hard they tried.

I knew I was different but didn't know exactly what to call it. What name to give it. What label. I was suppressing. Thinking about anything other than what I was feeling, ignoring that itch to scratch and find what that feeling of *different* actually meant. Distracting myself when the thinking started to turn into feeling. Running when the drinking turned into feeling again.

What was the first thing I did after he finally left my apartment? I texted a friend and bragged about my afternoon delight. Although I was disgusted, I was also relieved to have a chance to *bond, fit in* or whatever bullshit I was feeding myself to keep me hiding in straight sight. The friend texted back something like: "OMG. Finally! Can't believe it took this long!" I was confused by this…I had only been *dating* him for barely two weeks. How long is sex supposed to take between two people? Society got in my head when I was a child, and it would be over twenty years before I kicked it out for living rent free.

I was telling a lie because I eventually wanted it to be true, so I fit in somewhere in this heteronormative, sex- and alcohol-driven society. I guess the bigger question was: why did I feel the need to fit in so badly? Deep down, I know now there will be nowhere where I fit in perfectly.

As my friend texted me back to give her ALL the details later, I checked the time. It was later than I thought.

I was supposed to meet with a professor to go over an assignment that afternoon. Due to miscommunication on my part, he e-mailed me asking me where I was. I apologized immediately, horrified that I wasted his time and was not prepared. I thought we scheduled a phone call. How unprofessional of me. I did not like it when people wasted my time, so I tried my best not to waste anyone else's time, especially a graduate school professor. The professor was forgiving, but I punished myself.

I angrily cried after rescheduling the meeting and broke up with Afternoon Delight Guy a week later because he was getting in the way of my future. I was relieved not to have to deal with him but horrified that I let him get in my way.

You probably remember, reader, that promise I made to my fourteen-year-old self that I would never let anyone, especially a man, get in the way of my life's purpose, whatever that may be. This promise was made in eighth grade after a male classmate repeatedly hit me in the vagina during a class photo. He stood behind me. At first, he lightly skimmed my butt with his hand. Then his pace got quicker, and his hand moved between my legs, making my plaid skirt do a dance without me even moving. I was frozen, but then what did I do? I laughed right along with him. Ha ha ha. How funny! *Jackass.*

If any other classmates saw, they certainly did not say anything. The teacher couldn't see as she was too focused on taking the picture. If I hadn't laughed, I would've cried, and I was not about to cry in front of my entire class, especially not during a picture; how horrifying, my fourteen-year-old self being documented for everyone to remember me crying, me showing emotion! Even then, I didn't want to be weak. Nor did I or would I tell on this boy. Then I'd be a narc. No one wants to be a narc when they are trying to get through the last year before high school.

It was confusing and difficult for me to comprehend, my inability to speak up. How could I fight so hard on a soccer field, but it was nearly impossible to speak up for myself in my day-to-day life after hanging up my boots? It felt impossible, especially when it came to sex. It didn't occur to me that saying no to alcohol should have easily rolled over into me not rolling around sheets with someone I didn't want to.

I didn't think I could say NO out loud when it came to sex. That two-letter word got stuck in a thick invisible Wall. A different one though. A wall in my throat. A wall made of glass that, with each attempt to get through it, cut a little bit. Hurting me a lot. The more attempts I made to get through the glass wall, the more it hurt. The more it crumbled. The more it cut me. I didn't know that the glass would eventually not only come down but it would eventually stop hurting me and then would evaporate completely. Even after getting rid of ADG, I knew I would start drinking again sooner or later.

When I was drunk in Chicago, it was mostly only strangers who saw me drunk. I was scary good at keeping this promise. I knew these people were toxic and untrustworthy, but I hung out with them anyway: faceless, nameless strangers that I couldn't hurt and knew they would let me drink without question. They wouldn't tell me no or cut me off when I needed it. I learned very quickly who these people would be. I alternated between them. If I hung out with one or two all of the time, then they may have found out about me. And I was still not ready yet to let anyone find the truth. I was not ready yet to come out of hiding.

To distract myself even further, I picked up more shifts at work and dove deeper into the craft of screenwriting. I also wanted to meet and make lifelong friends with whom I could potentially navigate the industry someday. I did find some of those friends, but they came from unexpected places. I may not have gotten that close with my cohort during my time at DePaul, but I did leave with one kickass connection and met my closest friends in more classes and doing shows at The Second City training center. I wouldn't meet those close friends though for another several months. I'm proud to say that those connections, the ones I wanted to keep, never saw me drunk.

While I drank here and there with my grad school cohort, I never let myself have more than a few drinks with them, and I never ever—wouldn't even dare—have a drink at Second City. I was not about to burn any bridges with potential friends and colleagues. I did not think that I would be worthy of their forgiveness if a situation of Drunk Ally did arise. I finally cared enough about something to not want to screw it up.

Other than a single beer at iO in early 2016, I've never had a drink at The Second City or any other theater in Chicago. I was so often in rooms with people smarter and more talented than me.

Chicago held my present and most likely a big part of my future. I was not about to fuck that up by showing them a side of me I didn't even want to see. Better to hide her. Best not to let her out and run free.

Weeks after the baseball game and several days after that night out with my improv class, I was eating breakfast and paused to do something I normally did not do. I checked in with my body. After a quick scan, tears immediately hit my eyes and became a flood of relief and joy, spilling over my oatmeal and into my coffee.

The brain fog was gone, lifting me out of the mud. My head hadn't felt this clear in over a year...maybe even longer than that. The medicine finally kicked in. A few weeks later, I got my thyroid tested, and after a year and a half, it had finally been regulated.

Not wanting to send my thyroid back down the drain, I then went on and spent about three months without consuming any alcohol at all. My energy and clear head became so important to me.

I did not paint the nonconsumption as sobriety, though, or as an alcohol-free lifestyle. Any time I took a break from drinking, it was always, "oh, I'm not drinking right now" or "I'm just taking a break from alcohol." Alcohol was something I wanted to put down and be able to pick back up whenever I wanted. I wanted to fit in and be a normal person who could handle alcohol responsibly. I kept holding on to finally learning that—the responsible drinker thing—but what I eventually learned the hard way is that I never would. I am unable to. The only way to fix my drinking problem is to quit drinking altogether.

During my hiatus from the bottle, I was focused and working hard. My head was clearer than ever. I returned to Chicago after a week back in St. Louis for Christmas, learning and loving everything exposed to me in school.

I took the next two levels of the improv program at Second City, and after level C, we had our first show. It was in February of 2016, the first of many shows I performed at The Second City Training Center.

I had made some new friends. My plan was working, and felt I was in a good place.

I crushed the show. Totally, epically crushed it. It could not have gone better. Afterwards, most of the cast went up the street to Benchmark, one of Old Town's many bars.

The Wall started to become distant. I was comfortable...comfortable enough to not think about the fact that I was too comfortable. Comfortable enough that I felt I could have a drink after that first show.

Remembering that wine drunk is my "happiest" drunk, I opted for a glass of wine and just one celebratory shot. After that, I decided it was time for me to go home before I had anything else. Quit while I was ahead. Quit before I had too much. I walked to the train with my friend, Charlie, proud of myself for having a great show, and even prouder for not drinking so much. I was in control and walking away when I knew it was time to walk away.

Maybe I can do this responsibly? Maybe I will be able to fit in and connect comfortably.

Because clearly, I'd learned, right? Clearly, I had finally passed the test and knew how to only have a few drinks at a time instead of drinking until the point of no return: the Wall.

Just like school tests, though, we don't always retain the information we're tested on.

That night was a good night, and with warmer months coming and my birthday, too, there was no reason not to be happy at this moment. And I was happy. I really believed that I had cracked the code. If I did it once, drinking in moderation, then surely, I could repeat this moderation thing over again.

I felt on top of the world.

CHAPTER XLI

My coming out story started when I was a child, but my dark night of the soul came just before my twenty-fourth birthday in March of 2016, a month after the show at Second City. For Spring Break, I went home to St. Louis for a few days and then flew to Atlanta to visit my aunt and uncle for Easter.

One year and ten months had gone by since I had seen The Professor last. He was one of the few people from college that I kept in touch with after graduation.

A couple of weeks before, I asked him to meet for coffee while I was in town. We met at a Starbucks on Manchester Road in the Rock Hill neighborhood.

As I walked in, I saw him sitting at a four top. He looked the same. If anything was different, he looked more tired.

The Professor didn't have a drink, so I didn't order one even though he offered multiple times to get one for me. My anxiety used to kick in if I was the only person drinking…even if it was a nonalcoholic beverage. I wish I had ordered a hot coffee or tea to feel somewhat armed. I often wonder what I would have done if I had a hot coffee or tea in my hand as he professed his secret to me. I probably would've thrown it in his face, but I may have felt more secure had I ordered a hot beverage to arm myself with.

I hope that's what I would've done, but I'd honestly just use it as a comfort point, somewhere to lay my hands, something solid and stable to hold on to while my insides went off.

He had just published a novel, and as a future published author, myself, I wanted to pick his brain. I was there for business and a brief catch up, leaving out many details of my personal life. All I really wanted to know was what his writing process looked like and how he went about publishing his book.

I admired him, trusted him, and confided in him. I looked up to him both as a wise guide and literally as he stood several inches taller than me and carried extra weight in his belly.

After general hellos, I went on to tell him how much I loved Chicago and told him that I was just passing through town for the next couple of days before I headed to Atlanta for Easter.

It was a beautiful March day in St. Louis. I had on a turquoise sweater with a pink three-quarter-sleeve shirt underneath it. I wore jeans and converse sneakers, but it didn't matter what the fuck I was wearing. Does it ever really matter what you wear before or while you're assaulted? No, it fucking does not. In no way is a person ever asking to be assaulted by the clothes they choose to wear. It's probably truer that they are wearing what they're wearing for themselves. And I believe that there wouldn't be a shirt worn on purpose by any person with the words "Assault Me, please."

He told me he had to tell me something. He got very serious. So serious I truly thought he was going to tell me he was dying.

"I love you, Ally," he said.

My heart started pounding faster, and my initial thought was that he loved me the way a mentor loves a mentee—the love a teacher has for their students, the love a coach has for their team. At least that is the version I went with. So, I replied, "Yeah, okay. Love ya, too."

He softened yet perked up a bit as he said, "You do?" in a surprised and hopeful tone, one that told me I needed to get the fuck out of there as soon as possible.

"I'm in love with you," he said next.

He didn't fall in love with me at that moment. He fell in love with me while I was an undergrad student. He fell in love with me in his classes. Classes in which I wore soccer clothes. Classes in which I had just come from practice without changing my clothes, only clouding my outside sweaty odor with a Febreeze shower.

He had been waiting for *his moment.* He HAD to wait. He had to wait until I was no longer a student where he worked. He knew that. He knew exactly what he was doing.

I was coy about my departure. Even though I could've outrun his nearly sixty-five-year-old ass, my instinct told me to leave slowly. Ironically, I did not run.

He insisted on walking me to my car. Insisted. My car sat in a spot several yards from the entrance. It was broad daylight. I told him that "It's okay; I can walk myself." *CLEARLY. I can fucking walk myself.* But he insisted yet again.

Five seconds later, we got to my car, a 2014 Ford Escape. I opened the back door on the driver's side and tossed my bag in. Later, realizing that it was a dumb move to turn my back on this man, I then made a mental note to never turn my back fully when putting items in the car. To this day, that rule remains.

I turned around as the door shut, noticing that he stepped so close to me that I'd run into him. My back was now against the car because there was nowhere else for me to go. I said goodbye and tried to wedge my way away from him. I couldn't move much though.

He then pulled me in for way too long of a hug. He slowly released his grip and moved it to where he held both of my arms at the biceps. A grip that was way too tight. He stared into my eyes. I clenched my keys in my fist so tight that a tiny scratch on my finger later revealed itself.

I opened my mouth to say another firm goodbye, hoping he'd finally let me go. Before any words escaped my mouth, his beard scratched my face, and his tongue entered my mouth while he pressed his big belly against my toned torso. My back was heating up from my black car sitting in the sun for the last hour. The door handle pressed into my lumbar spine.

I didn't kiss him back. I thought of biting his tongue, but I was practically choking on his and couldn't make any minor movements, let alone fighting ones. I was just trying to breathe and not let his unwanted touch suffocate me.

I may have been breathing, but my body was frozen, the opposite of what played out in my mind as thoughts swarmed through it:

Please do not push me into this fucking car.

Please do not push me into this fucking car.

Please do not push me into this fucking car.

I was shocked.

Please let this be the worst of it.

Well, that was the worst of the unwanted tonsil hockey, but dealing with it and the ramifications that followed were worse and longer than the few minutes he clutched onto me. Right there in the middle of a Starbucks parking lot. In the middle of the fucking afternoon on a Tuesday.

From the time he professed his love to me to getting back in my car, less than fifteen minutes had passed.

After I got in my car, I watched him walk to his car, which was noticeably further away, at least a hundred yards from the Starbucks parking lot. So much further, in fact, that it was in a completely DIFFERENT parking lot. He purposefully parked there. Like I said, he knew EXACTLY what he was doing and what he was going to do that day. *You, bitch.*

This was the same professor who took me on a private tour of Lindenwood when it was on my list for grad school. Occasionally, I think of what might have happened if I had ended up as his student for another three years. I'm so grateful that I'll never know.

I let him start his car and drive away first. Once I felt safe enough that he wouldn't follow me, I still didn't leave right away. I just sat in the car, replaying the last hour of my life. Dumbfounded.

When I finally looked at the time, I still had two hours until I was meeting two friends and former teammates for dinner. So, I drove to the cemetery, crossing my fingers I wouldn't come across any humans. I only wanted to talk to the spirits that I couldn't see. To the spirits I could only feel.

I parked near my grandpa's grave but didn't get out. I rolled all the windows down, turned the car off, and listened. It was a beautiful day, but bad things still happen on beautiful days.

It was quiet except for the birds chirping, rustling branches in the wind, and cars driving by on the road just over a nearby hill. A few deep breaths later, I got out of the car and walked to my grandpa's grave.

Some pennies and a few jolly ranchers sat on the ledge above his headstone. He loved jolly ranchers and always had some with him. Blue raspberry was his favorite. It's mine, too.

I don't know how long I sat with him that day, but I didn't cry because I wasn't sad. I was angry and shocked, and I had every right to be. He knew exactly what he was going to do. It was not until long after I left that I realized he could have easily pushed me into my car and put so much more than his tongue inside me.

So, I just sat with my grandpa for a little while, praying that I'd get through the personal consequences a real scary and gross twelve minutes can bring to someone when it wasn't even their fault.

I wasn't planning on saying anything to Alyssa and Michelle at dinner, and I woke up that morning with the intention of not drinking. I wasn't sure if I should tell anyone, but after we ordered our food and sat down, I spoke up. I couldn't just sit there and pretend that this gross thing happened to me less than a few hours ago.

They may not have been as shocked as I was, but they couldn't believe it. It would've helped if they knew the exact professor it was, but we were all different majors and never had any of the same classes. Plus, that professor wasn't full time. He was an adjunct. Regardless, I'm glad I had some people there right after it happened.

Dinner went by too fast, though, and the last place I wanted to go was home. My mom was out, and my dad was traveling and wouldn't be back until the next night. I didn't want to be alone. So, I texted an old coworker, Bobby, and shortly after, I was in his basement drinking beer in his house on The Hill, St. Louis' Italian neighborhood.

As I drank with him, I told him what had happened earlier. Bobby was my escape from my realty. He was my go-to companion to pass the time the previous year before I moved to Chicago.

He was the only man I *think* I had fun sleeping with, but I was also almost always under the influence of weed and/or alcohol anytime we had sex. Four beers and some buzzed sex later, I chugged some water and headed home, not knowing this would be the last time I would ever see him. Bobby didn't die or anything. We just grew apart, and I think we both knew that our time together was never for the long run.

Bobby was much older than me, but the professor could've been my grandpa. Is it fucked up I slept with an older man after the whole senior citizen kissing me in a parking lot thing?

Maybe. I'm not ashamed of it though. I knew what I was doing there.

I knew exactly why, even though I didn't admit it until draft four of this book. I wanted a distraction. I wanted to forget what happened, and Bobby gave me that for a couple of hours.

Hoping the evening full of beers and sex would put me to sleep as soon as I got home, I took one look at my childhood bedroom and knew I wouldn't be sleeping in there that night…if I would even be able to fall asleep at all.

I hadn't been a child in some time, and sleeping in my bedroom that night felt like he would have tainted part of my childhood even though he wasn't a part of it.

Bobby was only a distraction for the time I was with him. I laid on the couch of my parents living room, eyes wide open. Alone with my thoughts. I considered grabbing more beer to wash them out—the repetition of asking myself *what the fuck?* as I replayed that coffee rendezvous from twelve hours earlier over and over again.

Memories of my nineteenth summer started flying in my mind. I specifically remembered the infomercials at 3 a.m. playing when I couldn't sleep. The repetition of them calms me. Remembering their soothing effect, I walked into the hearth room, where the first floor TV was. I turned on the TV and found an infomercial almost immediately, one that advertised one of those ab chairs where you extend your entire body and then move it forward for the crunch. After a couple of hours of staring at that, I moseyed back into the living room and sat on the couch, eyes staring forward but fixated on nothing but the darkness of the room.

It was almost 5 a.m. as I wrapped a blanket around me and sat in the dark, finding comfort that the dark and empty room matched what I was starting to feel on the inside once again. I couldn't tell that it had started to get lighter, though—darkness so heavy that it could not see the sun.

It was a feeling I felt not too long ago: my light started to fade away despite the sunrise just around the corner.

I dozed off for an hour or so and then was woken up by the sound of my mother in the kitchen making coffee. I walked into the kitchen with the blanket still wrapped around me and asked her to pour me a cup. Heidi walked over, the nudge of her nose on my leg as her way to say good morning.

Something in her eyes told me she knew. She always knew.

"How'd you sleep?" my mom asked.

Mom already knew the answer to that. I may not have slept on the couch many times, but when I did, it wasn't because I felt that it would've been comfier than my actual bed.

"Not well," I replied.

Most of that day was a blur until later that night when my mom and I went to a restaurant up the street from my high school. We had some time to burn before picking my dad up at the airport.

Before I told her what happened the previous night, I told the bartender: "I'm gonna need a drink. Budweiser. Draft." I finished it within minutes, and before I ordered the next, the bartender was already on it. He must have been listening to my story.

"Something happened yesterday..." I told her what happened, and she was just as shocked and pissed as I was.

Mom replied, "I was wondering why you slept on the couch last night."

Sure, I cried a bit because of what he did, but I mostly cried for the truth that couldn't stay hidden anymore. I cried for the fear he unlocked. I cried for the feelings he made me feel, and I knew I needed to make some hard choices. I cried out of anger because his assault on me made me never want to feel like a cis-man ever again. Not one forcing himself on me. Not one on me at all.

It felt as if each tear was a part of me starting to unhide. This time, though, instead of feeling like I was drowning, it was as though an empty lake started to fill, helping me rise back to the surface. As the tears came, I felt myself start to submerge in the truth. The words I had been running from started becoming as clear as the sky after a summer storm. The words came at me faster than a flash flood.

I am absolutely not straight.

Before those words were spoken into existence, however, they were just strung together as a fleeting thought. And before I chose to say them out loud, I drank. And before the biggest choice was made, I made some other questionable decisions. I still tried to drink the gay away, and I still tried to run away from coming out. I suppose I could call the next two months a victory lap.

I cried because in order to get to my true self and let her out, I had to admit certain things. I directed my anger toward him, and when I felt too much of the anger, of the sadness, of any of it, I drank. I came out because I was angry.

I cried for the months that followed because I knew they would be hard, scary, and lonely, and I didn't want to face them. I cried for the unknown, for the time when the truth would eventually come out. I cried because I had to face my fears, and I didn't want to, but I knew I needed to.

It'd be a few more years before Glennon Doyle started telling us that, yes, WE CAN DO HARD THINGS, but I wasn't so sure before then. The tears of fear were camouflaged, though, as the drunk tears of a beautiful, young, straight-passing white woman.

In May 2019, a story about another Webster student who was sexually harassed by a different professor from the gaming design department was published in the Riverfront Times, a local newspaper covering arts, culture, local news, and more. The student rallied and stood up for herself with the support of many others. She filed complaints multiple times.

Over a two-year period, nothing happened.

I wrote an official letter to the president of Webster demanding there be something done. I also gave a statement and filed a complaint with the school's Title IX office regarding my own incident, having felt empowered by the other student's situation.

I was told they couldn't do much because I was no longer a student, and I wasn't a student at the time of the assault. But, they said, at least they had it on record if and when he did this again, and that student spoke up, too. While I hope there are not others on *his* list, I know there are other survivors of assault. Thousands of us. Please speak up. In the words of the late, great Audre Lorde: "Your silence will not protect you."

That quote plays a profound role in my writing today, as well. Who am I to stay silent? I need to speak up if I want to heal. I must speak up if I want to meet my future self. I must speak up to help others.

I had been angry about what he did for a very long time. So angry that before I could punch or hit or pinch or even cut myself about it, and sometimes I did do those things, I'd reach for a drink instead.

A few years after the assault took place, I made a promise to myself: if I ever saw him again face-to-face, I would confront him.

Even though I have forgiven him, the anger still remains. Even though the anger is a mere needle in a haystack now compared to the bushel of needles it once was.

I thought I had let go of the anger completely, but I hadn't realized I was still angry until I ran into him at my local Costco in September of 2022.

I was living with my parents at the time, and I stopped there on my way home from lunch with a friend. Much like the day of the assault, the sun was shining, and the temperatures were warm. It was a beautiful day.

I only needed four things that day: gas, toothbrush heads, seafood, and milk. As I picked out my fish, I turned and walked towards the dairy fridge. And there he was, looking right at me but standing several yards away. He didn't recognize me.

He was with a woman, soon to be confirmed as his wife. They turned down another aisle, now parallel to where I stood. My hands shook as I grasped the cart handle and slowly pushed myself forward. My heart rate was through the roof. My mouth as dry as a dessert. Tingles of heat shooting up and down on the edge of my skin.

I pushed the cart forward and made eye contact with another woman nearby. She didn't pick up on my demeanor. I continued to the dairy fridge and casually checked the milk cartons. I learned many things that day, including that Costco milk is only a gallon. I always thought they were larger because the container is taller!

Anyway, for a brief moment, I tried to ignore the screams within me. Grateful for the chill of the dairy fridge, I set down the gallon of milk and said to myself: *this is my chance. This is my opportunity.*

I picked the milk jug back up and placed it in the cart. With my shoulders further back than they had been in months—years maybe—I marched out of the dairy fridge and back into the store to go find his ass so I could kick it…verbally.

You're okay. You can do this. You're okay. Just breathe. You got this. Just breathe.

There was no time to rehearse or go through the speech I would've liked to give him, the one I practiced dozens of times in my head while walking up and down the streets of Chicago on my way to work or class or shows.

I walked back through the seafood and meat section and headed toward the front of the store. Less than thirty steps later, the same number of steps it took to get from the entrance of that Starbucks to my car, I saw him again. He was in the clothing section this time, right between the socks and the sweatshirts. I took another deep breath and pushed myself forward once more. I turned into the aisle. He along with his cart were facing mine.

I stopped just before our carts touched and stared at him. He tilted his head to the side and said, "Do I—do I know you?" I nodded slowly, not breaking eye contact.

"From where?"

"From Webster," I said, strong and cool.

"Were you in one of my classes? Come on, help me out. I'm old." I didn't reply. I let him keep guessing.

"Were you in group communications? You were in group!"

"Yes, I was," I said. And a few other classes, too, but I didn't say that.

"Are you going to tell me your name?"

I took my hat off, revealing my much shorter hair from the last time he had seen me in person, nearly seven years earlier.

He stared at me for several seconds, then his jaw fell, his mouth wide open, just like the last time he was in front of me. There were only two things keeping me from ramming my cart into his. 1. I was still shaking so hard that I felt if I had maneuvered the cart in any other position other than standing still with my feet on the ground, then I would lose control of what he could see. I didn't want him to see how badly I shook. 2. Ever since soccer ended and my laundry list of health issues started, I choose to fight with my words and not my arthritic wrists. There is power in silence. There is power in not raising your voice. My inner Miranda Presley took over. The cold, unwelcoming tone of my voice was louder than any added volume. I took my time with the cadence of my voice, as well.

"Oh my god," he finally said. "Are you back in St. Louis? Why did you move back?" "That's not important," I said.

"When's the last time we saw each other?"

It was here that I noticed the woman behind him browsing the socks.

"We had coffee. We had coffee," he continued. Well, no, but we did meet at a Starbucks.

"Yeah, and you made a pass at me," I fired back.

"I did. And you never spoke to me again."

"You shouldn't have done that. It was wrong and you shouldn't have done that. You really, really should not have done that. I have forgiven you, but that doesn't mean what you did was right or okay. It was NOT okay."

"I'm sorry," he said nonchalantly without the presence of anger or remorse in his tone. It sounded neutral. He averted eye contact after saying, 'I'm.' I noticed his shoulders slightly dropped but then went back up when his eyes met mine again.

He wasn't sorry. It was one of those *I'm Sorry's* you say when it's the *right* or *appropriate* thing to say in a situation. If he were truly sorry, he would've reached out years ago.

"Okay," I said.

"Is there any else?" he asked.

"No, not really."

Assuming he felt a sense of her behind him, he then gestured to the woman and said, "Oh, this is my wife."

"I don't care," I replied.

"Do you want to meet her?"

"Seriously? No, I do not want to meet your *wife*," I said still not breaking eye contact.

A long moment of silence ensued as we stared each other in the eyes.

"Okay, then," he started and then his voice shifted five octaves to anger. "Can you please move then so I can get by?"

I rolled my eyes, turned my cart around, and beelined toward the registers but not at a pace that would attract attention to myself. My heart rate was still amplified. The sweat from my palms started to loosen my grip on the handle of the cart.

I eyed each checkout line, one longer than the next. I hurried toward the self-checkout area on the far right, notably furthest from the exit. I walked up to the only open register. A female worker stood next to it and smiled at me. I half smiled and diverted eye contact, not knowing that she was soon to become the second hero of this part in my story.

I looked behind myself cautiously as I scanned in my items. My hands still shook. The young woman asked, "Are you okay?" If I had to guess, I'd say she was in her early twenties.

I nodded, and said, "Yeah, I'm okay."

A few seconds passed and I recanted, "Actually, no. I'm not okay. The man that assaulted me is in the store, and I just ran into him."

"Oh my gosh. I'm so sorry. Do you want me to walk you out to your car?"

"No. No. He's not going to do anything, plus I'm pretty sure he's still shopping."

"Are you sure?"

"Yes, but thank you."

"Well, if you change your mind, let someone know at the front of the store, and they'll walk with you."

"I will. Thank you so much."

I finished ringing up my items, paid and walked toward the exit, only looking back once more before entering the parking lot. I turned left toward where my car was parked.

You're okay. You're okay. You're okay. I repeated to myself until I was safely in my car with the bought items in the trunk.

"Holy shit. I can't believe I just did that," I said to myself out loud. "You're okay."

I took several deep breaths and did a full body check in. My heart rate slowed down. My hands steadied. *You're okay enough to drive home.*

I stared and looked around the parking lot where I sat. I was shocked not only by running into him but by actually confronting him…in public nonetheless! But I was proud that I did so and kept that promise to myself that if I ever saw him again, I would say something.

I started the car and drove out of the parking spot. As most Costco parking lots, this one was huge, and as I turned right onto the next road that would lead me toward the highway, much of the lot was still to my right.

And there he was again, standing next to what I presumed was his car, in the middle of yet another parking lot on yet another weekday afternoon. He was looking around, waiting, and looking for someone. Unfortunately, he didn't see my middle finger in the air directed toward him as I drove behind him.

I focused on my breathing until I felt that I didn't need to anymore. I drove to my next errand: getting my eyebrows waxed. I paid in cash and was given a $10 bill in return. I told the nail tech to keep it, giving her a 100% tip. I needed to do a good deed. I needed to remind myself that goodness was possible in this ugly world.

I texted my mom to call me after her meeting, and she did after I had just gotten my eyebrows waxed. I told her what happened, and she told me she was proud of me. And then went on to say that she would've lit his ass up in Costco if she had been there.

My dad called the encounter an omen—a good one for me and a bad one for the Professor. I call it a gift from the universe, a meet-cute with a higher version of myself.

It was a beautiful day, and it was not just because of the gorgeous weather. It was a beautiful day because it was the day that I took back my power.

I didn't realize that's what I was doing when I confronted him until a few days later when my somewhat new therapist told me that's exactly what I did. I took back control. I took back my power.

I spent the next week baffled at how far I'd come. Baffled that I kept and followed through on my promise to myself all those years ago. Baffled that I wasn't immediately obsessed with this new version of myself, who I am still getting to know to this day. At that moment, I was incredibly proud of myself and felt a power that I'd never felt before.

Confronting those who've wronged me is something still very fresh in my daily, weekly activities. Speaking out loud about my feelings is not what I am used to. I am used to running, fleeing in the opposite direction. Fleeing to distraction after distraction.

Not anymore. But I'm still a work in progress.

That confrontation was the result of nearly six and a half years of inner work, persistence, therapy, self-love, and becoming.

It wasn't okay and will never be okay that he did that. And now, when I think about that hour at a coffee shop in the middle of a workweek (holy week, too, mind you!), anger is not my initial response. I was done being angry and started to feel proud of what I went through shortly before my twenty-fourth birthday. Of course, I had help and support along the way, but I owe the strength I gained to myself and myself only. It was because of me choosing to show up for myself and my mental health every day. The strength of surviving 100% of my worst days belongs to me and only me.

I'm not that angry anymore, but I do, however, have two more things to say to you, Professor. One: I forgive you…mostly. I forgive you in resentment, but forgiven in anger specifically? I'm not completely there just yet.

And two:

FUCK YOU.

According to the academic-sexual-misconduct-database, the gaming design professor at Webster ended up resigning in 2019. At the time of *I'm Gay and Drink Water's* publication, the Professor that assaulted me remains employed by both Webster University and Lindenwood University.

I didn't press charges against the Professor because it never crossed my mind. Shock, not retaliation overcame me. Shock then turned into anger, and anger eventually turned into this book.

No one asked me if I pressed charges or had evidence until I filed a complaint with the University's Title IX office. The only thing that I thought of finding was security footage, but that was a long shot.

Pressing charges was another uphill battle that I didn't want to climb. There was no evidence, even if he admitted to what he did. I knew how it would play out: it would be my word against his, without proof and knowing how sexual assault cases are handled in this country from A. Being a woman in America and B. Spending dozens and dozens of hours of research on sexual assault, I knew not much good would come from pressing charges. I know how it would've played out. The system is fucked.

CHAPTER XLII

The ending of my story is triumphant, but to say the least, I was a hot mess in the weeks that followed the assault.

I tried to throw myself into my schoolwork after the assault in March 2016, but it was harder and harder to distract myself in the weeks that followed. School was not a strong enough distraction—nothing compared to booze.

I felt lost. Confused. Heavy. Tired. Angry. I drank almost every day of the next thirty after The Professor forced himself on me. Any time I didn't feel hungover, I was drinking again.

I confided in one of my grad school professors, and I believe I was right to trust him with my story. He can be trusted. He apologized for what happened and told me to "lay off the sauce."

I said, "Okay."

I heard him, but I didn't accept his advice. Not yet, at least.

On my twenty-fourth birthday, all I wanted was to grab some beer and a burger and watch the Blues hockey game with my brother. He said he'd be by to pick me up at 5 or 5:30 that afternoon.

He called me just before 5…from the back of an ambulance.

My brother had a severe allergic reaction and was being rushed to the hospital. What hospital? I didn't know. He didn't get that info out before the call was dropped. All he told me was that he wasn't good and that he wasn't going to be able to hang out.

After a quick call to my dad, I got the information I needed and then hailed a cab. $100+, and fifty minutes later, I was walking into the hospital in an area outside of the city where I had never been. I found him in a semi-private room in the ER. He was shaking and sweating but cold to the touch.

I filled out the necessary paperwork, drove his car back into the city, picked up some items from his apartment, drove them back to the hospital, and then said goodnight. I got home with about thirty minutes left of my birthday. For dinner, I ate the only ready-to-eat food in my apartment: carrots and hummus. Then I went to bed.

He was not released until the next night, leaving me twenty-four hours for my mind to freely spiral into anxiety.

Two nights after he was admitted, we were finally at a bar watching another hockey game, and I got all the beer I wanted plus the burger. My anxiety was washed out temporarily by the beer. I didn't think about the anxiety that would come the day after an evening of drinking.

Less than a week later, I met a couple of friends for happy hour. I showed up in a skirt, ankle boots, a crop top, and an angry attitude—an outfit too fancy for a Wednesday night out and a mindset that should never be a reason to drink. I ordered an Uber on my way out the door.

Ever since the assault, I'd become hyper aware of my surroundings. So, as a white man pulled up in a silver Toyota Camry, I texted my friends a screenshot of the driver and car with my estimated time of arrival. I was ten minutes away. I was paranoid that anyone knew where I lived. I was paranoid of all my surroundings when I should've been checking in with myself more than checking in on the world around me.

I made sure to sit behind the driver's seat so it wouldn't be as easy for him to attack me directly. I held my keys in my left hand, with the biggest key end sticking out. I should have taken the bus, but it was warmer that day, and I didn't want to ruin my hair and makeup by commuting via public transit or by walking.

I got in the car. The driver turned right onto Madison Street, going east. He turned the music down and spoke.

"Ms. Ally?"

"Uh, yeah?"

"Are you a runner?"

"Yes." *Been one my whole life.*

"Oh good. Good. Your legs are so nice and long. Girls' night?"

"Something like that."

"You're gorgeous," he replied as he moved the mirror to where he could see me. He winked, parted his lips briefly and licked them.

You've got to be fucking kidding me. "Can you pull over please?" I asked.

"We're almost there."

"Pull over!" I growled.

Once stopped, I got out of the car and walked the rest of the way to the bar. Fortunately, I only had to walk a couple of blocks.

I didn't use Uber again for years after that. It wasn't the first time I had been harassed in one and wouldn't be the last. I turned around to make sure he was not following me. Not that it mattered; he knew where I was heading anyway.

There I was again—heading to a bar with a heated head. It was the best and quickest fix I knew. It was convenient. It was my only answer to feeling better for a while.

That night, I learned that a lot of places give women free drinks to keep them there. The night was slow, and not overly crowded, so my friends and I had many eyes on us as we occupied the corner of the bar.

Whatever I asked for, I got except water. I asked for water several times. Each time, I was given more to drink and convinced to drink that instead.

We left to go to another bar, where we met a random group of guys visiting Chicago on business. They were young, maybe mid to late twenties. I connected with one of them. I was totally trashed but accepted any drink he offered me.

At some point earlier in the night, I texted Charlie, a friend from my graduate program. After several messages of protest from him regarding coming to help me home, he showed up at the second bar. He was concerned and had every right to be. That wasn't the first time he showed up for me.

A few weeks earlier, I had wanted to feel something—anything aside from the numbness that alcohol coated me in.

I told Charlie what I was going to do. He insisted on coming over and I protested. I was asking for help but didn't really want it at the same; no, I really did want it but couldn't bring myself to say it directly. Charlie didn't give me a choice and told me he was coming over.

Before he got there, I took a knife from my kitchen knife set, a small bright green one, and dug it into my wrist.

I'm the only one who knows exactly where the scar is. I'm the only one who knows the groove there now was not one I was born with.

That night, a few weeks later, Charlie showed up for me again in the bar. The guy who'd invited me to his hotel left without me, and I instantly feel the urge to run after him. So, I did. I shoved myself past Charlie and into the back of a taxi. A few minutes later, it drove right by my apartment. Literally right in front of it.

I told myself: *Go home, Ally! Go upstairs and stay there. Tell them to stop.*

We drove beyond my building and got on the highway.

You can still go home. Tell him to turn this car around right now. It's not too late. Why are you doing this?

I didn't listen. I didn't speak up. I was on my way to make another bad decision. I was running as hard as ever before. I was on my way to prove that I could be just like the girls society favors. Although society is more accepting of queer people today and was growing to be more accepting at that time, the narrative was still very much that queer folks were othered and estranged from society. I was doing what I always did, convincing the world, convincing myself, that I did belong—that I was one of those girls.

The taxi pulled up in front of a hotel near O'Hare airport. I got out and strutted inside like I owned the place, except no one was there to see me. It was a weeknight. It was late. A little after 1 a.m.

I took the escalator up to the second floor. From there, I took a few steps toward the elevators. As I was about to press the button to go up, the guy from the bar exited one of the elevator cars. He looked tired, but his expression was kind. He put his arm around my waist and guided me into the elevator.

When we got to his room, I told him I didn't want to have sex. He said, "Okay. We won't have sex." I had followed him, really, because I just didn't want to be by myself when I got home, but minutes later, I felt his dick inside my vagina after slurring to him, "okay why not?"

After only seconds of him inside me, I pushed myself off him and walked into the bathroom. The door was odd. The bathroom was a perfect oval, and the door opened and closed on a swivel. Once I finished peeing, I leaned against the wall and slid down it. For a brief moment, I was relieved to have found the comfort of yet another cold bathroom floor.

I pulled out my phone and opened my email. I typed an email to The Good Professor, who told me to lay off the sauce just the week before. I hit send, and my phone died. If the message actually sent, I did not know until hours later.

I started crying and got up to leave, only to return a minute later because I left my glasses on the nightstand. I am thankful I remembered those because a. I couldn't afford a new pair of glasses and b. I loved those glasses. I looked fantastic in them.

If he tried to help me, I wouldn't let him. I didn't want him anywhere near me. One thing I actually don't remember for once is his name or face. He texted me the following day to see if I was okay. I lied and said that I was.

As I stumbled outside to the circle driveway of the hotel, the sun started to rise. There was a distinct chill in the air like most spring mornings in Chicago. I hoped to leave behind that night and forget what happened, but like almost every drunken night prior, I remembered almost everything.

There was not a soul in sight, so I slurred loudly, "What's a girl gotta do to get a cab around here?"

A valet appeared like an angel and said he'd get one for me. Minutes later, a taxi van was in front of me. I struggled to open the door. Once I was inside, I mumbled my address and prayed that my credit card went through when we get there.

It was 5:30 a.m. I was supposed to be at work forty-five minutes prior. *What a piece of shit I am. I'll probably get fired. I deserve to get fired. I hope I'm not, though. I need what every little bit of money I can get. I am still very, very drunk.*

I tried my best not to fall asleep in the cab, but my head bobbed up and down with the slow rocking of the vehicle in the stop and go traffic of an early weekday morning southbound on I-

90.

I don't think I have enough energy to fight off this cabbie if he were to try and take advantage of me. About thirty minutes later, the cab pulled in front of my building.

I swiped my credit card and paid with a tip, holding my breath. *Phew.* It went through.

I finally got into my apartment. It's a miracle I didn't lose my phone or keys that night. All I wanted to do was sleep, but I did not deserve to sleep. I deserved to be awake to feel every ounce of dumb shit that I had done…again. I plugged in my phone immediately and changed my clothes. Once my phone popped back on, I texted my co-workers and emailed my boss poorly explaining my absence. *I'll deal with the repercussions of that later. One problem at a time.*

My biggest problem right then was desperately wanting to make the Wall go away. I also didn't want to be alone. Thus began the hour-long drunken telethon. I wanted someone to hear me. I wanted someone to tell me I didn't have to drink alcohol anymore. I never wanted to feel the Wall or be near it ever again.

I sobbed through the phone to family and friends—my parents, my sister, a trusted family friend, and my therapist—looking to run away from myself by seeking external influences and knowing that every ounce of this drunk stupor was about to turn into a terrible, depressive, weeklong hangover. I knew I couldn't run away from that, and I knew drinking more wouldn't solve anything right then…or ever. I was searching for a quick fix to calm me down. Anything. But I found myself doing something I hadn't done in a long time. I found myself listening.

My therapist was the last person I called that morning. By the time I hung up with her, I decided I'd finally had enough. For real this time.

I was incapable of blacking out. If I continued drinking, I would've most likely been left with more drunken memories that I couldn't escape. They are in me forever. They are never going anywhere, I've even immortalized them to exist after I die…because I've written this book and all.

I do not want to keep living with the memories of being drunk. Alcohol has brought nothing good into my life. Why do I keep doing this to myself? How did I get here? How did I let this happen?!? I moved here for a purpose. If I keep this up, then it's goodbye to grad school and hello to living a life of drunkenness or dying from drinking. I cannot keep sabotaging my future by repeatedly drinking when I cannot cope with current issues that arise.

Just after 7:30 in the morning on April 20, 2016, I laid in front of my floor length mirror in my studio apartment by myself and pushed myself up as far as my body would let me. I looked at the person staring back at me: Puffy eyed. Depressed. Tired. Twenty-four-year-old Ally.

Oh, God. I was so fucking tired. Tired of doing this drunk shit. Tired of feeling like shit. Tired of being so fucking tired. I was in a place I desperately did not want to be. I'd been there before and was so afraid I'd keep landing myself back there again. I didn't ever want to be back there ever again.

So, I pressed my hands further into the floor and sat up a little further, even though I ached as the hangover had already landed. Through tears, I looked at myself in the mirror and said, "I can't do this anymore. I am done. You are done."

And just like that hot summer day in the garage five years earlier, something whispered back to me…

"Get up, Ally. Get the fuck back up."

So, I did.

CHAPTER XLIII

I still felt like I was hiding when I started coming out as bisexual. I felt I was ready to stop hiding…at least a little bit. Coming out as bisexual wasn't so much for me but more so for the story I wanted to tell for that thesis. Whatever my reason, though, it was a pivotal moment in the direction of whole truth.

A few weeks into sobriety, I had to give a pitch for my thesis film script in front of my class. That morning, I was going over the notes for my pitch. As I said each word in my floor length mirror, I watched my lips telling my story. The feature length drama I wrote was about a college soccer play who presses charges after being sexually assaulted by the head coach.

Something sounded off as the words left my mouth. Something was missing from my unique point of view. Something that needed to be said to connect myself to this story more.

I went to the gym to clear my mind. I hopped on the treadmill with my headphones blasting the music of a random Spotify playlist. My skin began to sweat about half a mile into my run.

I looked around at the other gym members, briefly wondering what their stories were. We all have a story to tell. I wondered how many of them have told or will tell theirs, whatever they may be. I asked myself: *Who do I want to be? What do I want my story to be? Why this thing? Why now? Why me?*

I decided I wanted to be someone who spoke up. I was someone who had become so sick of hiding and not fully talking about my feelings. I had started trying with my new therapist, and while that was hard, I was making progress. Even with the difficulty of speaking out loud, I wanted to speed things up. The impatience in me wanted to fast forward to being more outspoken. My thesis class was a safe environment to start doing so outside of my therapist's office.

I had always felt safe in the environment of grad school at DePaul. The professors were welcoming, enthusiastic, topnotch in their craft, and above all else, kind. It was a place where we were encouraged and supported to explore and experiment our stories. My thesis professor, told us many times to answer these three questions when deciding on a story to write:

1. Why this thing?
2. Why now?
3. Why me?

I was the second or third person to pitch in class that night, and after I went over the plot, I said, "As a survivor of sexual assault and as a bisexual woman, I feel that this story is important and needs to be told."

I swallowed hard after announcing I was bisexual. Even as I was saying the word bisexual, it felt like a lie. I was proud of myself for saying I was anything other than straight. Some of that glass wall I mentioned earlier had evaporated, but I swallowed some of it, too, which was then sitting in my gut, nicking it.

I assumed I was bisexual because I had slept with both men and women...well, one woman. I'm not the best at math, but putting that together, I concluded bisexual was the logical solution. However, I only enjoyed sex with women, and 90% of the time I slept with a man, I was high and/or drunk. Saying those words out loud, "As a bisexual woman..." sounded far away, like it was underwater or someone else was saying it behind a door not fully open nor closed. Ajar.

It was another lie, but it was closer to the truth. And I knew it was a lie because saying it was too easy. But it would become harder to say the more I said it. After school ended for the summer, the pit in my stomach remained. I quit drinking; I kinda came out, so why wasn't I feeling better yet?

I started asking myself more questions: *when was the last time I was happy and my true self in a romantic relationship...and with sex?*

I silently answered: *Lauren.*

Less than sixty days after I quit drinking, I finally admitted to myself that I am not straight. I am gay. The acceptance of that admission came right after. Like I solved a twenty-four-year-long puzzle.

Quitting alcohol was a major puzzle piece in putting the pieces of my true self together. Alcohol covered up a huge part of myself that was vital to reaching my highest self. The only way to reveal the higher parts of me was to quit the thing that was masking them, suppressing them. Not that I blame alcohol. I was the one making the choice to drink, but I was also the one that made the choice to stop.

The more sober I became, the more memories became clearer. I'd been gay that whole fucking time. I remembered things I hadn't thought of in years…

I was eight years old. It was a weekend afternoon, and my family and I went out to run errands. At the end of these shopping trips, if my brother and I were lucky, we'd stop to rent a movie on the way home at the neighborhood Blockbuster, but only if it wasn't too late.

We were on the highway heading toward the mall. Dad was driving, and Mom sat shotgun. My brother sat in the passenger seat, and I sat behind the driver's seat.

It was quiet until I broke the silence by asking, "Mom, am I gay?"

She replied, "Well…um…are there boys on TV that you think are cute?"

"Yeah."

"Then you're not gay, sweetie."

I love my mother, and I'm sure she was shocked that her little girl asked this without warning in the spring of 2000. Maybe what they really meant was Y2GAY, not Y2K.

To this day, I still think guys are cute on TV and IRL but that doesn't mean I am attracted to them. The feeling of feeling different still lingered inside me despite trying my best to believe my mom. When you're eight years old, though, at least in my experience, adults are the ones with all the answers.

Nowadays, my style reflects how I feel. Some days, it's more masculine, and other days, it's more feminine. But when I was a kid, I was a total tomboy who, at times, was proudly mistaken for a boy. However, on many occasions, I wore the dresses my mom bought for me. I didn't hate them, but I honestly didn't want to think about my style. It was easier to say yes and be grateful for whatever clothes were put on my back.

I did not know how to stand up for myself as a child, either. It took decades for me to learn that. The only place I ever felt I could fight and argue without societal or parental repercussions is on the soccer field. Fighting with and sticking up for your team is acceptable in sports. It is praised.

Fighting for your truth off the field, alone, as you've witnessed in my story so far, is a hard pass out of bounds.

My mom remembers me asking this question differently. She remembers me asking during dinner one evening when my dad was out of town.

In the kitchen, we had a small, boxy, white TV in the corner where the two counters met. When the USWNT was in the World Cup Finals in July 1999, we brought the TV on the deck, and we watched it. I wore my Mia Hamm jersey.

Other than that game, usually one of three things played on that TV: *Young and the Restless*, *The Oprah Winfrey Show* or the News: local or *The Today Show*.

On July 1, 2000, the first state to announce civil unions was Vermont. There was a news segment on this announcement, which expanded into a conversation about same-sex marriage. My mom told me that this was when I asked her if I was gay. Maybe I did. I have no memory of this out of the ordinary dinner conversation, but perhaps I asked her twice.

She was caught off guard and recently told me she wished she had handled that conversation differently and had been more aware. I don't blame her at all; it's not like there was a convenient manual for parents in the 90s whose children questioned their sexuality. I kept a lot to myself when I was a kid. Mostly because I didn't want to get in trouble if I spoke up. Mom says I'm not gay, then I'm not gay.

Sometimes, though, kids and parents are wrong. You know yourself. Don't let anyone else tell you who you are, especially if they are telling you something you are not.

Four short years after asking my mom what my sexual orientation was, we were at another mall on another Saturday. A lot of the time, growing up, most people thought I was shy. But I usually only was when first meeting people.

Ever since I came out of the womb, I studied people and situations long before I opened my mouth. I wasn't necessarily shy. I felt the need to observe the world around me before I decided what to say or who I wanted to be around.

I observed my parents' behavior. My mother always has a purse or wristlet with her.

Always. When I was younger, my dad typically kept his wallet in his back pocket. The older he got, the more he forgot it at home or in the car or brought a credit card to wherever he was going. My mom kept her wallet in whatever purse she used at the time. Two different types of wallets. Two different types of genders. Two different people. Two different heterosexuals. Two completely acceptable ways of carrying a wallet. Not only do I see my dad and brother slip their wallets into their back pocket, but I also occasionally see other women place their wallets in the back pockets of their jeans, too.

It was a fall day, at twelve years old, I was wearing my Busch Soccer Club team jacket. It was an Adidas blue and black track jacket with my number sewn into the sleeve near my wrist. I was obsessed with that jacket. The team was the best in the state then, and I was honored to be on it. Of course, I wore my jacket as much as possible. It had two zip-up pockets and one pocket on the inside. On the bottom, I wore jeans. My wallet at the time matched my jacket. My favorite color was blue, so months before, I easily picked out a blue wallet with a black trim clasped closed by a three-inch Velcro strip. I carried a little bit of cash and every gift card the wallet could hold without sacrificing the grip of the strip. It was practical for the small wallet to be placed in my back pocket. I'd be doing a disservice to the inventor of the back pocket for neglecting its function. I thought it was a subtle way to express myself.

I admired the practicality and freedom of carrying a wallet in my pocket overhauling a purse around. My brother and dad, especially, were not as observant as I am. As soon as we get out of the car, I put my wallet in my back pocket. It was there for over an hour before my dad noticed and said I could not keep my wallet in my back pocket. I asked why, and he said, "that's what dykes do." My brother laughed. My dad said this in a normal tone, with no idea that what he said was so offensive—he meant no harm. I took it as a compliment.

I felt seen by the word *dyke*, but I was also aware that I would need to keep that a secret. The word *dyke* is short for bulldyke...

My favorite word origin that came up when researching the history of the word is that: "the word

Dyke was possibly from Boudicca (Bou-dyke-ah), a Celtic queen who organized a revolt against the Roman Empire in 67 A.D. Boudicca was seen as a threat to the power structure. Later, as its connotation changed to refer to lesbians."

Why yes, I am a queen who organizes revolutions.

I was okay keeping this label to myself because now I knew what *those* women were. Just knowing meant a lot to me.

I made sure to smile at any dyke presenting woman from that day forward. *I see you, girl!* I always wondered if they saw me, too: a baby dyke in the making. I was always only wondering, though. Always keeping quiet and only letting myself present enough to where I would be seen by a gay person but hiding enough that I could also pass as straight.

The word dyke never seemed like a bad thing except for the time someone in high school called me Dyke in my Facebook honesty box. Yeah. Back in the early 2000s, Facebook had something called an honesty box where users could anonymously write to other users. What could possibly be wrong about that?

Seeing Dyke appear in my honesty box stung because I felt that I had been outed. I felt that I would need to try harder to hide. My epically short hair and athleticism didn't help either.

That word has a history of being a homophobic slur toward lesbians, but it was the first term I learned that was more specific than the word gay. Therefore, it holds a special place in my little gay heart.

My parents, along with most people, just assumed I was straight. Society says: "you look and act straight, so you better start looking even more like a hetero and acting like one! We don't want to confuse people!" I find that last sentence humorous. My brother and I are just sixteen months apart, and most people often mistake us for twins. A lot of times, I was mistaken for a boy growing up, and I found this complimentary every time and proudly corrected the person who misgendered me. Even looking like a boy many days growing up, I never thought that made me less of a woman, nor did I ever feel less of a woman dressing like a boy. Boy clothes, soccer clothes, were just so much more comfortable to me than dresses. To this day, I dress for comfort over style, and I'm happy to say that I believe I've found a balance of cute and comfy attire.

Boys get to pee on the side of the house! Why the hell can't I pee outside, too? I find it incredibly inconvenient for my adolescent female self to have to run inside to pee when I could have easily just gone behind one of dozens of bushes outside. All because I don't have a penis. Boys got to whip out their baby dicks and pee wherever, whenever they damn well please, without punishment, but when I did it, I would be frowned upon by my peers but mostly disapproved by the adults around me. I was one of the guys as far as I was concerned. I made up for the lack of peeing outside during childhood when I was in college, drunk and peeing outside during all seasons. And guess what? So did a lot of my other friends who have vaginas.

Homosexuality was never really taught to me, only mentioned briefly at church and then when I learned about the "Don't Ask, Don't Tell" policy in the U.S. Military. The knowledge of that policy left a mark on me that kept me on high alert. Even after its repeal in 2010, I was still on high alert. And by high alert, I mean I mustn't ask, show, or tell my sexuality. I subconsciously internalized it as *girl, you better hide.*

Another instance my young mind did not understand was on one blistering hot summer day. My brother and I, along with our neighborhood crew (all boys), stood on the deck of our house eating popsicles. Each of us wore shorts and T-shirts. We just finished playing a baseball game or capture the flag. Those were our two go-tos. Well, those and flashlight tag, but we only played that at night.

So, we're all eating popsicles. St. Louis summers are hot. Tyler or Mike complained about the heat. Meanwhile, my shirt had become partly tie-dyed in cherry red. One of the boys took off his shirt, and soon, so did the rest of us, myself included. I barely had my shirt above my head when my mom helped me pull it back down. I was confused because, at that time, my chest looked exactly like their chests: flat with two nipples and maybe a third on Mike. I didn't have titties yet! What did it matter? Why couldn't I do what they were doing? Free the nipple.

I lived and have lived a blessed and privileged life. My childhood was no exception. Adventures, games, and toys were more than enough. My childhood was full of outdoor and indoor adventures with minimal technology in front of our eyes, especially from 1992-2005. My brother and I were free to wander innocently in our neighborhood and the woods that surrounded it. It was blissful most of the time.

My childhood was not without dolls, either. Every girl I knew growing up had dolls. I was given a plethora of Barbies. I never seemed to care what Ken had under his clothes. Not only was I not interested, but it never occurred to me to think about what was underneath his clothes. I didn't even wonder about it. Not a single thought of it crossed my mind. In my own private retaliation from the Popsicle T-shirt Incident of '97, my Ken doll is NOT allowed to take his shirt off. Ever. I then freed all my Barbies from their shirts (and bottoms) to let their breasts and other bits roam free like the good Lord intended.

I already knew what a lesbian household looked like without it being shown to me, and I have my Barbies to thank for that. I did, though, make the Barbies wear some clothes while cooking because no one wants to get burned! And they only cooked if they felt like it. Ken cooked the rest of the time.

I made Ken be the girls' driver, too. His only job was to drive the Lesbian Barbies around to go play sports or go shopping or go wherever the fuck they wanted! Just completely clothed Ken and naked Lesbian Barbies strolling around town, also known as my childhood basement.

Ken was their bitch (also probably like the good Lord intended). I was clearly changing gender roles from a very young age.

Being gay is something I felt within myself and saw in others, and I did my best to fill in as much as I could along the way. I did not need to teach it to myself because that's the way I was born.

Unlike today, there was far less representation of gay folks when I was growing up. Sure, it would have been easier if an older, wiser adult had conversations with me about homosexuality, but it was not talked about in my house or school. While I'm happy for the next generation, I'm a bit annoyed that there weren't as many books, people, and stories out there as there are today. However, there's still a long way to go, and I'm less annoyed knowing my stories will be out in the world. And that's why we're all here, right? To leave things better than how we found them? To leave the world a better place for the next generations?

Homosexuality was briefly mentioned here and there in church or religion class and in the news, but there was no way in hell young Ally would dare open her mouth with a counterargument or at the very least: a question from a confused, queer adolescent. At least not after she found her answer when she asked her mom that one evening in 2000.

I knew long before my eighth birthday what gay meant. My mom's brother was gay, and my father's brother was gay. My uncle living with his boyfriend was as normal to me as my dad living with my mom. I realized even then that while their life looked a little different, love is love.

Five-ish years after asking my mom if I was gay, at age twelve, I was still unaware that two women who are intimate are called Lesbians. Sadly, I didn't learn the term "lesbian" until long after my Lesbian Barbie Dream House days. I only knew them as gay men and gay women. I didn't play LBDH very often. In fact, I only played it a few times. I stopped before anyone found out my secret, knowing even then that while I enjoyed what I was doing, it wouldn't look right to others. I was terrified of getting yelled at by adults when I was a child…still am most days. I was a good kid that rarely got in trouble. I listened to my parents most of the time, except when it came to keeping my room tidy. Eventually, I outgrew the Barbies and found ways to tear off their heads and other limbs. Oops. Sorry, ladies…that may have been where my hiding and suppressing escalated. *Damn.*

The first time I remember hearing the word "lesbian" was when a lesbian couple moved in next door when I was in sixth grade. Both were back pocket wallet carriers. I was even more fascinated that they attended the same catholic church that we did. *They go to church?!* I stared at them as they walked up to communion together. *That's brave*, I thought, to enter a catholic church together d. To my awe, no fires were started. They didn't turn to dust or melt. The priest didn't condemn them or kick them out. In fact, I was the only one that weirdly reacted: I kept trying to sneak looks at them, just to make sure what I was seeing was real. Two lesbians in a church?! My twelve-year-old mind was officially blown.

That summer, I spent as much time in the backyard as I could, accidentally on purpose kicking my soccer ball into their backyard for an excuse to talk to them. I always asked for my ball back but never engaged in any other conversation, no matter how much more I wanted to know.

Fast forward two years, and I was fifteen years old. Another neighbor and I were chatting in the backyard. He was my age, and a few weeks later, he would be my very first kiss that was accompanied by his boyhood boner.

That afternoon in the backyard, our women-loving women neighbors finished up some yard work. I waved at them and noticed the look on his face. He raised his eyebrows at my friendliness toward them, and then I jokingly told him that I was a lesbian. It was the first time I ever said those words out loud, and the last time I'd follow them up with: "I'm just joking!"

I wanted to see people's reactions. Over the years, I came out on several occasions, but everyone thought I was joking. I didn't confirm it nor deny it, so I left them to believe their assumption that it wasn't true.

My lesbian neighbors moved shortly after I "came out" to my other neighbor, long before I could have a real conversation with them and crushing my dream of a Miss Honey-Matilda situation, even though I didn't want to leave my own family. I mostly just wanted to know about *theirs.*

Fast forward fourteen years from when I first asked my mom if I was gay. I was twenty-four. I wanted to tell my parents in person. The timing comes down to Father's Day weekend of 2016. This would either be a nice Father's Day weekend, or it was going to be the end all be all of Father's Days from here on out. I called my brother and told him first because I knew he would not give a shit whether I liked men, women, or anything else in between or beyond. He was surprised but not at the same time. It was just unexpected news on a weekday afternoon, I presumed.

I called my uncle next, who lived in Florida with his longtime partner. He is the most generous man in my family, with a heart of gold. On the phone, he told me that my parents would love me regardless of how I identify and reassured me that he's gay and they love him, too.

Everyone does. He's the kindest, sweetest man!

Those two phone calls took place on my walk home from my shift at the gym, at roughly fifty-six days alcohol free.

By the time I called my mom, I was standing at the corner of Jefferson and Washington in the West Loop. It was late morning. The sun was shining. Construction workers yelled over saws and cranes. She answered. I stopped walking.

She knew something was going on with me. I let her know yesterday that I wanted to talk to her and dad about something.

"What else could it be? You already told me you're bisexual."

"Can you wait until tonight? I really would like to tell you in person."

"Please, just tell me. I haven't been sleeping!"

"Okay."

I took a deep breath and repeated the words out loud that, up until that day, I'd said only to myself: "I'm not straight. I'm not bisexual. I'm gay." Her voice breaks as she replies, "Are you sure?"

"Yes."

"Really sure?" she asks again through full tears this time.

"Yes. I am 100% sure." At that point, I was crying too.

"I wouldn't wish that life on anyone. Do you know how hard your life is going to be?"

"Well, yeah. It's not like I chose this. Plus, mom, life is already hard."

"I thought you were going to tell me you're pregnant."

"Nope! Just gay."

I never looked around to see if anyone saw me crying on that street corner. It was just me, the phone, the sky, my mom, and the ground on which I stood. Everything else was unclear. Everything else did not exist.

"Have you told anyone else?"

"Yes. Eric knows. So does Uncle Jerry."

"You haven't told Dad?"

"I'm going to today."

"Okay. Well, I'll see you at dinner."

"Yeah."

"I love you."

"I love you, too, Mom."

I stopped crying before I entered my apartment building. It was the only time I ever cried about being gay. I cried because I thought I'd upset my mom, and that was never my intention. That's the last thing I ever wanted to do.

An hour later, my dad picked me up. He was in town for business, so I had a ride home for the weekend.

With my stomach in knots for the next four and a half hours, I managed to show no signs of worry or fear during the entire car ride from Chicago to St. Louis. I had only seen my dad angry on two occasions and drunk on less than three. Still, though, I did not know how he would react.

I know how I'd gotten there. I wanted to be there. I needed to be there. That was how I'd move forward. That was how I'd grow. That was the first step in getting better. That was how I'd get stronger. But there I was, scared of his reaction. Worst case scenario: they'd cut me out of their lives. I didn't want that scenario to pan out, but it's something I thought of every day for the few weeks leading up to telling my parents.

Five hours later, we were just two miles away from the restaurant where we were meeting my mom for dinner. I wanted to tell him before we got there. Just me and him. Finally, I said, "Dad, there's something I need to tell you—"

"You're pregnant?!" he interjected.

"No. I'm gay."

Per his usual spirit, he placed his hand on my shoulder and replied with a dad joke: "No wonder you're so good at sports."

I sighed, relieved to break the tension I'd been feeling for the last several hours.

Feeling the best I had felt all day, the best I had felt in months (years probably), I replayed the speech in my head that I wanted to say at dinner. A whole speech never given. The meal was like any other, aside from the glittered debris from the rainbow of truth I just dropped upon them.

They talked about work and their days, catching up from being away from each other for the last several days. I kept trying to chime in with lines from the speech I prepared for them. I was ready to talk about it. I needed to talk about it. Coming out was a big deal, but not as big as the years leading up to that moment were a huge deal! I ended up being quiet most of that dinner.

They didn't tell me to get out of their lives. They didn't disown me. Although I wanted a cake and maybe some balloons, I wasn't expecting it. I was, however, expecting at least a hug. Honestly, they provided the most boring reaction I could've gotten.

I shocked them. They needed time to process. My mom told me years later that she was sad for me but also relieved. I later learned, too, that my dad told my mom, "That's MY kid.

Doesn't change a thing. That's. My. Kid."

I went over to my brother's apartment one afternoon weeks after coming out to my parents and met him by the pool. He had a few drinks in him, but despite his state (maybe encouraged by it), he treated my coming out as something to celebrate. He was proud of me. We cut our pool day short, and he took me to a fancy dinner with a four-course meal.

I finally got my cake. Well, it was just a slice of cake, but I'll never forget that gesture from him.

So, I came out. I did it! However, I naively thought coming out would set me free from my depression. I thought sobriety would set me free from my depression. I thought moving to Chicago would set me free from my depression. But for me, it is only a matter of time before another episode of depression disrupts my life. I will never be fully free from a depressed mind. It may be quieter at times. I may be happier at other times, but depression will always be waiting on the outskirts of my life, waiting for a door to open to sneak back in again.

That is my reality. That is the mind I was given, the body I was given—a great mind that has not so great things happen to it. The only thing I know for sure is that if I keep going and pushing through, I'll get better eventually, even if it's for a little while. That little while certainly makes up for the time I spend depressed. Cliché, I know, but I've learned to appreciate the better times as opposed to fearing the bad ones coming.

I am used to it by now. Depression is as normal for me as two women kissing. Depression is as normal as a man and woman kissing. Depression is as normal as the sun rising every morning. It is normal to me, and although that normalcy can suck so hard, the sun will rise again. SOOOO CHEESY! But it's true. Life goes on, and I will go through periods of depression, however many times again. And that's okay.

Things may not ever be easy, but does it get easier? I believe that it does. I believe that we can and will learn how to cope and accept that life is fucking hard. It's supposed to be.

I will always rise back up. Nowadays, whenever I am depressed or having a shit day, I say, "well, at least I'm not hungover." It can always be worse. Everything is worse with a hangover.

My sexuality is so simple; it's stupid. My mental illness is the complex part. My health is the complex part. A tricky bitch. However, my depression is also not who I am. Depression is just part of the mind I was given, just like being a lesbian is the sexuality I was given.

The only part of my journey that was a phase was playing straight. Once I figured it out, nothing had ever been so clear. I honestly only cared about how my family and a few close friends felt about my sexuality. If anyone else had or has a problem with it, then they aren't worth my time, even more so: they aren't worth my energy.

Ever since my Lesbian Barbie Dream House days, it has always made more sense to me for girls to kiss girls and for boys to kiss boys, with consent, of course. I just never told anyone because the judgement and potential isolation from my world held me back. Heterosexuality does not connect as normal to me in my brain, in my gut, or in my heart. This is my mind, my body, my soul.

I figured out who I am and who I want to be. Turns out, she was in there the entire time.

And for who I am yet to become, she's in there, too, and I won't leave her behind.

Hold on, sister. I'm coming back for you. I'll pull you up until it's normal for me to carry that higher version of myself and then I'll continue to repeat it until I am at my utmost highest and utmost truest self.

Just got to keep digging deeper and keep peeling back those layers. Just got to keep going.

CHAPTER XXLIV

After drinking away my savings, I found that I couldn't afford to continue with improv classes or anything outside of school and work for a while. I didn't spend every penny on alcohol. My downfall was the money I spent while hungover.

My hangovers were the worst. Whatever high I got from being drunk the night prior threw me for a terribly depressed, self-loathing crapshoot in the days following.

The hangovers were accompanied by my most depressed times. I'd wake up from a drunken slumber, absolutely hating myself for getting drunk again. I sipped a little bit of water, used the bathroom, and looked at my face, but I didn't wash it. I didn't deserve to wash it. I was punishing my body more instead of nourishing her back to her badass self. A lot of hangovers looked like that.

For example, on some hangover days, I took a Xanax in hopes of fast-forwarding to feeling better, aka sleeping it all away, but the Xanax only granted me a few more hours of sleep—far from the coma I was hoping for.

I allowed myself only more water until hunger pains took over my stomach. When the hunger pains grew louder, I told myself that I deserved the sharp pains after my behavior lately. I rolled off my couch, thinking *I have to eat something, but my kitchen is empty.* I was too tired to cook for myself, even if I did have food to cook with anyway. I ordered Ramen San on Grubhub to have it delivered ASAP. $20.00 for the food. $5.00 delivery fee + 20% tip. I devoured it while watching another episode of something on Netflix. I took another Xanax and set five alarms for the next morning, making sure my alarm was on the other side of my apartment, forcing me to get my ass out of bed.

My hangovers lasted for days. Often, I'd be scheduled to open the gym the next morning and felt just as shitty as the previous day. If I was lucky, I'd start to feel better by the night of day two. To be on time for work, I needed to clock in by 4:45 am. I'd wake up at 4:20 am and order an Uber to take me to work. $8.00.

When I'd clock out of work, I ordered yet another Lyft. I knew I should've walked home because fresh air would do me good, but I couldn't muster up any energy, and I told myself that I didn't deserve the fresh air. I paid the Lyft $10.00 plus a surge fee for a busy time of day.

I'd leave for class two hours early to finish reading and to grab food beforehand. I was exhausted, but I managed to walk ten minutes to the Clinton pink line stop. On the platform, I realized I left my water bottle at home. On campus, I'd get a salad, a bottle of water, and a snack for later. $22.00. While that total didn't add up to much on any given day, it added up quickly when I was doing that three or four times a week.

This was my pattern most days in the spring of 2016. I spent half of the last of my money on getting real groceries. I held my breath until I saw APPROVED on the card monitor that read $142.88. I exhaled loudly enough for the cashier to notice. She handed me my receipt. I grabbed my bag and walked home. Only walking because the grocery store was only three blocks from my apartment.

My bank accounts and credit card saw improvement just after a month of not drinking. Just like putting my credit card back in my wallet, I needed to sit in stillness and go inward myself. I only allowed a few trusted others in my bubble at the time.

I was newly sober, and alcohol was and still is aplenty in the comedy community. I wished I was ready to go back, but I wasn't. I wasn't sure when I would be either. I hoped soon, but I really didn't know. I seriously considered giving up comedy in order to remain alcohol-free. Instead of quitting cold turkey, I decided to just take a break from comedy for the summer. Without any financial resources to return to classes, now was the right and perfect time to take that break. Plus, I had to make up the work for a class I had withdrawn from during the spring quarter at DePaul.

I spent my first sober summer since I was sixteen writing, working, exercising, and continuing to see my therapist on a weekly basis. I rode my bike along the lakeshore. I hung out with my brother and a few of his friends at the pool. I went to the library. I took care of myself the best I could despite not digging deeper into my feelings.

After I made up the work for the withdrawn class, I put most of my energy into researching sexual assault and law for my thesis script. I was obsessed with it. I had an intense need to learn all I could about the topic and tell the best story possible. And I did that, but what I was really doing was channeling all my anger from my own assault into that script. I thought writing about it would've set me free. While I talked quite a bit about my feelings in therapy on the assault, I was far from forgiving him or anyone at the time, including myself. A year later, when I stopped going to therapy weekly and started going twice a month, I still felt anger toward him. The situation would persist for years, as you've heard from the Costco confrontation.

As my body began to detox from my month-long bender, I thought about sex. A lot. I asked myself: when was the last time I not only had sober sex, but it was also meaningful and safe and freeing and right and natural to me? Then, I begin to count up my age from eighteen to twenty-four...six years?

It's been SIX goddamn years? Holy Virgin Mary. I gotta fix that...but not yet.

By the end of that first sober summer, I felt like I could finally start dating women. I went into the gay dating game thinking it would be easier now that I wasn't drinking, but I was completely fucking wrong.

I felt empowered in my newfound sobriety and after coming out. I wanted to hold on to the empowerment, so I did. The downside of holding on to empowerment, though, meant I was not dealing with the harder, not-so-fun feelings that still came with those things. Like not being fully accepted in a community in which alcohol largely flows.

I knew how to swim, but it was hard to keep up with the current and find my footing as a fresh out of the closet twenty-four-year-old in Chicago. It took me a while to finally address that because I wanted to hold on to the empowerment. I thought that if I addressed my concerns that I wouldn't be *gay enough* and that the empowerment would fade too soon. I'd eventually find sober queer folks and other LGBTQ friends who didn't mind my not drinking, but it did not happen overnight.

Alcohol was a massive suppressant of my sexuality, and I thought that because I finally came out, it meant I was in the clear for depression. Just like I thought quitting soccer meant I'd finally be free from mental health issues.

Coming out was great, but I naïvely believed that would take care of my mental health. While it helped, coming out, it didn't mean that I would be free from a depression-prone mind. I still needed to talk it out in therapy. I still needed to take my anti-depressants consistently. I still needed to be kind to myself.

I stopped dealing with the emotions from the betrayal that led to some of the darkest days of my life. The betrayal of me not coming out sooner or ever thinking I could never live truthfully. I didn't want to mourn the loss of my love for the taste of whiskey and beer. I didn't want to mourn the loss of a normal social life. I didn't want to mourn the loss of being more accepted by society. I didn't want to add that to the list of things to mourn that I hadn't gotten to yet—soccer being at the top of that list.

I was and still am so proud of myself for speaking a truth that had been bottled up for so long. I deserved to reap the rewards of speaking up and living as my authentic self. But I also owed it to myself to take care of my mind like a child home sick with the flu.

I might have finally learned how to stop drinking, but I still hadn't learned how to talk about my emotions…at least not on a consistent level when I was in my mid-twenties. I could write about them all day long, but speaking them out loud into the world on a daily basis? That took more time.

I dealt with most of my emotions through therapy and in my art. I wrote stories and did performances based on my experiences. I even wrote and produced a short film that won an LGBTQ+ award at a Chicago film festival and was nominated for several other awards across the country. It took several years after coming out to be more active in speaking more truths outside of my art. To speak them to and with friends, family and other loved ones.

It wasn't until the Spring of 2022 when I started regularly speaking up sooner and more frequently in one-on-one settings. Moving back home unexpectedly in October of 2021 was a pivotal turning point. I had just gotten out of a nearly three-year relationship that made me feel small, unheard, unseen and silenced.

At times, I spoke with shaking hands and trembling words, and my hands broke out in a cold sweat. I moved back to St. Louis with intentions of eventually leaving again, but just as I've mentioned in this book, the universe has intervened with plans of its own. Those plans are beautiful and better than I ever could have dreamt for myself.

The Cardinals Opening Day in 2022 was cold and rainy. My parents, along with some family members, all went together. I donned a winter coat and beanie with jeans and boots. The Clydesdales and opening ceremony distracted me from my pain until my mom and I were sitting in post-game traffic on the down ramp of the parking garage. I couldn't keep it in any longer, and I quietly said with the words caught in my throat, "I am in so much pain." I cried tears of fearing the unknown but also tears of relief.

Two days later, at Jacq's bridal shower, I received a text from a former Chicago neighbor letting me know my ex's father had suddenly passed.

Tears hit me like a wave crashing onto the shore. Fast, cold, and messy. At the time, I was under-weight and in tremendous pain physically due to chronic health issues. When my emotions heightened, so did my physical pain. I tried to catch my breath as I looked at my mom and told her I needed to get out of there immediately. She quietly guided me outside as I sobbed. My Godmother and mom's sister, Patti walked out right after with a glass of water. They both hugged me and made sure I drank every last ounce of the water in that glass. When we got home that afternoon, I slept for three hours.

Between my health issues that year, leaving Chicago suddenly, my ex's dad dying, and a few other family matters, I swear I came into therapy each week with another major life curve ball. I was back in an incredibly dark place. My health issues left me walking with a limp and taking steps two feet at a time, both up and down stairs. I was afraid to be fully honest with how sad my mind became. I was afraid I'd be sent to a facility or carted off in an ambulance, making a scene for others to gawk upon. I wanted to start drinking again more than ever during the last six years without it.

I walked into therapy one day, promising myself that I would be 100% honest and upfront with my therapist. I broke that promise and walked out, mentally kicking myself. I was so pissed at myself the rest of that day and the next.

That's not who I want to be. I want to be someone who does say how she feels and who does speak up even when it's hardest. I wanted to be that person as she entered the next decade of her life.

The next week, I told him I was having suicidal thoughts. While they had been fleeting over the years, this time, ideation started to slither inside my mind. To my relief, no dramatic scenes happened. No one barged in to stare at me. No one else knew at the time other than him, and shortly after that, my other best friend, Nashaemun. No one else knew before I wrote down these words in these sentences.

When I first spoke up about those thoughts, it was just me and my therapist who met me with grace and compassion. From there, I felt myself start to swim safely out of the rip current.

In the fall of 2022, I had my second surgery for endometriosis, aka the main cause for my physical living hell. Endometriosis is a medical condition "in which similar tissue to the tissue that lines the uterus grows outside the uterus in places where it doesn't belong." The surgery took place a couple of weeks after I confronted The Professor in Costco.

I woke up groggy and hungry. After I urinated and drank some apple juice, I was released to go home. On the way, my mom stopped to pick up dinner. By the time I finished eating on my parents' living room couch, the anesthesia had mostly dissipated. My mom looked at me and told me the results of the surgery.

The doctor removed my left ovary. The endometriosis tangled itself in and around my ovary, eventually created a web glued to the left side of my abdomen wall. The tissue was pulling my reproductive organs closer to the left side of my body.

After seeing the photos from my insides, I couldn't believe that something as small as that tissue was causing me so much pain. I wasn't upset about losing half of my egg supply. I wasn't upset about being down an ov. I was upset because of *why* I lost it. For years, endometriosis has taken time and energy away from me. I lost my ovary because of a disease. A disease with no cure. A disease that is unpredictable and invisible on the outside. I couldn't help but think, *what else will it take away from me?*

Immediately after I thought that, with a fresh batch of tears in my eyes, I said it out loud to my mom. She replied, "You can't fixate on that mindset, Ally. Look at the positives here: you're going to be in less pain at least for a while. Yeah, the endo may spread, but you're okay for now. And that's a big win, sweetheart."

I let some more tears fall as I grabbed my water bottle. I drank out of it, took a deep breath and set it back on the coffee table, nodding in agreement with my mom.

With my stronger set of mental health coping mechanisms and my support system, I am more equipped to navigate my health issues and the curve balls life throws at me.

I reevaluated most of my life after that surgery, and what I really wanted out of it. My soul-searching led me to fully commit to a career in law while continuing to write and create art on the side. I'm currently working toward a kickass score on the LSAT, and I plan on applying to law school in the next couple of years.

I wouldn't go as far as to say that timing *is* everything, but it's damn close. If I hadn't taken care of my physical health along with my mental, I wouldn't fully be able to enjoy the final stages of publishing *I'm Gay and Drink Water*. I wouldn't fully be able to enjoy and embrace the love my partner gives me every day. And I certainly would not have been able to fully feel and enjoy the emotions and excitement that came in July 2023 when I received a phone call from Webster University's Athletic Director.

I had started working at a law firm in downtown St. Louis two months earlier when my phone rang. I didn't recognize the number, so I didn't answer. However, as soon as I could listen to the voicemail, I did so immediately. With his thick East Coast accent, the Athletic Director asked me to call him back, leaving a few details in his message. Curious and impatient, I dialed him back within minutes.

He answered on the second ring and congratulated me on being chosen as an inductee for Webster's Athletic Hall of Fame Class of 2023. I thought somewhat frequently over the years about being inducted into their Hall of Fame, but I had never expected it to come less than ten years after graduating. It was my second year on the ballot.

As I sat in an open conference room at work, overcame with many emotions, I thanked him and professed my gratitude for Webster's program and the opportunity to be a part of it. My cadence quickened so he couldn't hear my voice stumbling on the tickle in my throat.

I walked into the bathroom after we hung up and cried like a baby in one of the stalls. Tears of so many emotions: relief, happiness, and gratitude mostly. I was able to fully feel the greatness of this major recognition, and it truly felt like my past had been recognized. After all, I was back then. After all, I did back then. After the hurt, the championships, the loss, the persistence. It feels damn good to be seen and be honored along with many other incredible athletes.

You may not be able to see things for what they are until a decade later when they're shown to you in other ways, in different perspectives. Everything holds some significance, no matter how miniscule or massive. A short sentence said out loud could have a giant impression.

I'd say now that I'm much more used to speaking my mind, but it still is uncomfortable a lot of the time. It takes practice each day.

Along with regular therapy, it would also take several failed relationships with ex-girlfriends in my 20s. It would take navigating the push and pull of a career in law. It would take learning to live with chronic pain. It would take not just going to therapy on a regular basis but going to see the right therapists that were the best fit for me. It would take daily affirmations, journaling, exercise, and surrounding myself with the right people.

I have learned how to deal with my feelings. I have learned to sit with the discomfort of them. I have learned to feel them. It took nearly thirty years, but I am becoming the person I want to be more and more every single day.

I have learned to stop running. I sit and stay now just like my puppy, Stella! Well, I stay more often than not, and Stella is still working on the *stay* part herself. My instinct is to still run, but the main difference now is that I know how to stop finally. If I do end up running, it isn't very far and it isn't very long, and I always, always, always come back to myself. And when I do, I come back to a better, higher version of her.

LOOKING BACK

Part of me wishes I could unlearn all of this. All the bad stuff. I wish I couldn't remember. But if I were to erase these memories—if I were to erase my past—would I still be the person I am today? Probably not. There is a reason I cannot black out. There is a reason I am to remain sober. A reason bigger than anyone can see, including myself.

I'm good at a lot of things, but I suck at drinking safely. So why keep doing it? Why keep constantly trying to prove to myself that if I could drink in moderation once, then I could try to drink like that again instead of binging? I should never have gone into a night or day or drinking with the *hopes* of it turning into an okay night when evidence should have shown me that the odds were never in my favor.

With as many health issues as I have now, I cannot imagine a life in which I consume alcohol. Plus, I treat my alcohol-free life as a game, a game I intend to keep winning. For eight years and counting, I have been winning this game, and I will be the champion with plans to remain undefeated.

The champion in each of us has multiple layers. I believe my success in winning this alcohol-free game comes from getting to know each layer and being brave enough to explore each one in the first place. We all have dozens of layers, like an onion or a decadent cake. I am sad for those who do not explore to find the many layers that are within them, but I do not dwell on that sadness, as that is their choice. It's their life, not mine. I can only merely encourage others through my words but mostly through my actions.

Cakes and onions may be simple, but humans are complex individuals. We all can do so much more than we think we can do. But most live in comfort and choose not to live beyond that. I am not *most* people. I do not want to live in my comfort zone.

Therapy and writing were my two biggest paths to stop running. I finally accepted that there is no quick fix when it comes to dealing with the harshness of mental health. As we all do, I needed an outlet to process and the time to do that, as well.

Just like my writing routines with each project, my ways to cope change, too, when going through a bout of depression. Most likely, because I am a different person between each episode, what works one day or one week may not work the next, and that is okay! I've grown and changed and will continue to do so as I age.

I don't think I would've published this book or have started the *I'm Gay and Drink Water* podcast without finally ending the what-seemed-to-be-never-ending marathon of running away from myself.

As for college, there would be a lot I would do differently if I had the chance to do it again. I should have studied harder and more. I should have ventured out to challenge my mind academically as much as I challenged my body. I should have taken the time in high school to reflect on what I really wanted out of my college experience. I should have looked at more schools. Sought out different programs. Maybe taking a gap year would have been best, but I kept going because I didn't want to be left behind. Nowadays, I don't dwell much on my soccer career. I do, though, spend time here and there watching YouTube videos of insane goals from Abby Wambach, Mia Hamm, and other players new and former members of the USWNT. I watch them for inspiration. This is a reminder that anything is possible with a lot of hard work, talent, and luck if you believe in that sort of thing. Glorious moments come from hours of preparation, sweat, and tears. Then, of course, I fall into the rabbit hole of more insane goals. My favorites are the ones scored by younger players, who you can see their pure love for the game created a magnificent piece of art. Each goal is special, each game is special, and each moment is special because it will never be the same ever again.

So, maybe I should have done a lot of things. But the "shoulds" are not something to dwell on. What was and what will be is meant for me. What is meant for me will not pass me up, and at the end of the day, I suppose I wouldn't change a thing.

Onward.

When I look back at pictures from college, I am me. I was just a lesbian playing straight. I don't regret not coming out sooner. I had a lot of weeds to pull before I figured out what was in my soil and how rich it really was. Our hardships make us grow. That's just the way of the world. It's changing and will continue to change for the better...if you let it.

I often imagine how much suffering I would have dodged if anyone spoke to me or one of my classes or teams about sexuality and/or mental health. BONUS if they happened to talk about them hand in hand because according to a 2020 study done by the Trevor Project on LGBTQ+ youth:

"48% of LGBTQ+ youths reported engaging in self-harm in the past 12 months, including over 60% of transgender and nonbinary youths. 68% of LGBTQ+ youths reported symptoms of generalized anxiety disorder in the past two weeks, including more than 3 in 4 transgender and nonbinary youths. 1 in 3 LGBTQ+ youths reported that they had been physically threatened or harmed in their lifetime because of their LGBTQ+ identity."

In May of 2022, the NCAA reported that from a survey of 9,800 NCAA student athletes:

"When asked whether their coaches took their mental health concerns seriously, 59% of the men's sports participants agreed or strongly agreed, and 50% of the women's sports participants did so."

In my honest opinion, those numbers should be 100%. Do better, coaches. I, and I'm sure many other people, were left to figure out a lot on their own. A little support and kindness go a long way.

My biggest advice to all is this: ask your loved ones questions! I no longer feel the need and want for someone to ask me as if to prompt me into saying how I feel. I've worked on speaking up without that prompt, and with practice, I am becoming someone who just says what's on her mind despite what others may feel about what I have to say. It's not about them.

I am happy to see growth in mental health resources for student athletes, my alma mater included! If you do not see this happening in your community, your school, or your team(s), I encourage you to find a way to integrate it into the curriculum and training. It is worth it even if only ONE person needs it.

Soccer saved me many times. I was the happiest when I was playing because it was my escape. It was a blast, and I was great at it!

I loved the road trips because a lot of the time, they were on weekends, which meant a weekend when I was not drinking. I was my true self on the soccer field, even without knowing or completely acknowledging who my true self was and is.

On the field, the only words coming out of my mouth were positive affirmations, the occasional talk back to the referee, and petty comments to my opponents...yeah, I wasn't above smack talking. I yelled at my teammates often, but only because I really, really wanted to win, and I knew what they were capable of doing. I knew their great potential.

Winning validates who I am even more, distracting others from asking me questions about my true self—as if they would.

For the record, I never had any feelings for my teammates or friends other than Lauren. In case any of you are reading this and wondering if I had a crush on you. Sorry. I didn't. I was also so good at pretending I was straight that a lot of the time—enough for me to actually think I believed it. I never saw my teammates and friends in college in a romantic way. And 90% are too damn straight.

After I came out, I rarely needed reassurance of my sexuality from others, but looking through old photos, I am pleased to see myself in them. I've been gay this whole fucking time. It just took a while to accept it and even longer to fully embrace it. I'm still me, but even more so now.

There is so much more to my coming out story than just: I am gay. As you can see, I wrote an entire book about it. So, next time someone comes out to you, keep in mind how far they've come to say those three words. The same goes for bisexual, trans, queer, pansexual, demisexual, asexual, gender binary, and the orientations that are still being discovered. Don't be an asshole. It's much less energy of yours to be kind.

I felt a need and want to come out. I felt that it was necessary for my overall well-being, and I wanted to come out because so many people saw me as a straight person. I wanted to come out so I could be seen for who I really am. I wanted to tell people because I needed to say it, and I needed them to hear it.

Coming out is up to the person. Whether they choose to or not, it's okay either way. What's not okay is outing someone. So, HETS (aka heterosexuals) and Allies don't do that. Please, please, please do not do that. Whatever you decide, please know that you are not alone. And as for the late bloomers, it's better late than never, and you, my dears, are right on time.

Now, I peel off layers of myself like an onion about to be cooked. I am raw, and so much more lies within me and a world I do not yet know. My endless curiosity both blesses and curses me. However, the curse-like feelings fade once I discover where those curiosities lead.

Depression takes away my hope and positive emotions and replaces them with despair, sadness, and exhaustion. It is a struggle almost every day, even when a depressive episode is not in its prime. I choose to believe my intellect is not a liar. I choose to believe that my intellect is the truth. It would be so much easier to listen to depression, and some days I do.

But intellectually, I know that depression is a liar. Why would I listen to a liar?

It drags me down because these lies come at me 24/7 when my depression is full throttle.

Imagine your worst enemy in your mind feeding you lies about yourself almost every minute of every day. Distractions work, but only for a while. It's depression's game.

As for the days, I do believe the lies depression feeds me; I have friends, family, and a great therapist to tell me otherwise.

Each time I find myself in an episode of depression, some things come up that were not there before. But still, I keep going. This is one of the few things I know how to do. "Keep going" means something different to each person. To me, it means that I try my hardest to do the bare minimum on the days I don't want to do anything at all. I go to work when I want to call in sick; I'm not physically contagious unless you count the negative energy that feeds and pours onto others. I take a shower even though the mere thought of cleaning my body makes me exhausted.

The list goes on and on and on. If I can do one of the things on my list, especially go to work, then it makes me feel less like a bum piece of shit and more like a functioning member of society, even if that feeling only lasts an hour or the morning or just a few minutes. Even so, I'm all for taking a mental health day if I truly need it.

As I write about my late teens and early twenties as a woman now in her thirties, I am still peeling back those layers. More now than ever before. This book was at a standstill for a couple of years.

I kept revisiting it, but there was still something holding me back. I couldn't quite add in the necessary emotional reflection because I didn't know exactly what that was yet. I hadn't named the emotions. I hadn't reflected on them on a certain level of depth I wanted this book to have. I hadn't spoken up enough verbally to know what to write or how to write it in words. But I put in the work. And a few months after doing the work regularly, those written words became clearer. I'm still a work in progress and always will be, but I have never been prouder of myself for showing up and daring to be vulnerable day in and day out. I am doing it, and you can, too.

Stay hydrated. Stay gay, or however you identify.

I am me.

My name is Ally.

I'm gay and drink water.

ACKNOWLEDGEMENTS

I'd first like to thank my editor, Dana, who helped me give this book what it needed to get across the finish line. Your eye for consistency and detail is truly appreciated, and you helped me pull out more emotions that this final draft needed. To my parents, thank you for supporting me in all ways and taking me to and watching soccer practice and games for most of my childhood. Thank you to my beta readers for giving me honest and caring feedback. Thank you to my Chicago LGBTQ+ Writing Group for your notes on the early drafts of this book. Thank you, Brad, for challenging me to find different ways to write, and thank you for being there for me in the good times and bad. To my brother, Eric, thank you for celebrating my coming out all those years ago. Your support during those times is one of my favorite memories with you. Thank you to two of the best therapists I've ever had: Sharon and Scott. You both have helped me see more of who I am and helped me become a person who no longer runs away. Thank you for showing me what true consistency looks like. To Tsuki (SB), while I didn't write much about our friendship in these pages, you are a pivotal player in my story, and I am so glad you're still a part of it. You always keep me going, and you especially did back then. To Nashaemun, I am so grateful for you and the creative support you've always given me. Heidi, my childhood dog, you were one of the best. Thank you for showing me what it's like to love and be loved by a soul with four legs and paws. Lastly, thank you to my soon-to-be spouse, Leslie. Without your love and encouragement, I don't think this book would have made it out when it did. Thank you for loving and embracing all the parts of me.

All of you hold a very special place in my heart.
Xoxo,
Ally.

Don't miss out on updates for speaking engagements, future books and more! Also, if you feel inclined and felt this book helped you in any way, a review is always welcomed and appreciated. Scan the QR code here to leave a review now:

WORKS CITED

"Estimated Probability of Competing in College Athletics." *NCAA. Org*, NCAA, www.ncaa.org/sports/2015/3/2/estimated-probability-of-competing-in-college-athletics.aspx. Accessed 12 July 2024.

"Incident 8259 - Resolved." *Incident 8259 | Academic Sexual Misconduct Database*, Dec. 2020, academic-sexual-misconduct-database.org/index.php/incident/8259.

"Mental Health Issues Remain on Minds of Student-Athletes." *NCAA.Org*, NCAA.org, 24 May 2022, www.ncaa.org/news/2022/5/24/media-center-mental-health-issues-remain-on-minds-of-student-athletes.aspx.

NCAA Recruiting Facts, www.nfhs.org/media/886012/recruiting-fact-sheet-web.pdf. Accessed 8 July 2023.

"OK Definition & Meaning." *Dictionary.Com*, Dictionary.com, dictionary.com/browse/ok. Accessed 8 July 2023.

Shakespeare, William. *A Midsummer Night's Dream*.
"Th e Trevor Project National Survey 2020." *Th e Trevor Project*, www. thetrevorproject.org/survey-2020/. Accessed 8 May 2023.

Printed in Great Britain
by Amazon

50010438R10182